Preaching and the Holy Mystery

The Eucharist as Context and Resource for Proclamation

reprinted with corrections 07/2019

Preaching and the Holy Mystery

The Eucharist as Context and Resource for Proclamation

reprinted with corrections

Richard L. Eslinger, OSL

OSL Publications
Ashland City TN

Preaching and the Holy Mystery

The Eucharist as Context and Resource for Proclamation

reprinted with corrections

Copyright ©2016 Richard L. Eslinger
All Rights Reserved

ISBN: 978-1878009722

Produced and manufactured in the United States of America by

OSL Publications

The publishing ministry on The Order of Saint Luke
1002 Hunters Lane
Ashland City TN 37015

Every effort has been made to acknowledge sources and to trace copyrights. If any right has been inadvertently infringed upon, we ask that the omission be excused and agree to make necessary corrections in subsequent editions.

> The Order of Saint Luke is a religious order dedicated to sacramental and liturgical scholarship, education and practice. The mission of the publishing ministry is to put into the hands of students and practitioners resources which have theological, historical, ecumenical and practical integrity.

To Elise,

Gift of song to God's people

and gift of covenant love to me.

Cover photo courtesy of St. Andrew's Episcopal Church, Maryville, TN; Fr. Steve Mosher, photographer.

Table of Contents

About the Author — iv

Acknowledgements — v

The Service of the Table (Graphic) — vii

Introduction — 1

Chapters

1. The Offertory — 18
2. The Sursum Corda — 33
3. The Preface — 40
4. The Sanctus and Benedictus Qui Venit — 69
5. The Post-Sanctus Narrative — 107
6. The Institution Narrative — 130
7. Anamnesis/Oblation/Epiclesis — 154
8. Doxology and Amen — 198
9. The Lord's Prayer — 216
10. The Agnus Dei — 241
11. The Communion — 267

Endnotes — 290

About the Author

Richard L. Eslinger is *Emeritus* Professor of Worship and Homiletics at United Theological Seminary, Dayton, Ohio, where he has served since 2001 including three years as Academic Dean. A scholar-pastor, Dick has served United Methodist congregations around the country including Boston, Massachusetts, Seattle, Washington, and Cincinnati, Ohio. He has enjoyed seasons of teaching at Duke University Divinity School, Mount St. Mary's Seminary of Cincinnati, and Vancouver School of Theology in Vancouver, British Columbia.

He is the author of eight books on preaching include the seminal *A New Hearing: Living Options in Homiletic Method* and its sequel, *The Web of Preaching: New Options in Homiletic Method.* Other publications include *Narrative & Imagination: Preaching the Worlds that Shape Us* and *Pitfalls in Preaching.*

His denominational and ecumenical involvements include serving in the national worship office of the United Methodist Church and membership in the Commission on Worship of the Consultation on Church Union and the North American Committee for Calendar and Lectionary.

Dick and his spouse, Elise, are members of the Order of St. Luke. His professional affiliations include membership in the North American Association for the Catechumenate, the Catholic Association of Teachers of Homiletics, and, since 1986, the Academy of Homiletics by which he was honored in 2012 with the Lifetime Achievement Award.

Acknowledgements

I am grateful to the Order of Saint Luke not only for publishing this volume, but for the Order's support, encouragement, and wise counsel throughout its gestation and writing. Abbot Daniel Benedict has been first among equals in these ministries and I give thanks for his virtues of compassion, love of the church's liturgy, and kindly shepherding of this writer. My Abbot's deep interest in the relationship between a theology of creation and the sacramental life has both inspired and informed me. Thank you, Br. Daniel. Also among members of the Order, several other members must be named. Sr. Rychie Breidenstein guided my manuscript through to completion both through her on-going editorial care and her knowledge of the church's liturgical traditions. Sr. Elizabeth Moore then saw the manuscript through its production process with precision and creativity. Sr. Elise Eslinger, my beloved, served as "continual encourager," wise woman of worship matters, and best critic of my writing. I dedicate this book to her.

I am also deeply grateful to several communities of colleagues who have provided encouragement for this project. Dean David Watson and the faculty at United Theological Seminary along with faculty emeritus friend, Kendall McCabe have been strong supporters of the book throughout its development. My colleagues in CATH, the Catholic Association of Teachers of Homiletics, likewise, have offered encouragement as well as homiletical and liturgical insight. Other friends in the Academy of Homiletics (AH) similarly have provided support, both through kind encouragement and homiletical wisdom, including Robert Howard, David Schnasa Jacobsen, and Joni Sancken. I give thanks to God, week in and week out, for such family, friends, and colleagues.

Ascension Day, 2016

The Service of the Table

Offertory

Blessed are you, Lord God of all creation...

The Great Thanksgiving*

Sursum Corda

The Lord be with you.
And also with you.
Lift up your hearts.
We lift them up to the Lord.
Let us give thanks to the Lord our God.
It is right to give our thanks and praise.

Preface

It is right and a good and joyful thing
  always and everywhere to give thanks to you,
  Almighty God, Creator of heaven and earth.
  Our souls proclaim your greatness, O Lord. Our spirits rejoice in you,
  our Savior. For you, the Almighty, have done great things for us, and
  holy is your name. Your mercy reaches from age to age for those who
  fear you. You have shown strength with your arm. You have
  scattered the proud in their conceit. You have deposed the mighty
  from their seats of power and raised the lowly to high places.

And so with your people on earth
  and all the company of heaven,
we praise your name and join their unending hymn:

Sanctus and Benedictus qui Venit

Holy, holy, holy Lord, God of power and might,
Heaven and earth are full of your glory.
Hosanna in the highest,
Blessed is he who comes in the name of the Lord.
Hosanna in the highest.

Post-Sanctus Narrative

Holy are you, and blessed is your Son Jesus Christ,
  your beloved in whom you are well pleased.
Your Spirit anointed him
  to preach good news to the poor,
  to proclaim release to the captives and
    recovering of sight to the blind,
  to set at liberty those who are oppressed, and
  to announce that the time had come when you would save your people.
He sought the lost, and welcomed home the wayward.
He healed the sick, fed the hungry, and ate with sinners,
that there might be joy in the presence of your angels
over each sinner who repents.

By the baptism of his suffering, death, and resurrection,
   you gave birth to your church,
  delivered us from slavery to sin and death,
  and made with us a new covenant
  by water and the Spirit.

Institution Narrative

On the night in which he gave himself up for us
  he took bread, gave thanks to you, broke the bread,
  gave it to his disciples, and said,
"Take, eat; this is my body which is given for you.
Do this in remembrance of me."
When the supper was over he took the cup,
  gave thanks to you, gave it to his disciples, and said,
"Drink from this, all of you; this is my blood of the new covenant
  poured out for you and for many
    for the forgiveness of sins.
Do this as often as you drink it, in remembrance of me."

Anamnesis/Oblation

And so, in remembrance of these your mighty acts in Jesus Christ,
we offer ourselves in praise and thanksgiving
 as a holy and living sacrifice,
  in union with Christ's offering for us,
as we proclaim the mystery of faith.

Acclamation

Christ has died. Christ is risen. Christ will come again.

Epiclesis

Pour out your Holy Spirit on us gathered here,
 and on these gifts of bread and wine.
Make them be for us the body and blood of Christ,
 that we may be for the world the body of Christ,
  redeemed by his blood.
Help us to hold these mysteries fast in our hearts
 and to bear fruit with patient endurance
that we might be neighbor
 to the least, the last, the little, and the lost.
By your Spirit make us one with Christ,
 one with each other, and
 one in ministry to all the world,
until Christ comes in final victory and
 we feast at the heavenly banquet.

Doxology/Great Amen

Through your Son Jesus Christ,
with the Holy Spirit in your holy church,
all honor and glory is yours, almighty God,
now and forever.
Amen.

The Lord's Prayer

The Fraction (Breaking the Bread)

Agnus Dei (Lamb of God)

Lamb of God, you take away the sin of the world.
  have mercy on us.
Lamb of God, you take away the sin of the world.
  have mercy on us.
Lamb of God, you take away the sin of the world.
  grant us peace. **

The Communion

---

* "Lukan Liturgy of Word and Table, Great Thanksgiving Two," *The Book of Offices and Services* (Akron, OH: OSL Publication, 2012), 15-18.
** "Agnus Dei", *The ELLC Texts: A Survey of Use and Variation*, accessed July 17, 2013, http://www.englishtexts.org/Documents/Survey0of0use#content

INTRODUCTION

Imagine being asked to attend a wedding in another church by a friend or family member. You locate the church, pull into the parking lot and enter the worship space. All of the visual cues are present that you are in the right spot: ushers hand out the wedding bulletins, the paraments are all a festive white, flowers flank the Table, and the musicians are already playing Pachelbel's "Canon." Finally, with a flourish, the music for the procession begins and the bridal party enters along with the cleric. Yes, you think, this is really going to be a wedding!

The opening greeting and prayers quickly pass and the betrothal vows are made. Then, after a solo, the liturgy moves on to the Service of the Word. Nicely, a relative of the bride has served as a reader in his parish church and does a fine job with 1 Corinthians 13. The preacher reads the John 2 story of Jesus' first sign at Cana in Galilee. The congregation is seated and the preacher now begins the sermon. But, in this imagined wedding scenario, something strange, even bizarre, now happens. The sermon does not mention Christian marriage at all, not a word. No reference to covenant or even faith, hope, and love.

Instead, the sermon seems like an old Monty Python routine—a serious and passionate, but irrelevant, discourse on the Maccabean Revolt or something equally out of touch with the context. Finally, having come to an end, the pastor/preacher now moves back to face the couple who are left standing there in perplexity. The vows are exchanged and the announcement made that these two are now within the holy covenant of marriage. Then, a brief prayer, a benediction, and the recessional. Later, at the reception, there are the usual toasts (including some funny stuff by the best man) along with the compulsory dancing of the Macarena. But, at table after table, the wedding guests repeatedly ask each other the same question: "What in the world did that sermon have to do with a wedding?" No one can come up with any plausible reply.

The Call for Balance: Interplay of Word and Sacrament

There are numerous occasions for which the preacher shapes his or her sermon so that it leads to a particular liturgical outcome. Or, to reverse the formula, preachers are familiar with a variety of specific occasions which provide abundant resources for the sermon. When there is a righteous "fit" between the proclamation and the liturgical context, the sermon leads the gathered community toward the rite and, conversely, the rite provides all kinds of resources for the shaping of the sermon. In our imagined wedding scenario, we have come at least to expect one of those "generic" wedding sermons. On the other hand, when text and context mesh particularly well, it is a delight to be in the congregation; to listen as the well prepared preacher shapes the sermon to both fit the liturgical function and lead the couple towards the exchange of vows and the giving and receiving of rings -- proclaiming the gospel while speaking to the distinctive virtues and character of the two who are covenanting in Christian marriage. The homily points toward the rite while the words and actions of the rite infuse and enrich the homily. This is all as it should be!

A similar dynamic obtains in many other worship settings. When a preacher prepares the sermons for a revival series, the journey in each of the messages is carefully assembled so as to lead to an invitation to follow Christ, or more fully serve the Lord. Or consider the labors of a priest who is preparing a homily to preach to the catechumens during the Fourth Week in Lent. The story of the Man Born Blind (John 9:1-41) will be carefully exegeted and interpreted for this profound occasion—after all, the catechumens are on their own journey towards the waters of their baptism at the Easter Vigil. On the other hand, the particular ritual context, the exorcism and the scrutiny, will never be far from the homilist's imagination. Likewise, a bishop's or presbyter's sermon at a service of ordination will certainly speak to this Spirit-filled occasion and will be designed to lead both the ordinand(s) and the assembly toward the historic rites that will follow. Moreover, those rites of ordination will become an important resource, a "liturgical bible" for the preacher.[1] Perhaps a doublet line of the *Veni Creator Spiritus* will be quoted in the sermon, or the sacramental act of the laying on of hands will evoke other times when there has been a caring, healing, laying on of hands (such as at Holy Baptism). In these instances, the particular ritual event becomes not only the context for the sermon, but its words and actions become a rich and fruitful resource as well.

Now consider the liturgical occasion of the full Sunday Service of Word and Sacrament. It is a widespread and ecumenically-pervasive reality that the majority of sermons preached at the Eucharist are rather innocent of the sacramental context. When preaching at the Service of Word and Table (United Methodist terminology for the Eucharist) the reality that the liturgy will move *from* proclamation *to* the Holy Meal is simply ignored. Such inadequate approaches to preaching and Holy Communion brought Edward Foley to ask the question directly: "In concrete terms, when have we heard a preacher take the text of the eucharistic prayer seriously?"[2] And to expand on Foley's good question, we could ask: How often does the homilist seriously engage the actions of the Eucharist, as well as its words? How often have we heard a message on the Scriptural foundations of those texts and actions? When have we heard the preacher drill deeply into the theological complexity of the Eucharist which is the liturgical action which so fully embodies the faith of the church? Or when have we been moved by the preacher's recital of the poetics of Eucharistic praying, including the ancient song echoing "Holy, Holy, Holy Lord. . . .?"

Put simply, the congregation is too often hearing sentimentalized "Communion meditations" on one hand or, more pervasively, sermons in which the Eucharistic Meal could just as well not be celebrated for all the homiletical difference it makes. Instead, notes Patricia Wilson-Kastner, we should expect a sermon that connects the word and table in the liturgy, both by bringing the Scriptures alive for the congregation, and by evoking the desire for redemption and change possible only through transformation in Christ."[3] Wilson-Kastner adds that such a sermon "invites the congregation to be nourished for this transformation in the Eucharistic meal."[4]

Both the centers of gravity within the Sunday liturgy, those of Word and Sacrament, are essential for the fullness of the assembly's life in Christ; they comprise "the double feast."[5] It is important, then, to explore more fully the distortions that occur when one center of gravity envelopes and obscures the other. Whenever such distortion afflicts the Holy Mystery of the Eucharist, the lively, Spirit-infused interplay between Word and sacrament is thwarted. Therefore, it is "meet, right, and salutary" that these issues be plumbed more deeply on behalf of the reform of the Sunday service in the Western Church. It should be noted that the context of our explorations is the Sunday service where Scripture is read and a sermon is offered and where the Lord's Supper is observed. Clearly the distortions we have endured in Western Christianity are to be viewed in their extreme: (a) on the Protestant side in congregations where on most Sundays the "celebrations" are bereft of the Holy Meal; and (b) within the Trendentine Catholic Church prior to the Second Vatican Council when the Mass was frequently celebrated on the Lord's day with only a minimal reading of Scripture and without any homily whatsoever. Our concern, however, relates to distortions that can be discerned even when Word and sacrament are present within worship on the Lord's Day. These distortions, put directly then, occur when the Word overrides the sacrament or when the sacrament overrides the Word.

Option A
Word overrides Sacrament

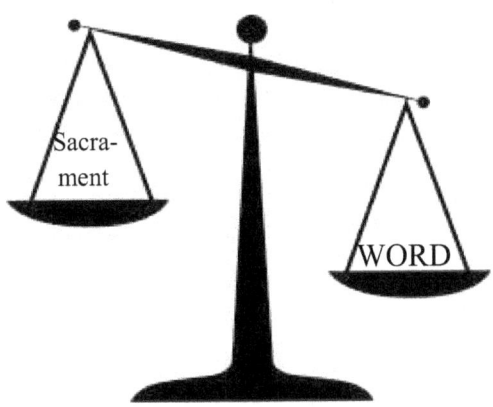

Oddly, even when the congregation observes both the Word and Sacrament within the Sunday service, the balance can be tilted so much toward the former that the latter is deemphasized—almost to the point of insignificance. The issue here is not that of St. Augustine of Hippo who provided the church with his famous dictum that the sacraments were "visible words."[6] What is problematic is not the infusion of the Word within the Sacrament, but malpractices of various sorts whereby the "Preaching Service" comes to override the ritual of making Eucharist.

Various long-standing practices within some Protestant traditions provide the most obvious examples of such dominance of Word over Eucharist. For example, it remains easy to find churches where the standard "preaching service" is augmented on "Communion Sunday" by a service of the Table that gives every evidence of being a temporary appendage to the main liturgy. In some cases—especially in large member congregations retaining impressive 1950's-style "Protestant Hour" services—the "preaching service" still takes "the allotted hour" and on Communion occasions a service of the Lord's Supper is conducted after the benediction is given at the main event. Within the span of churches following this pattern, a remnant will conduct the Service of Holy Communion in a chapel, again after the Preaching Service has been concluded.

Even in denominations blessed with a commitment to the full Sunday Service of Word and Table—such as the Disciples of Christ and their Restorationist siblings—the patterns of a full Preaching Service to which is appended a minimal Lord's Supper may be discerned. In all of these variant expressions, the Service of the Word is regarded as the center of gravity of Lord's Day worship, while the Eucharist is given the status of an attachment which, in due course, will once again be detached and put aside until the next Communion Sunday.

A further practice by which the Service of the Word comes to dominate and minimize the Service of the Table, is the persistence of a notion of a moment of consecration that involves no fully developed Eucharistic Prayer, but only the recital of the "Words of Institution" by a member of the clergy or designated lay person. Frequently in these contexts, the brevity of the consecration provides the preacher further opportunity to remark on the themes and images of the sermon. The Preface becomes a further "point" of the sermon! Other variations on this practice include words spoken prior to the Institution Narrative that ruminate on the importance of the Lord's Supper or on Jesus' intent and even his feelings and emotions at the Upper Room Meal. Perhaps the most lamentable expression of this "Preface as homily" practice is the, fortunately, rare occasion where the minister tells the congregation during this moment what the ritual of the Lord's Supper *is not*. The congregation will grow accustomed to hearing admonitions from the clergy that what is about to occur is not "magic" or "superstition" or "transubstantiation." In every variation of this "Preface as homily," the Preaching Service has intruded into the context of Eucharistic praying in an unhealthy and aberrant manner. Moreover, these practices retain the focus on the person of the preacher at a time in the liturgy when she or he needs to become more transparent as the whole assembly makes Eucharist.

Further overshadowing of the sacrament of the Table, relates to preaching on special occasions such as the feasts of the saints or, in Protestant contexts, denominational special Sundays. In the former instances, there is a temptation for the preacher to shift away from the calling to proclaim the gospel and, instead, to delve into the biographical data of the respective saint's life and death. Providing such a history lesson may be of educational value, but also leaves the saint very much in a past tense relationship to the assembly, "removed and often elevated above us."[7] The issue here is not that of a quantitative overriding of the liturgy of the Table; rather it is that of a sermonic approach that blocks the inherent movement of the assembly from proclamation to Eucharist. James A. Wallace re-focuses our attention on what should be the normative connection between preaching and the sacrament: "[T]he end of the sanctoral homily is not knowledge of the saint, but insight into the dealings of God with this [present] community."[8]

The old line Protestant version of this mistaken approach to preaching the feasts of the saints relates to another version of "sanctoral calendar"—the denominational special days. These Sundays devoted to fine social causes and noble thematics (such as "Laity Sunday," "Human Relations Sunday," and "World Communion Sunday") serve in a similar fashion to block the inherent movement of the assembly from proclamation to the Holy Meal. Sermons offer information on the special program of the day—helpfully provided by the denominational office—and encouragement toward the accompanying special offering. Ironically, this blockage of the movement from Word to sacrament can even occur on Worldwide Communion Sunday! In place of a homily that is biblically grounded, the preacher may focus the sermon on the span of this interdenominational event across the globe and upon the good works to be achieved by this special offering. Finally, just as with an excessively expansive sanctoral calendar, these denominational special days have a tendency toward constant multiplication as new social causes need to be accorded their own occasion. The result is an erosion of the liturgical calendar with its rhythms grounded in the Incarnation and the Paschal Mystery of Christ's death and rising. Regarded from a constructive point of view, "the liturgy of the word is evocation and confirmation of faith, leading to faithful participation in the sacramental mystery."[9]

Option B
Sacrament overrides Word

The most extensive eclipse of proclamation within the Sunday service of Western Christianity is found in the general situation of the medieval era. The factors that contributed to this long decay of preaching, according to Reginald Fuller, involved "mass conversions, the multiplication of presbyterial masses, the decay in educational standards, the Western development of low mass" which led to a condition whereby "the sermon ceased to be a normal part of the liturgy."[10] While the factors cited by Fuller did, in fact, lead to decay in the state of proclamation during the medieval era, his conclusion is wildly overdrawn with regard to faithful liturgical preaching. As noted by James F. White, "The Middle Ages gives evidence of a series of revivals in the amount and quality of preaching" because, the development of lectionaries for mass in both the East and West were "of first importance."[11] It was at that time that the pericopes for each liturgical occasion—Sunday or special feast—came to be aligned with the propers for these respective masses. This early medieval organization of the liturgical texts served as an important foundation for the later developments and reforms of preaching in the West.

The eleventh and twelfth centuries in the Western Church were a period of renewed interest in biblical interpretation and in homiletic reflection. Guilbert of Nogent (c. 1055–1124) appended to his commentary on Genesis a work he titled, "A Book About the Way a Sermon Ought to be Given."[12] The homiletical supplement to his commentary represented, according to O. C. Edwards, Jr., "the first new homiletics textbook since Augustine's *De doctrina christiana*."[13] About one century later, Alan of Lille (c.1117–c.1202) produced yet another textbook on preaching, *The Art of Preaching*.[14] Topics covered in Alan's text included an extended definition of preaching ("an open and public instruction in faith and behavior, whose purpose is the forming of [persons]; it derives from the path of reason and from the fountainhead of the authorities"[15]). Alan then ranged through other core issues of homiletics including sermonic form, considerations of rhetoric, and the character of the preacher.

The center of gravity of this renewed emphasis on preaching and on the art of preaching was found in the monasteries, and the "greatest practitioner" of early medieval preachers was Bernard of Clairvaux (1090-1153). Within Bernard's remarkable corpus of homiletic writings and collected sermons, many of the latter are published versions of the homilies he preached at the liturgies of the hours at Clairvaux and elsewhere, along with liturgical homilies based on the lessons of the calendar.[16] Regarding the next two hundred years of the medieval era, rather than the condition depicted by Fuller in which the homily almost ceased to exist within the liturgical setting, the thirteenth and fourteenth centuries saw a remarkable blooming of interest in preaching as well as in the recently awakened field of homiletics. At the heart of this "explosion"[17] of preaching was the emergence of the two core mendicant orders, the Franciscans (founded in 1209) and the Dominicans (founded in 1215).

Especially for the latter friars, the Dominicans, the emergence of the universities provided a new resource for educating preachers in the West. In a related development, O. C. Edwards, Jr. notes the dramatic rise in urban centers as a new context for the evangelical preaching ministries of these mendicants. Toward the latter portion of this high medieval era, the "university" or "scholastic" sermon came to dominate among the better trained preachers, a highly organized, topical scheme of sermon organization that merited the designation of "artistic sermon."[18] However, at the parish level, preachers mostly left the tree-shaped organization of their homilies for the scholastic-minded and turned to the newly burgeoning printed resources for preaching (the fourteenth century versions of our internet homily resources!). To be sure, Reginald Fuller's assessment of medieval preaching in the West is applicable within the daily masses said by most priests outside the monasteries, and in numerous parish settings as well. It is among these liturgical settings that the Service of the Word became seriously diminished in relation to the Service of the Table.

If the medieval diminishment of proclamation distorted the full liturgy of Word and Sacrament, the severely reduced frequency of the Eucharist in many Protestant contexts also resulted in the divorce of Word and Sacrament. Among many traditions (Methodist, Presbyterian, and even Lutheran churches for example) when Holy Communion is observed, the preacher often shifts from a biblically grounded kerygmatic and prophetic word to a "Communion meditation." Thus, when the sacrament was celebrated, the Word was not proclaimed! In its place was a fond rumination on the Lord's Supper that was topically shaped, mostly lacking a Scriptural basis. The practice continues today, even within congregations of the Wesleyan, Lutheran, and Reformed traditions.[19] The contours of such Communion meditations can be easily discerned through an internet search of that category. Several characteristics seem to be rather persistent across a diverse span of ecclesial traditions.

Many such Communion meditations, for example, address the individual in her or his own solitary spiritual condition. To be sure, some of the meditations posted online do turn to Scripture for images of life together in Christ. However, a significant percentage of the Communion meditations, ironically, bypass the Communion shared within the Body of Christ as the one loaf is broken and shared. The Apostle Paul's affirmation in 1 Cor.

10:16-17 regarding the mystery of our being the one body in Christ as we share the one bread is lost within many such Communion meditations.[20]

Additionally, many online Communion meditations seem to harken back to a time when the Service of the Table was shaped by the themes of Christ's atoning work for his people and the people's profound unworthiness. The liturgical ellipsis embodied in the sacrament prior to the Second Vatican Council, and the reforms following it, tended to orbit around the atoning work of Christ at Calvary and the penitential words and actions of the worshippers. In the Methodist Ritual prior to the Eucharistic reforms of the 1992 *Book of Worship*, for example, the only vestige of thanksgiving in the Communion rite was the one statement in the Sursum Corda, "Let us give thanks unto the Lord."[21] Many Communion meditations seem stuck within this pre-conciliar era of the non-eucharistic Eucharist.

Finally, it is striking how closely many Communion meditations mirror the difficulties encountered in "children's sermons." In addition to the shared affinity for thematic orientation, a number of Communion meditations trade on the same sort of mega-stories that are to be found in so many children's sermons. When such a large illustration is deployed in either format, the text of the talk no longer derives from Scripture, but becomes that of the mega-story. In both contexts—the Communion meditation and the children's sermon—the story aims at some analogy with Jesus or, more generically, with God. So Jesus becomes a children's book hero or God's grace is equated with the Marshall Plan following World War Two.[22] In all of these retreats from proclamation, it would appear at first glance that the Service of Holy Communion has intruded back into the Service of the Word in inappropriate ways. What has really transpired, however, is that the inherent role of the sermon in leading the assembly to join all creation in thanks and praise and the breaking of bread has been thwarted. Oddly, the Communion meditation may wind up serving more as an obstacle to the Table than a vehicle toward the Holy Meal.

Option C
Finding the Balance:
Word and Sacrament in Dynamic Relationship

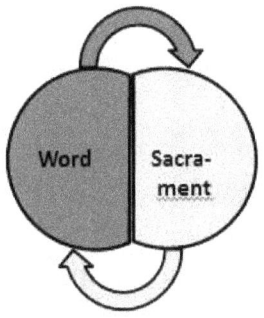

The relationship between the sermon and the Eucharistic celebration involves an on-going interplay between the two centers of the Sunday liturgy. The Word is heard and proclaimed and the community is fed; the Word does not return empty as it is faithfully proclaimed and the risen Christ "will give to all the faithful his own self for heavenly food."[23] One direction of this interplay between the sermon and the Eucharist is that the former is preached in order that the assembly may have sufficient virtue and readiness to enter into the mystery of the Holy Meal. Put simply, the preaching of the Word has as one of its solemn roles the shaping of a people who eagerly and knowingly come to the Table to meet the Christ who is proclaimed. Wallace states this liturgical role of the homily as follows:

> The homily prepares the community for what is about to occur, evoking the faith of those gathered so that the prayers and hymns of the rite truly become those of the community and the ritual action expressed in the rite is affirmed by the body of Christ here present.[24]

The homily, then, serves as a vehicle by which the community of faith will even more faithfully engage in the mysteries of the sacrament, and, thereby, the entire sweep of the liturgical celebration will more fully prepare the assembly for their work in the world.

This liturgical function of preaching thus extends to its missional function; the gifts of the Spirit serve to both build up the body of Christ and to equip the community in Christ for its ministry in the world (see Eph. 4:11-13). The statement of the National Conference of Catholic Bishops, *Fulfilled in Your Hearing*, summarizes this central function of the liturgical homily by pointing to its sacramental outcome: the Word is to be preached in such a way that the hearers[25] will be able to say with faith and deepened conviction, "It is right to give him thanks and praise."[26]

This complementarity of Word and Sacrament is emphasized nicely in the United Methodist statement on Holy Communion, "This Holy Mystery:"

> Word and Table are not in competition; rather they complement each other so as to constitute a whole service of worship. Their separation diminishes the fullness of life in the Spirit offered to us through faith in Jesus Christ.[27]

However, the dynamics of preaching and the Holy Meal are not to be construed solely in this linear fashion (as we affirm that the former prepares the congregation for the Eucharistic celebration by deepening its faith and conviction). Rather, the Eucharistic Feast provides a rich and diverse context for the preacher related to its words, signs, and actions.[28] The assumption underlying this book is that the congregation's response to the question, "When did the preacher take seriously the Eucharistic context of the sermon?" will be "Oh, frequently, most all of the time!"

A Homiletical Mystagogy

The church's Trinitarian faith is embedded in the dynamics of Eucharistic praying and the words and actions of the sacrament speak to issues such as the environment, Christian life and work, the difference between orthodoxy and "bad religion," as well as numerous other foci of theology and Christian practice. Given this assumption—that the Eucharist is the normative context for the sermon on the Lord's Day as well as a core resource for proclamation—the issue emerges as to a method whereby these implications may be explored. Fortunately there is a precedent in the tradition, as 4th and 5th century bishops engaged in mystagogical preaching to the newly baptized (focusing chiefly on instructions concerning the sacraments and sacramental life since these were not conveyed to the catechumens prior to their Christian initiation).

For Bishops Ambrose of Milan and Augustine of Hippo in the West and Cyril of Jerusalem and Theodore of Mopsuestia in the East, the pedagogy at these post-baptismal instructions was straightforward.[29] The various words and actions of the Eucharist were interpreted in sequence, and applied as regards the life together in Christ of these new babes in Christ. What was performed by these bishops was a mystagogy for discipleship. The lectures and homilies of these episcopal leaders of the church have remained seminal sources for Christian praxis and doctrine. Unfortunately, the early medieval era saw a turn toward an allegorizing of the actions and texts of the Mass. But almost a millennium has transpired now for the church to recover from those excesses.

This project, then, is shaped as a variation on the methodology of those 4th and 5th century bishops. The Eucharist's sequence of ritual acts and particular components will be interrogated for their implications for proclamation. We will begin at the Offertory and continue through the classic shape of the liturgy to the Communion itself. Along the way, we will both trace the origins and development of each respective element within the Eucharist and explore its implications for 21st century proclamation. This exploration of the roots of the various elements of the Eucharistic Rite along with their development, deformation (if any), and reform will be engaged in depth and with ecumenical expanse. Only by such serious engagement will those of us called to preach be capable of interrogating the words and actions of the Holy Meal with regard to their implications for the proclaiming of the gospel.

Our liturgical explorations, moreover, will be conducted primarily within the sacramental traditions of the Western Church. This is not to say that this project is intended to exclude sisters and brothers within Memorialist traditions[30] of the West. First, prior to the Sixteenth Century Reformation, the course of Eucharistic praying is our common heritage. Second, preachers within various Memorialist traditions do, in fact, share many of the elements of the Liturgy of the Table with Christians in sacramental communions. And finally, my prayer is that through such explorations of the church's traditions of Holy Communion, we will come both to preach toward the Table as well as find greater unity at that Supper.

What follows, then, is an offering of homiletical mystagogy. By this is meant the careful interpretation of the Eucharist, both in its component elements and in whole, designed to bring those of us called to preach into a more profound awareness of the Holy Meal's implications for our proclamation. The opposite side of the coin also obtains. If we find some homiletical pay dirt in our explorations of the anaphora and its component elements, we may conclude as well that some of these insights and reforms in the ministry of preaching will be left unattended as long as the sermon continues to be detached from its Eucharistic context. But even in traditions where the full Sunday service of Word and Table is the weekly norm, it may be salutary to explore more deeply the ways in which the Eucharist provides rich resources for the preaching of the gospel.

A homiletical mystagogy, then, involves a sequential engagement with the respective component aspects of the Eucharist—from Offertory to Communion—first with regard to issues of origin and development of each rite, and then with regard to the implications for the liturgical act of the sermon.[31] The process, of course, is grounded in a theological claim: It is the same Word that is read and heard in Scripture that is proclaimed in faithful preaching, and then is celebrated and experienced in the Meal. Small wonder, then, that such living, Spirit-filled connection is discovered among these liturgical encounters with the Word of God in Christ.

1

THE OFFERTORY

"Blessed are you, Lord God of all creation . . ." [32]

The youth group had a terrific time on Saturday baking all those loaves of bread to take to the homeless shelter downtown. But one of the loaves was set aside for another holy purpose. So at the Offertory the next morning, one of the youth and her parents present the bread and the wine as the congregation sings. It is time to give thanks.

Investigating the Rite

The Eucharistic offertory is the cardinal rite in the Sunday service of Word and Sacrament. That is to say, the offertory is the hinge (as N.T. Wright notes, "*cardo* in Latin means "hinge"[33]) between the liturgies of the Word and the Holy Meal. On one hand, the offertory sums up the various responses to proclamation—such as a creed, the intercessions, the Peace, and occasional rites such as Holy Baptism and baptism-related rites. On the other hand, the offertory sets up the very possibility for the Supper; at the heart of the offertory is the offering of the bread and wine. Hence, the offertory "belongs" to both feasts— the feast of the Word and that of the Eucharist. It is both the congregation's response to the proclaimed Word and the initial act in the four-fold action of the Eucharist. Since Gregory Dix's magisterial work, *The Shape of the Liturgy*,[34] various traditions have become familiar with Dix's argument regarding the relationship between the Dominical actions at the Upper Room and on other occasions (the Multiplication of Loaves and the breaking of bread with the risen Christ). Jesus first "takes" bread, which becomes embedded in the church's liturgy as the offertory, and gives "thanks," ritually expressed in the Eucharistic prayer. He then breaks the bread (the Fraction) and "gives" the bread and wine to the disciples (the sharing of the Bread and Cup). It is at the hinge of the Offertory in the Sunday worship of God's people in Christ that the proclamation of the Word has a crucial stake.

For about eight hundred years following the close of the New Testament, both the Eastern and Western church manifested the same ritual actions that constituted the Offertory. The faithful would bring various gifts to the Eucharist and present them at the Offertory—bread, wine, and even other foods as they were able. The deacons received the gifts following the sharing of the Peace, and bread and wine sufficient for the Eucharist was brought to the Altar Table while the surplus was set aside and delivered to the shut-ins, the sick, and the poor following the liturgy.

The practice is well in place by the time of the earliest core of the Apostolic Tradition in which it is noted that "Those to be baptized are to bring no vessel with them other than the one they must bring for the Eucharist, it is fitting that he who is worthy of it should make the offering."[35] Although Lucien Deiss interprets Hippolytus' instructions here as pertaining to a vessel to "carry the Eucharist home,"[36] the more obvious purpose of the dictate is that the catechumens have not been allowed to receive the Eucharist until their baptism at the Easter Vigil and therefore could not participate in the assembly's practice of bringing (offering) the Eucharistic Gifts until they had received Holy Baptism.

The essential role of the congregants at the Offertory, however, diminished and died off in the early medieval period in the West (the Eastern Church has retained the practice with no diminution to the present day). Several factors conspired in the medieval West to suppress the people's participation in the Eucharistic Offertory. First, as Michael McGuckian notes, the gradual shift to the use of unleavened bread—between the ninth and eleventh centuries—meant quite practically that "the people could no longer bring their own bread from home to offer at Mass, as they had done before."[37] Second, McGuckian adds that the multiplication of private Masses meant that the people were not even present for the Eucharist and therefore could not offer anything. With the rise of the missals that provided all texts and music, "Mass could now be celebrated by a priest with only a few people, or even with only a server."[38] Additionally, with the growth of monasticism, the notion of an assembly of the faithful became redefined in most every cathedral setting; no offering of the Eucharistic Gifts was expected from the people. They were now spectators at best.

In the medieval Mass, however, the Offertory did accrue significant expansion as regards the priest's prayers, the *Sucipe, sancte Pater* . . . ("Holy Father, almighty everlasting God, accept this unblemished sacrificial offering . . .") and addresses to the assembly, finally leading to the Secret prayers mostly offered in silence.[39] The dogma of the sacrifice of the Mass becomes embodied now in this increasingly complex series of rites that take the place of the offering of the people as an acceptable sacrifice. Adolf Adam notes that in the early medieval church, the Eucharistic gifts of bread and wine "were considered almost cultic sacrifices" in which the procession of the gifts "was also called a sacrificial procession. . . ."[40] Adam adds that the prayers and ceremonies that accrued to this "offertory procession," "could give the impression that we were already at this point in the Mass dealing with the transformed gifts."[41]

Actually, the gifts themselves had been transformed, not by any preliminary consecratory rite, but by an evolution of the bread deemed appropriate to be offered at the altar. From the earliest sources of the liturgy, the bread was made from grain "scattered upon the hills, and was gathered together and made one" (a metaphor in the Didache that became the petition to God for the unity of the church).[42] Both Eastern and Western churches used leavened bread at the Eucharist for almost a millennium, with Orthodoxy continuing in the practice. During the same historical period in which the people were losing their participation in the Offertory, the Eucharistic bread also suffered loss. However, the depreciation of the sign of the one loaf, gathered from the wheat of the field, became ever more serious. Adolf Adam summarizes the process:

> Over the centuries, the custom grew of baking increasingly thinner wafers that were more and more white. These wafers were imprinted with religious symbols using an iron implement. All of this has unfortunately led to a significant loss of the symbolic power of these hosts, since people can hardly recognize that they are still bread.[43]

Of course, it is all too evident that the efforts of the sixteenth century reformers or later conciliar reforms have not restored the Eucharistic practice of the early church. The very white wafers with religious imprints are used both by many Roman Catholic parishes (real baked, although still unleavened, loaves are to be found mainly within monastic communities) as well as numerous Protestant congregations. Moreover, some of the latter congregations have turned now to "Holy Communion Chicklets," hard tiny loaves the size of a grain of puffed rice. With reference to all of these moves away from the one loaf of early Christianity, the quip of one liturgical scholar best summarizes the outcome: "I have more trouble believing it is bread than believing it is the Body of Christ!"

Martin Luther was far less gracious in his attacks on the offertory and its ceremonies that, in his view, all amounted to works righteousness rather than grace and priestly sacrifice instead of covenant promise. In his commentary (1523) within his "An Order of Mass and Communion for the Church at Wittenburg," Luther savaged these perceived sacrificial accretions to the Mass.

> [T]hat utter abomination follows which forces all that precedes in the mass into its service and is, therefore, called the offertory. From here on almost everything smacks and savors of sacrifice. . . . Let us, therefore, repudiate everything that smacks of sacrifice, together with the entire canon and retain only that which is pure and holy, and so order our mass.[44]

Not only were the rites themselves to be excised from the Mass, but also a doctrine of priestly identity that cohered to this sacrificial "abomination." The offertory, for Luther, is to be purged of all that "smacks" of sacrifice and priestly offering which, he insists, is a blatant example of works rather than faith.

The Eucharistic reforms initiated by the Second Vatican Council of the Roman Catholic Church and, subsequently by various Protestant communions, sought to move beyond the impasse of the sixteenth century while recovering practices and theological insights from the early church. The recently replaced Missal labeled the "Offertory" as "The Preparation of the Gifts," although the text of the presiding minister's prayer has received considerable criticism for its seeming retention of the notion of priestly sacrifice at the offertory.[45]

Other Western communions also emphasize the core function of the offertory as the offering and preparation of the Eucharistic gifts. The Episcopal *Book of Common Prayer* (1979), for example, provides a rubric indicating that "Representatives of the congregation bring the people's offerings of bread and wine, and money and other gifts, to the deacon or celebrant."[46] An analogous rubric in the United Methodist *Service of Word and Table* directs that, "The bread and wine are brought by representatives of the people to the Lord's table with the other gifts, or uncovered if already in place."[47] The *Lutheran Book of Worship* provided the most succinct rubrical direction: "The OFFERING is received as the Lord's table is prepared."[48] However, *Evangelical Lutheran Worship* expands the directive somewhat to add that the Offering "is gathered for the mission of the church, including the care of those in need."[49] None of these Protestant liturgies retain any notion of sacrificial offering or priestly sacrifice, but, once the children of the Reformers (including the Anglican liturgical tradition) mostly lost the practice of the Lord's Supper on the Lord's Day, the offertory was diminished to a monetary collection.

This was especially true in those churches influenced by nineteenth century revivalism, when, coupled with infrequent Communion, the offering was relocated from its "cardinal" position and placed now within the "opening exercises" leading the congregation to the sermon and the invitation. Ironically, this Protestant non-eucharistic offertory in many congregations has come to acquire as much pomp and circumstance as the medieval rite. The minister, for example, will receive the offering and turn to the altar, extending his or her arms dramatically outstretched with the plates as the Doxology is sung. Luther would probably have thundered, "works righteousness!" if he witnessed such excess!

More recently, there has emerged a striking ecumenical consensus that the Eucharist in general, and the Offertory in particular, are intertwined with a theology of creation. What is offered at this hinge act of the Offertory involves in every respect the good gifts of creation; what is given thanks for in our Eucharistic praying, is grounded, literally, in our existence as human beings whose very existence comes from God. The joint Roman Catholic and United Methodist statement on Eucharist and Ecology, "Heaven and Earth are Full of Your Glory," grounds the relationship between the Holy Mystery of the Table and the mystery of creation in such conviction:

> Creation is God's *first* gift. Creation is the first sign of God's glory and God's love. For humans, the world is not simply a stage for human action; our relation to the world, to creation, is constitutive of our very identity as persons. In the Eucharist, we encounter the fullness of Christian revelation, the reality of existence as gift, for the gift of redemption includes the prior gift of creaturely existence.[50]

Given this foundational statement of the juxtaposition between creation and Eucharist, we may assemble several theses regarding the significance of the Offertory for a robust doctrine of creation. These include the following:

1. *Perfect gifts of Creation from God*—As is made explicit in both words and actions, what is presented at the Offertory are the good gifts of the creation, God's *first* acts of creation and expansive love. The psalms and the prophets proclaim the biblical witness that "the earth is the Lord's and the fullness thereof, the world and those that dwell therein" (Ps. 24:1, KJV). The Gifts of bread and wine are from God's creation and are offered to the

Creator by us human creatures, also of the earth. All of the creation is dependent upon God and at the Eucharist, all creation joins in praising and thanking its God. Various hymns and songs on the Eucharist continue to witness to this thanks for creation as well as thanksgiving with all creation to our God. Composer Ruth Duck expresses the first pole of this dialectic:

> Give thanks to the Source who brings forth earth's goodness;
> The bread on our table, the fruit of the vine.
> Give thanks to the Love who welcomes the wand'ring,
> Invents new beginnings and calls us to dine.[51]

The other pole is creation's response to the goodness of the Source, the Creator of all that is. All creation praises its God, including those "sea monsters" as well as "wild animals and all cattle, creeping things and flying birds" (Ps. 148:7-8). All creation praises the Lord.

2. *Imperfect gifts of creation to God*—At the offertory, the Eucharistic Gifts of bread and wine, then, are the good gifts of creation, offered again to their creator. But the sacrament of the Table is different than that of Holy Baptism as regards the sacramental signs. Water, as has been frequently noted,[52] is received from the creation; it is brought to the font in its natural state. Bread and wine are different. We do not process wheat grain and bunches of grapes at the Offertory. Rather, these gifts of creation are already the end result of human agricultural expertise and labor. Both the fruit of the vine and the seed of the stalk of wheat have been domesticated over innumerable generations and each is brought to harvest after long

seasons of maturation and careful tending. Then, the processes that follow the harvest involve human industry and careful sequences of preparation until the bread and the wine are readied and presented at the Altar Table. Once more, the Joint statement of the Roman Catholic and United Methodist team exploring Eucharist and ecology puts it nicely:

> In the Eucharist, we use manufactured signs, bread and wine. By using bread and wine we revere both creation and human work. Bread and wine are blessed not only because they are taken from the earth, but also because they are the work of human hands.[53]

Of course, the work of human industry represented in the Eucharistic Gifts may be tainted by post-Edenic corruption as well as blessed by righteous and joyful enterprise. On one hand, most of us have known a bread baker, perhaps in our own family, whose special delight is in the creation of a wonderful loaf of bread fresh from the oven. Others of us have had our appreciation for certain wines deepened by a vintner whose joy and wine-making savvy seem to overflow from that person. At best, the gifts of these bakers and vintners should be those offered for the Holy Meal. On the other hand, the factory-like agricultural practices that abound in North America may be represented in the very Gifts we offer to the Table. "Wheat and grapes may come from oppressive agricultural practices," note the Roman Catholic and United Methodists![54] Issues of social justice are co-mingled with the "gifts of finest wheat."[55]

3. *Sacraments as loci for all Creation's gifts*—A widely held assessment is that the creation is in some manner or other "sacramental." That is, it reflects the hand of the One who created all there is. "The heavens are telling the glory of God," proclaims the Psalm (19:1). Thus, the sacramental quality of creation is lodged in its ability to point toward its Creator, to attest to the goodness, the sense of order, and the expansiveness of God's creative work. However, there are also numerous post-moderns for whom the universe certainly evokes curiosity and even awe, but in no sense does it point toward any creator beyond itself and its own generative dynamics. So, for example, physicist Stephen Hawking intensely explores questions as to the origin and destiny of the universe, but explicitly rejects any need for a God at all by way of explanation.[56] Put simply, the status of the universe as "creation" is ambiguous, especially in a postmodern context. Some will, with Hawking and others, insist that the universe will not yield any status as creation wrought by a Creator, while on the other hand, many faithful still proclaim that "the heavens are telling the glory of God"(Ps. 19:1a). Perhaps the usual line of reasoning as regards creation and Eucharist needs to be inverted. What if sacramental practice is the primary location for a vigorous theology of creation—thus taking seriously the *"lex orandi, lex credendi"* (the rule of prayer leads to the rule of belief) dictum? Or, more directly, what if sacramental practice and growth in faith are preconditions to a mature theology of creation? The sacraments model the right use of creation; the Gifts reflect the Giver of all the good gifts of creation. A sacramental lens provides the best optics for viewing the universe as the creation.[57]

Homiletical Implications

When proclamation is juxtaposed with the Eucharistic offering, several implications embedded in the latter are evident for the former. When the sermon is preached within the full Sunday Service of Word and Sacrament, it anticipates this essential "hinge event" at which the people offer bread and wine and their other gifts. Most directly, this interplay of sermon and offering strongly undergirds the preacher's role in making an offering to the Lord when the Word is proclaimed. At the Offertory, the congregation—including the preacher—offers their gifts for the Holy Meal. Following the readings from Scripture, it is time for the preacher to offer her or his "gift" of the homily, the sermon. Being a gift of the preacher, the implication is clear that an unattributed first person illustration "borrowed" from somewhere on the internet or, indeed, a "borrowed" entire sermon nullifies this sense of offering. The preacher, rather, offers a word that should have the aroma of a freshly baked loaf of bread presented by a family in the congregation. No stale sermon measures up to this homiletical offering!

Much of contemporary homiletics focus on the sermon as an address *to* the congregation. A preacher will muse and struggle with what needs to be said to the assembly. However, there is more. The inductive method of Fred Craddock, for example, is grounded in an empathic participation in the experiences of the congregation. "One preaches *in* and *out of* as well as *to* that community."[58] Preacher-scholars interested in rhetoric will carefully note what kinds of pulpit speech will be heard by the congregation and which ways of speaking will simply not be retained in the congregational consciousness.[59]

Other commentators will glean hearer response criticism for cues as to how best to shape the sermon.[60] Moreover, some homileticians have pushed the significance of the listeners beyond that of "the hearers." In the "roundtable church," the congregation is a vital participant in the birthing of the sermon itself.[61] In all of these approaches, to some degree or other, the sermon's gestation and proclamation involve a mutuality and synergy between preacher and congregation. Just as at the Eucharist, the congregation offers the gifts which will be sanctified and received, so in the preparation and delivery of the sermon, the assembly's gifts are received and woven into the sermon. The juxtaposition here is striking and evident.

Rooted in a theology of creation, the presentation of the Eucharistic Gifts offers the preacher homiletical resources regarding both sign and act. The presentation of the Gifts offers rich pastoral and homiletical opportunities. For example, if families, including children, are chosen and trained for this important lay ministry, the homilist is provided with a powerful counterpoint to the disciples' attempt to prevent the children from coming to Jesus (Mark 10:13-16). This liturgical action by children as well as adults at the Offertory is then reinforced when the children later join with the other faithful in coming to receive Holy Communion.

A deep pastoral note is also sounded in these complementary liturgical actions of presenting the Gifts and receiving the Gifts at Communion. Once anyone is invited to serve in the rite of the presentation of the Gifts, that member of the household of faith is thereby welcomed to the Table along with the other members of the assembly. The "marvelous exchange"[62] of which St. Augustine spoke is rooted in the dual procession of the faithful: representatives of the laity offer the

Gifts to the Table; the entire assembly then comes to the Table and receives the feast of Holy Communion. Such an "exchange"—from Offertory to Communion—may serve as a powerful image of the ways in which our own meager gifts are accepted and hallowed by Christ.

The image of the Eucharistic bread is of singular importance as the homilist preaches through the Year of Grace. The Synoptic accounts of the Miraculous Feedings all provide the opportunity for the preacher to invite the congregation to join in the abundance of the feast the Lord offers to the hungry. An ironic twist in Mark 8:14-21, following the second feeding of a crowd, also invites the preacher to focus the attention of the assembly on the Eucharistic bread. In this pericope, the disciples, having just assisted Jesus in feeding the four thousand in the wilderness, are filled with anxiety on the sea crossing which follows. "They had only one loaf with them in the boat" (Mark 8:14). An anxious congregation can now be reminded that they, too, have only one loaf in their ship of the church—Jesus the Lord.

The Johannine account of the Miraculous Feeding, as we would expect, offers several distinctive features beyond those in the Synoptic accounts. The missional implications of the Eucharist—through which the congregation is repeatedly reminded of its ministry of feeding the hungry as it has been fed at the Holy Meal—is now nicely inverted. Here, in John 6:1-14, Andrew comes to Jesus and tells him, "There is a boy here who has five barley loaves and two fish," adding "But what are they among so many people" (John 6:9). Wes Howard Brook comments that, "The little boy's supplies are both bountiful for one his age and ridiculously small."[63] Howard Brooks pushes his insight more deeply: "The detail that the loaves are 'barley' emphasizes the poverty of the crowd, as this kind of bread was even cheaper than the more common wheat."[64]

The Johannine account of the Miraculous Feeding turns our usual perception as to who is the helper and who is the needy one upside down. In this respect, the narrative in John 6 functions much like the Parable of the Good Samaritan (Luke 10:25-37). The poor little boy with the barley loaves is revealed as the one who possesses the virtues of grace and compassion for others. A sermon on this text, preached at the Eucharist will explore this reversal of the helper and the needy; we in the congregation are those in need and the bread of the poor is offered to us with generosity.[65]

Conclusion

The initial, and most basic observation regarding the interplay of Offertory and proclamation is that these rich and evocative resources for preaching are subverted if the signs and action of the Eucharistic offering are distorted, or simply non-existent. In churches where a "preaching service" allows only for a money collection at the Offertory, the deep insights of the United Methodist and Roman Catholic bishops' statement on Eucharist and ecology are denied to the preacher and to the congregation. One of the rich sacramental resources for proclamation is denied to the preacher by an on-going absence of the Eucharistic offering within the preaching service. However, a diminishment of the Offertory persists in traditions where the practice at Holy Communion is to have the bread and cup already prepared on the Table.

Offertory, in this usage, is constrained only to the act of uncovering the elements by, typically, the presiding minister. What is lost by such enduring Protestant practice is the vital engagement within the early church of the assembly's active participation in the Eucharistic offering. What is lost homiletically are images of the active ministry of the laity in the preparation and presentation of the Gifts. For example, the connection of the sign act of members of the community of faith presenting the Eucharistic Gifts and those same lay persons then being invited to receive the blessed and broken Gifts at Communion continues the mystery that St. Augustine termed "the marvelous exchange."

A further irony emerges within United Methodist churches where the "open Communion table" emphasis prevails. In many of the same parishes the laity have little or no role in the offering of those Gifts. The marvelous exchange is subverted. The marvelous exchange is subverted. The hope, however, is that preachers will be renewed in their ministry of proclamation as the Eucharistic offering is restored within the Sunday Service of Word and Sacrament. The Offertory is the cardinal event that links Word and Table together.

2

THE SURSUM CORDA

"Lift up your hearts" ⁶⁶

As a child, I was drawn into the mystery of the Service of Holy Communion in my Methodist Church (though not actually being invited to commune until my later Rite of Confirmation). Four times a year an elder in the church would visit our country parish in Maryland and preside at the Lord's Supper. The difference between the language and style of prayer of the other forty-eight or so Sundays of the year and those of the Communion Service were strikingly apparent even in my childhood. But what else I remember was how the call to thanksgiving in the dialogue I later came to know as the Sursum Corda led not to thanks, but to a solemn meditation upon the work of Christ on the Cross and to a further prayer that assigned us with the dogs under the Lord's Table, completely unworthy "so much as to gather up the crumbs."⁶⁷ What echoed from ancient Eucharistic praying led no longer to a Great Thanksgiving, but to a Service of Penance instead.

Investigating the Rite

Early evidence for the opening dialogue of the Eucharistic Prayer is provided in the *Apostolic Tradition*.⁶⁸ The Prayer of Thanksgiving for the ordination of a bishop—one of two such prayers Hippolytus relates—begins in a familiar way:

> And when he has been made bishop, all shall offer the kiss of peace, greeting him because he has been made

worthy. Then the deacons shall present the offering to him; and he, laying his hands on it with all the presbytery, shall give thanks, saying:

> The Lord be with you;
> *And all shall say:*
> **And with your spirit.**
> Up with your hearts.
> **We have them with the Lord.**
> Let us give thanks to the Lord.
> **It is fitting and right.**[69]

While the Prayer lacks a Sanctus and any notable Preface, most church traditions in East and West have continued the practice of this opening dialogue between presider and people. The Sursum Corda calls both the assembly and presiding minister to lift up their hearts and give thanks and praise, the act of making Eucharist (giving thanks). Ironically, even when most any word of thanks was lost to the Prayer of Consecration, for example, in the Anglican and Methodist traditions, the Sursum Corda remained at its usual location. Its call to thanksgiving, oddly, was ignored in favor of a consecratory prayer focusing chiefly on the atoning work of Christ and the acknowledgement of the congregants' sinfulness. The reforms of the Eucharist following the Second Vatican Council have both retained the Sursum Corda as the opening dialogue of the Prayer and, more importantly, restored the Prayer's modality of thanksgiving. Once again in the Western Church, coherence has been recovered between the call to thanks and the Prayer of Thanksgiving.

A rarely noticed dynamic is at work within the Sursum Corda as the presiding minister at the Table extends the invitation, "Let us give thanks to the Lord." The people then respond, "It is right to give God thanks and praise." There is embodied in this couplet a subtle, but real, transaction between priest and assembly whereby the former extends an invitation which is then ratified by the assembly. In fact, when the Sursum Corda's dialogue is begun, a caution should register in the mind of the presider: "If God's people do not concur with my invitation to give thanks and praise, I must not continue in the Prayer." The final line of the dialogue expresses the authorization of the assembly for the presiding minister to proceed by offering thanks and praise. Reflecting on call and response within the African American sermon itself, Evans Crawford's reflection also obtains for the dialogical opening of the Eucharistic Prayer:

> The call and response or sharing of the proclamation of the word by the people was an effective expression of the priesthood of the entire group in the presence of God.[70]

Now a more intimate juxtaposition is revealed, that between presiding minister and the assembled faithful.

Whereas older Roman Catholic and Reformation polemics sought to locate "priesthood" in one or the other of the parties—priest or people—the Sursum Corda's deep interchange is really between priest and priestly people of God. The latter, the assembly, by completing the quartet of the dialogue with the words "It is right to give God thanks and praise" commends two priestly liturgical functions to the presider. The minister at the Table is acknowledged as one set apart to lead the Prayer on behalf of the congregation and he or she is commended to offer the Prayer by way of a poetics of thanksgiving. Of course, as the World Council of Churches has proclaimed, "It is Christ who invites to the meal and who presides at it."[71] Yet at the outset of Eucharistic praying an intimate exchange of liturgical action and authority resides in the depths of the Dialogue. No wonder presider and people should be about a lively antiphonal call to thanks and praise.[72]

Homiletical Implications

Thus, the liturgical journey leads from the Word to the Table by way of the Dialogue. There is, we remain convinced, a symbiosis between the proclamation of the Word and the celebrating of the Eucharist, and this interplay is significant in its liturgical sequence and in detail. From the perspective of an interest in proclamation at the full Service of Word and Table, the Sursum Corda is a reminder of the dialogical quality of the preaching of the Word. The Word goes out and does not return empty (Isa. 55:11). God's people in Christ have an "*antwort*," in German, a "word back."

Of course, this preaching-as-dialogue has been a hallmark of African American preaching since the days when those in bondage in the South were invited to "Steal Away to Jesus." Melva Wilson Costen writes of the importance of call and response in slave worship that reflects its African heritage in general and its orality in particular. Regarding the preaching in both contemporary African American worship and that of the slave church brush arbors or "praise houses," she says, "Dialogical communication skillfully takes place between preacher and the community, *thus both must listen ardently to the other* (italics mine)."[73]

There is an antiphonal rhetoric in the DNA of African American preaching that is essential to its "homiletical musicality."[74] The Sursum Corda is also grounded in the dynamics of an oral culture and its "antiphonality."[75] No wonder, then, that the Sursum Corda, calling priest and people to give thanks, was chanted in the ancient church. It, too, was grounded in an oral liturgical musicality. Further, the call and response pattern in African American preaching and worship is an expression of the relationship between a loving and liberating God and a people called into covenant. As Evans Crawford notes, the sound of this homiletical musicality "was a celebration of the richness of the life in Christ, the wonder of having life more fully, a wonder touched off by the hum thought of the preacher."[76]

With confidence in the grace and power of the Father of the Lord Jesus, early Christians engaged in a dialogue with their presiding minister. That the Great Thanksgiving opens in an antiphonal liturgical act is both rhetorically important and theologically instructive. The liturgical act of proclamation, too, is at its depth an antiphon between preacher and people. It is a dialogical communication in which both ardently listen to each other, forging the course of the sermon as they proceed. Most obviously, then, as we consider the character of preaching that calls God's people to the Holy Meal, the former will have a dialogical quality of its own. The call and response pattern within African American preaching and worship has been noted and praised. But others now have taken upon themselves the challenge of calling preachers to be in partnership with their listeners as well.

A prophetic voice for this new hearing of the Good News, Fred Craddock's critique of deductive preaching, with its points and propositions, was argued precisely at this point. It was "a most unnatural mode of communication, unless, of course, one presupposes passive listeners who accept the right or authority of the speaker to state conclusions which he then applies to their faith and life." [77] Craddock then adds his memorable image to this critique: There is "no listening by the speaker, no contributing by the hearer. . . . If the congregation is on the team, it is as javelin catcher."[78] David Cunningham provides a succinct summary of preaching that is hobbled by this lack of dialogue with the hearers. He states that the rhetoric of the sermon is "incomplete without the active participation of those who *receive* revelation."[79]

Sadly, all too many examples of "the congregation as javelin catcher" homiletical monologues are to be heard; their number is legion. Whether in thundering "prophetic" social pronouncements of some liberal or conservative preachers, the delivery from the pulpit of some self-help or church growth verities, promotional appeals for denominational "special days" or the "lectures" handing out the ideology of some mega-church, the absence of an active participation by the listener is a common denominator of them all.[80]

One further interplay calls for exploration with regard to the Sursum Corda and the sermon. If the latter has become for the assembly an incarnation of the Word experienced in ardent co-listening, then what follows (the Dialogue) will become a thankful response. This response echoes that of a biblical people throughout the biblical narrative. As noted by Guerric DeBona, one account of this dynamic of the Word being proclaimed with a response of communal thanksgiving is found in the Book of Nehemiah when the people of Jerusalem respond to Nehemiah's words by going forth "to eat and drink and send portions and to make great rejoicing, because they had understood the words that were declared to them" (Neh. 8:12). DeBona continues,

> The people of God participate in God's saving work even as they hear and understand; they give praise and thanksgiving, and so at the Preface Dialogue in the Eucharistic liturgy the president of the assembly invites the hearers to "lift up your hearts." That is what is "truly right" because "our desire to thank you is itself your gift."

> If the homily has been a life-giving bridge from Word into sacrament—naming the wonderful works of God—then the people have reason to rejoice.[81]

The gift, and consequent challenge, of preaching at the full Sunday service of Word and sacrament, then, includes this incarnational issue: Has the proclamation of the Word so filled the listeners with joyful praise that they are urgently looking forward to lifting up their hearts in thanksgiving at the Holy Meal? Put simply, the Eucharistic Dialogue expects that the Good News has become enfleshed in the sermon and its own dialogical proclamation.

Conclusion

The Sursum Corda is both the dialogical entryway to the Great Thanksgiving and embodies fruitful resources for proclamation. Several of these resources for the preacher are now evident. First, the Sursum Corda grounds the dialogical character of faithful preaching. Whether by way of vocal feedback or unspoken "feelback," the congregation is a partner in the liturgical act of the sermon. Second, the Dialogue emphasizes the role of the assembly in shaping the Word that will be proclaimed. The lived experience of the congregation and its ongoing life and work are essential to the formation of sermons that are pastoral, evangelical, and prophetic. Finally, implied in this call to thanksgiving is a clear word to the preacher: "Proclaim the Good News, naming grace and inviting joyful discipleship."

3

THE PREFACE

"It is very meet, right, and our bounden duty..." [82]

How the presiding minister will offer the Great Thanksgiving is usually discerned by how the opening sentence of the Preface is embodied and spoken. Will he get it garbled, even while grasping the worship book in both hands, or will she, unencumbered from holding any text, lift up her arms and voice, intensifying the call to give God all thanks and praise? Will the presider mumble the words or begin the Eucharistic praying in a sweet and unctuous manner far removed from the meaning and intent of the Prayer. All you need, most of the time, is a careful attention to the first line of the Preface to learn whether the presider will be "strong, loving, and wise"[83] *or simply confused, shy, and awkward.*

Investigating the Rite

The single most critical point of clarification at the outset is to understand that the Preface—that liturgical material bookended by the conclusion of the Dialogue and the beginning of the Sanctus—is not a preface. That is, this initial portion of the Prayer over the Gifts by the presiding minister is not a preface *to* the Prayer but the opening sequence *of* the Prayer. In fact, prior to the insertion of the Sanctus within the Eucharistic Prayer—a development first made in the East and later in the West—the Preface could be discerned as that opening material following the Sursum Corda embodying the dynamics of thanksgiving.

In this respect, the Preface may have its origins in the opening portion of the tripartite Jewish after-meal prayer, the berakah. The initial section of the berakah focused on a joyful thanksgiving to God for the gifts of creation and for covenant.[84] Once the Sanctus was located within the seam between the first and second sections of the anaphora, the Roman rite began to speak of this opening section in Latin as *praefactio*, which "does not mean a preliminary, but a proclamation."[85] Lamentably, the title was misunderstood and the Canon itself (only in the West) was increasingly thought to consist of the Post-Sanctus.

Once this notion of "*praefactio*" as "preface" gained currency, it was reinforced in the West by such practices as differing stances for each, the assembly standing for the Preface and kneeling for the Post-Sanctus. The Continental Reformers of the Sixteenth Century simply deleted the Preface entirely, typically beginning the prayer with the Words of Institution. The standard practice among American Methodists was for the minister, "facing the Lord's Table" to say two sentences for a Preface, the first responding to the last line of the Dialogue ("It is meet right, and our bounden duty . . .") and the second introducing the Sanctus ("Therefore with angels and archangels, . . .")[86]

Following the reforms of the Second Vatican Council of the Roman Catholic Church, the first three core Eucharistic Prayers of the Mass were provided with numerous Proper Preface options (numbering into the dozens) which related to various seasons, festivals and occasions. Eucharistic Prayer IV, based upon an Eastern pattern, was the only one to provide an invariable preface. The further revisions of the New Roman Missal of 2011 provided for over eighty prefaces, again specified for various days and festivals within the temporal and sanctoral calendars, as well as other pastoral and liturgical occasions.

Many begin with an opening phrase that essentially repeats and intensifies the last line of the Dialogue. The Tridentine Latin Mass expressed this intensification and repetition simply:

> Response: *Dignum et justum est.* ("It is meet and just")
> Priest: *Vere dignum et justum est, Aequum et salutare,*
>   ("It is truly meet and just, right and profitable...")[87]

Now, in the Missal of 2011, many of the prefaces open with the following:

> It is truly right and just, our duty and our salvation, always and everywhere to give you thanks, Lord, holy Father, almighty and eternal God, through Christ our Lord.[88]

Generally, then, a proper preface retains the opening that repeats and intensifies the last line of the Dialogue and closes with a rather standard introduction to the Sanctus. However, the material sandwiched between the opening and closing lines is "proper" to an occasion, day, or season and is therefore noted, not only by its essential brevity, but also by its changeableness, its variability. For example, in the Church of England's *Common Worship*, the Proper Preface for Trinity Sunday is as follows:

> And now we give you thanks because you have revealed the glory of your eternal fellowship of love with your Son and with the Holy Spirit, three persons equal in majesty, undivided in splendor, yet one God, ever to be worshipped and adored.[89]

Within this brief proper preface, we note qualities that obtain for most prefaces as well as elements that are distinctive to the occasion (in this case, Trinity Sunday). With reference to the enduring qualities, it is particularly evident in this Preface that it along with the entirety of the Eucharistic Prayer is addressed to the First Person of the Trinity. The reference to "your Son and the Holy Spirit" is a carefully worded phrase retaining this address to the Father.

Another enduring quality of any preface conforming to the Western Church tradition is that it is offered by the presiding minister at the Table in concert with the entire people.[90] Certain prayers at the Offertory within Western tradition are shaped to express the first-person petitions of the presider/priest. (Hence, the *"Suscipe, sancte Pater, . . ."* of the Tridentine Mass of the Roman Catholic Church.) However, the preface within a Eucharistic Prayer, though offered by the presider, is offered on behalf of the whole assembly and the prayer is consistently in the plural "we."

On the other hand, the variable foci of the proper preface are immediately evident. A Eucharistic Prayer beginning with this proper, expressing the mystery of the Holy Trinity, will not be offered, say, on the First Sunday of Advent or on All Saints. There is no question as to the particular day or occasion to which this prayer is "proper." One interesting note, though, is the way in which the church has seen the applicability of a particular proper to another occasion. So, for example, in the resource published by the Anglican Church of Canada for the propers of the liturgical year, the prefaces for most of those commemorated as saints are specified as: *"Preface of an Apostle;" "Preface of a Martyr;"* or, simply, *"Preface of a Saint."* However, when the occasion is specific, such as "The Birth of Saint John the Baptist" (June 24), the *"Preface of Advent"* becomes the proper preface of the Eucharistic Prayer.[91] In United Methodist Eucharistic praying, one text suffices for "All Saints and Memorial Occasions." If a biblical saint was to be recalled and celebrated, for example, a different preface is not available to provide focus to that occasion. Rather, a version of the ancient diptychs is located within the Post-Sanctus and the saint would be memorialized there.[92] This feature of some Eucharistic Prayers in the early church was the location where brief intercessions were made or specific saints were recalled and celebrated. The practice continues in some Western rites.

Most of the Western traditions which inherited the variable preface organization of the Eucharistic Prayer, including the Anglican, Lutheran, Presbyterian, and Methodist communions, also paralleled the Roman Catholic reforms after the Second Vatican Council. For example, the Episcopal Church provided for an increased number of Proper Prefaces in the *Book of Common Prayer* revision of 1979. The Episcopal Church also continues to offer occasional supplemental liturgical resources and the 1998 publication, *Enriching Our Worship*, provides three additional Eucharistic prayers, each containing distinctive prefaces.[93]

Lutheran revisions of the Eucharistic Prayer have followed similar trajectories. The *Lutheran Book of Worship*, 1978, provided two settings of the Sunday Service of Holy Communion. In both liturgies, the Sursum Corda is followed by the opening line of the preface with an accompanying rubric, "The preface appropriate to the day or season is sung or said."[94] In *Evangelical Lutheran Worship*, 2006, ten musical settings of Holy Communion are provided with Setting Two providing distinctive full texts of the Great Thanksgiving for "Advent— Epiphany of Our Lord" and "Ash Wednesday—Day of Pentecost."[95]

Along with other denominations during the 1970s and '80s, the United Methodist Church issued provisional liturgical texts for the Sunday Service as well as for the Service of Holy

Baptism and those for weddings and funerals. In 1980, the General Conference of the United Methodist Church approved the latest versions of these services for alternate use in local congregations (the Ritual of the 1965 Book of Worship remaining, for the time, in place along with that of the former Evangelical United Brethren Church). The final version of "Word and Table" along with the other services, was approved at the 1988 General Conference and then published in the *United Methodist Hymnal* and *The United Methodist Book of Worship*.

Throughout the series of revisions during the "test run" of the Sunday Service, the overall shape of the Sunday liturgy was fully in harmony with that of the broad ecumenical reforms begun by the Second Vatican Council. However, when the Eucharistic Prayer was examined, it was evident immediately that the United Methodist text had diverged from that of the Roman Catholic, Lutheran, Episcopal, and even the prior Methodist pattern. The Western practice of employing a proper preface for the various days, festivals, and occasions had been abandoned in favor of a through-composed prayer specific to each liturgical event. The preface was no longer the proper; rather, the entire Eucharistic Prayer became the proper. This shift in liturgical organization of the anaphora did not affect the opening and closing phrases of the United Methodist preface. All of these Great Thanksgiving propers began with a version of the familiar, repetitive, and intensifying statement following the last line of the Dialogue:

> It is right, and a good and joyful thing, always and everywhere to give thanks to you, Father Almighty, creator of heaven and earth.[96]

The final statement of the preface also followed ancient tradition, as well as the contemporary ecumenical practice, of providing a smooth segue to the Sanctus:

And so, with your people on earth and all the company of heaven we praise your name and join their unending hymn.[97]

However, between the opening and closing lines of the new United Methodist preface, the terse rhetoric of the other Western prefaces was loosened and the preface became more of a narrative of the paradigmatic events of covenant history, chiefly focused on those events related to God's covenant people Israel.

In this format, the narrative aspects of the Post-Sanctus focused mainly on the Incarnation of Jesus Christ and the Spirit's work in the church. Again, these narratives emphasized distinctive occasions and festivals both in the Preface and the Post-Sanctus. Numerous Eucharistic Prayers in their entirety, therefore, were needed to provide for the different "proper" occasions within the liturgical year and among various pastoral occasions.[98] The Roman Catholic Missal of 2011 provides both alternatives: Three of the Eucharistic Prayers follow the usage of the Proper Preface while Eucharistic Prayer IV—derived from Eastern traditions—is through-composed thereby obviating any variable Preface.[99]

These liturgical retrievals and reforms related to the expansion in proper preface texts included the development of a significant corpus related to days, festivals, and occasions. Also evident has been an unambiguous emphasis on a rhetoric of thanksgiving within these prefaces ecumenically. That venerable resource, *The Catholic Encyclopedia*, noted that two qualities distinguished the earliest extant prefaces in the Latin Church, their "shortness and changeableness."[100] We may also add a third quality, that of the sequential logic of the texts. The opening and closing lines of most any preface serve as predictable bookends, leading from the Dialogue and leading to the Sanctus. Sandwiched within these frames, the variable material focuses on the occasion, day, or festival. A sequential logic obtains within most every proper preface.

Homiletical Implications

Continuing a homiletical mystagogy, we will explore these three enduring qualities—brevity, variability, and sequential logic—of the Preface of the Eucharistic Prayer with regard to their implications for proclamation. Again, we are assuming an interplay between the qualities of the liturgical acts of the Eucharistic rites and the dynamics of the sermon. The three qualities resident within most every preface after the reforms of the liturgy include the succinct nature of the rite, its "changeableness," and its reliable pattern of sequential logic. Additionally, these lead to a question about the implications of lectionary use when viewed in relationship to these enduring qualities that have such important implications for the sermon.

1. *A compact, succinct content*—There are traditions, chiefly Roman Catholic and Anglican, in which the liturgical homily is typically marked by a brevity or "shortness." This emphasis on the "brief homily" is, in some ways, the outcome of teaching what the homily should not be. Such "definition by negation" is grounded, for these traditions, in a theological understanding of the gathered faithful at the Eucharist. *Fulfilled in Your Hearing* (FIYH) sets up one parameter for the liturgical homily this way: "The liturgical gathering is not primarily an educational assembly."[101] Moreover, the assembly gathered for Eucharist on the Lord's Day is not a group of non-baptized inquirers; neither is it a political party or a caucus for some ideological cause. The baptized who assemble for worship at the Holy Meal are Christ's Body and

have come to receive deeper faith, to be fed with the Bread of Life, and to be strengthened for their mission in the world.

Preaching on other occasions—that is, at times and contexts other than that of the Sunday Eucharistic feast—and preaching to other communities—such as the catechumens who are seeking faith in Christ and Holy Baptism—may well be more educational, evangelistic, or prophetic. FIYH states the case directly: "A homily presupposes faith."[102] William Willimon speaks of this distinctive quality of the liturgical homily as "baptismal preaching." It is "not so much a matter of being didactic, of explaining something, as it is of testifying to something, struggling to describe an event that has already happened to the congregation, bringing into view the significance of our baptism with words."[103] Bounded by such concrete and distinctive purpose, it becomes increasingly clear what the homily at Eucharist is not to be. A liturgical homily's brevity, then, is a function of its context, its purpose, and its rhetorical and methodological parameters. Discerning what the homily *is not* brings clarity regarding its brevity. Becoming aware of what the homily *is*, then leads to a brighter vision of its depth.

We have alluded to a rhetorical dimension with the insistence on a "brief" homily in some liturgical traditions. This critique here leads to an insistence on the brevity of the homily which is applicable across the span of preaching styles and ecclesial traditions. "We tend towards overkill in our use of words and towards neglect in our use of silence," insists James Wallace.[104] However, the issue of linguistic overkill is not solely a quantitative matter. Rather, there are certain kinds of words that provide the listeners with "empty calories," spoken entities that bloat the sermon while actually lowering the ability of its language to communicate.

These empty calorie words have been explored extensively and in depth by David Buttrick.[105] For example, Buttrick finds that popular pulpit words such as "very," "truly," "really," and "indeed" add little to oral speech and serve to "make language thick and less accessible to consciousness."[106] Moreover, Buttrick argues that adjectives serve mostly to obscure and weaken our speech, in spite of their overdone usage in Romantic literature. Verbs, on the other hand, are the grammar of vivid and concrete communication. "Excitement in preaching is usually created by verb *color* and *precision*."[107] A graphic depiction of the rhetorical alternatives may be conceived as follows, with the "color and precision" verb-heavy side providing the terse, compact preface-like prose.

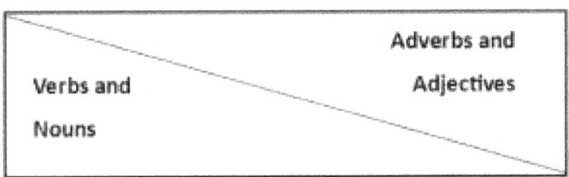

Richard L. Eslinger, Pitfalls in Preaching, Grand Rapids, MI: William B. Eerdmans Publishing Company, 1996, 11.
Used with permission.

Once again, the issue is not simply that of the quantity of words employed while developing a single thought in the sermon; the congregation's retention of the language in the first place depends upon more qualitative issues such as the presence or blessed absence of "empty calorie" words and an over-abundance of adjectives.

Of course, there are other preaching traditions in which the performance of the liturgical homily is not highly valued in contrast to temporally more extended sermons. To be sure, an African American Baptist or Pentecostal congregation would probably be shocked if their preacher delivered a homily-sized sermon on a Sunday morning. This is not to say that African American sermons should be stereotyped as all lacking "preface-like prose." Rather, Cleophus LaRue notes, there are a number of factors that make for longer moves within the black sermon. These include,

- o The black sermon as performed word usually runs longer than the traditional mainline sermon.
- o The black preacher often engages in prolonged and precise detailing of some text, image, metaphor, or slice of life centered around one thought.
- o The listening congregation expects and has grown accustomed to following an elongated story plot without losing sight of the defining thought that occasioned the move.[108]

Even given the more extensive time-frame of many sermons in the African American church, there remain widely-held protocols as to the rhetorical boundaries of the preacher. For example, LaRue raises a cautionary note regarding the practice of inserting a closing reference to Jesus in a sermon on an Old Testament text where "Jesus appears as an afterthought tacked on to the end. . . ."[109]

Moreover, an extension of the length and rhetorical amplitude of sermons expands beyond those of the liturgical homily in many contexts apart from ethnic minority or majority considerations. One significant factor, of course, is that the schism between Word and sacrament in many North American churches has resulted in the sermon becoming "a kind of homiletical ocean liner preceded by a few liturgical tugboats."[110] Given the dominance of the non-eucharistic model of the Sunday service, the sermon in such a liturgical context tends to expand to fill the void left from non-celebration of the Holy Meal.

Among the numerous factors involved in the temporal expansion of the sermon in some Protestant quarters, two in particular need special scrutiny, one having a long season of exposure while the other is of much more recent origin. Both, interestingly, have been mislabeled as "narrative preaching," although their more accurate description would be misuse of story.

The older pattern has been described as the "necklace" approach to sermon construction. Here, the preacher has obviously been about the business of collecting stories that have some moralistic or pietistic content and, equally obvious, the preacher has become quite skilled in performing them. The sermon, in this "necklace" model, becomes a series of these "pearls" strung together as they are told in sequence, all presumed to be connected to some common theme (the string for the pearls). In the necklace sermon, the number of such "pearls" is somewhat irrelevant to the extent of the sermon's duration. Since there is no plotted sequence to the stories, the sermon can be extended to fill any time frame by way of dipping into the barrel and retrieving more pearls to be strung on the necklace. Any Scriptural text in this model becomes distilled down into a theme that strings the pearls together or, in another variant, finds itself placed in the barrel along with the other pearls to be deployed as needed.

On the other hand, a more recent trend—again mislabeled as "narrative preaching"—involves a strange metastasizing of illustrations within the sermon. Within the past two decades, certain preachers' sermon illustrations have been growing in length to the point that they occupy up to thirty or forty percent of the sermonic material. This "elephantitis" of illustration is most certainly an unfortunate by-product of the internet's ability to circulate such expansive stories and they mostly share common traits. These mega-stories tend to be individualistic tales of triumph through adversity and achievement through tenacity. Moreover, the mega-stories are replete with pathos and have an obvious "big idea" payoff that can be exploited homiletically. Given that latter quality, such mega-stories will take over for the biblical lesson and become the sermon's actual text. Once more, the economy and concretion of the preface within the Eucharistic Prayer serves to caution wise preachers against such excesses. The issue is not one solely of the length of such stories; their "gospel" is typically a romantic and individualistic distortion of the Gospel.[111]

2. *A changeable focus*—As has been noted, most prefaces within Western Eucharistic Prayers are "proper," that is they change in focus and theme from liturgical season to liturgical season, and from occasion to occasion. Considering this core quality of changeability within the preface of the Eucharistic Prayer, the homiletical implications immediately focus on practices where a lack of that trait degrades the hearing of the Word. These practices range from matters of sermon delivery to issues related to the deployment of illustrative material and on the questions related to sermon method itself. Each element constitutes a situation where a certain changeability is needed by the listeners but is not provided by the preacher. Some of these "stasis-issues" (characterized by a chronic lack of dynamics or mobility) are as follows:

A. Regarding the preacher's inflection within a sermon, I will predictably encounter one or two students in my introduction to preaching class whose vocal inflection in other contexts is normal and appropriate to their subject. Then, when they rise to preach during the sermon lab, their pulpit speech becomes "preachery" as, for instance, it drops vocal tone by a musical third or fourth at the end of most sentences. The effect is dulling and detracting. It is not that someone in particular has advocated for this unnatural inflective habit in preaching. Rather, there seems to be an abiding consensus among some colleagues that pious and religious speech should sound this way. It then becomes habitual until some caring mentor or homiletics professor takes the preacher aside and calls attention to this vocal pattern. (The habit also infects the offering of public and liturgical prayer, again usually susceptible to intervention and analysis.)

A similar issue dealing with sermon delivery relates to the preacher's entire persona accompanying her or his sermons. Once again, a stasis obtains, though in this case it deals with the emotive "preacher" voice that is presented from the pulpit. Persons who otherwise exhibit various affective moods and expressions in other contexts, turn on a pulpit persona that is stereotyped and unchanging. Thus, I have experienced charming and expressive persons who, when coming to preach, adopt a consistently stern facial expression and deep, solemn voice. In other instances, I have experienced pulpit personae of chirpy merriment and constant celebration.

All of these pulpit "voices"—the solemn, happy, angry, etc.—share several characteristics. First, they are stereotyped, perhaps derived by imitation from some pulpit personality. Second, they are static and predictable in their deployment. Third, these personae will override the particular affective quality of the biblical text and specific sermon content. The liturgical preface, on the other hand, changes with context and occasion. The delivery of the sermon—its inflection along with the voice of the preacher—similarly must be "proper" to its text, context, and occasion.

B. A series of issues related to some sort of homiletical stasis can also afflict the material in the sermon intended to bring concretion to its conceptual material. Generically labeled "illustrations," these materials actually include brief illustrative narratives, one or more examples, and, finally, the depiction of imagery.[112] A number of problems cluster within the deployment of the conventional sermon illustration—that anecdote intended to reinforce or make vivid the "point" in the message. One changeability issue emerges when the preacher offers the same illustrative subject on a recurring basis. Whatever else may change—the liturgical season, the biblical texts, the events of church and world—one note of deadening consistency obtains, the congregation will hear yet again about the preacher's pet topic. So, one congregation will not be able to hear any sermon without the knowledge ahead of time that a golf story will illustrate something or other (or weaving, sailing, or collecting Belgian lace, etc.).[113] The chronic playing of the same illustrative category that has become beloved by the preacher will no longer serve to illustrate anything but that preacher. Consequently, the ethos of the preacher will suffer from such self-illustration.

With preachers having at their disposal such a broad and diverse suite of concretion strategies—story illustration, examples, and imagery—the sermon suffers a rhetorical diminishment if only one type of concretion is deployed again and again. Once again, the preface's changeability is an encouragement to seek the "proper" strategy for bringing lived experience to the sermon. However, some preachers will serve their listeners only an unvaried diet of illustrative material. So, in sermon after sermon, some congregations will hear only story illustrations when the preacher turns to specific application. Other assemblies may only hear lists of examples as the reiterative concretion scheme. A few preachers, perhaps those with vigorous and undisciplined intuitive personality preferences, will boggle the congregation with a myriad of imagery whatever the occasion.

The foundational issue here is that the strategy for bringing a move to concretion within the sermon is weighted with theological as well as rhetorical import. Particularly if the story illustrations all derive from one cultural context or historical era, the sub-text of these stories will be that the Gospel is best lived out within that idealized narrative world. Moreover, a subtle bias is conveyed that the individual and communal life of the hearers is best lived out by way of orderly narrative.[114] The matter of gender bias also infects the choice of illustrations by some male preachers. Not only are illustrations the chief diet served to these congregations in order to provide concrete experiences, the characters in the stories are likely to be males who display agency and heroic virtues. By contrast, those same illustrations will depict women as passive or dependent upon the male heroes. Once again, the proper preface embodies changeability, and that quality can provide a caution to men in the pulpit not only to vary their concretion strategies within the sermon, but sometimes to shift the gender focus of illustrations when they are deployed.

A companion transgression often accompanies an undo dependence on story illustrations within the sermon. In this case, the congregation is also served almost exclusively storied types of illustrative material, but those stories will be almost entirely about the preacher and his or her family! In such cases, it is not a by-product of the rhetorical strategy that the sermonic stories serve to illustrate the preacher rather than the conceptual issue at hand. To the contrary, it seems to be the intended purpose of the first-person tales that they illustrate the preacher. (Otherwise, what is the rationale for such predominance of these personal references from the pulpit?)

With an excessive dependence on such first-person narratives, the preacher may unwittingly convey several profound distortions of Christian faith. First, there is an unsubtle message conveyed that the Christian life is most fully lived by the ordained rather than by the laity, the whole people of God. So the message is clear in these over-done first-person narratives: "Want to be a complete Christian? Become ordained and serve as pastor and preacher." Moreover, the second class status of the laity is reified in the insistence that they must access the means of grace and the virtues of the faith in ways mediated by and translated through the experiences of their preacher. If the subject at hand is God's call to persons to be about faithful discipleship, then the congregation will hear the story of the preacher's call to ministry. Or, if the message is dealing with perseverance in a season of adversity, the congregation will hear the story of the preacher and the preacher's spouse when they were struggling with a very ill child. And if, on All Saints Day or Sunday, the sermon focuses on the lives of some recent saints, the preacher will relate the stories of a beloved grandmother or grandfather. It all stays in the family!

After a steady dose of these first-person illustrations, most any congregation is very ready for changeability to redeem this predictable habit. If used at all, first-person story illustrations should "go communal" with ease and rapidity. Otherwise, the illustrations should be congruent with the conceptual content of the particular homiletical move. Thus, if the conceptual focus is ecclesial—a matter of the Body of Christ—then any individualistic illustration is a wayward tactic and a first-person individualistic story doubles the transgression.

3. *Sequential Logic*—The Preface, throughout its "default" or proper variations, maintains a sequencing that links it in place between the Dialogue and the Sanctus. As we have noted, most any preface opens with a statement intensifying the last line of the Dialogue. Thus, in United Methodist euchological practice, the concluding line of the Dialogue ("It is right to give our thanks and praise.") is followed in the preface's opening phrase by an intensified restatement of the *"dignum et justum est"* ("It is right, and a good and joyful thing, . . ."). At the aft end of the preface, a statement transitions from the particular focus and thematic content of the prayer to an introduction of the Sanctus, also serving to cue the assembly to their entrance into the Eucharistic Prayer. This statement in the 1662 *Book of Common Prayer* expresses the rhetorical and liturgical genius of the writer of the first prayer books, Archbishop Cranmer:

> Therefore with angels and archangels, and with all the company of heaven, we laud and magnify thy glorious Name; evermore praising thee, and saying:[115]
> *(Here follows the Sanctus.)*

Between the dependable opening and closing lines of the preface, the specific thematic and imagistic material embodying the action of making Eucharist is developed.

The resonance between this dynamic of the preface and that of the sermon centers in their held-in-common grounding in a plotted logic. Reflecting on the homiletical plot from this distinctive narrative perspective, Eugene Lowry notes that plot "deals with some kind of *sequential ordering,*"[116] Lowry continues by depicting "sequential ordering" as a narrative plot that "typically includes an opening conflict, escalation or complication, a watershed experience (generally involving a reversal) and a denouement (that is, the working out of the resolution)."[117]

Other homileticians would concur with Lowry concerning the essential quality of sequential ordering, but would look elsewhere than the dynamics of narrative for the sermon's plot. David Buttrick, for example, insists that the sermon must embody some sort of sequential ordering. "Underlying the movement of a plot is some sort of 'logic' by which parts are assembled and travel."[118] (Buttrick here could be depicting the sequential ordering of the Eucharistic preface!) In some cases, especially when preaching *in* the mode of immediacy[119] and preaching *from* a biblical narrative, the sermonic plot will trace the Scripture's narrative scenic progression. However, Buttrick also extends the notion of plot to include the "logic" of most any pericope; an ordered sequence will still shape the homiletical plot. That plot—whether derived from a biblical narrative or, for example, the Pauline epistolary logic—always tries "to bring out some structure of meaning within a field of consciousness."[120]

By way of contrast, the old "point"-based preaching assembled a series of propositional statements which contained no underlying sequential ordering. For example, a quick internet search spotted the following sermon points for the Parable of the Good Samaritan:

> A neighbor is one in need whom we can help.
> The incongruity of divorcing neighborliness from religion.
> The cost of compassion.[121]

As with the majority of such sermon-building points, there is no necessary sequential ordering of the thematic. A preacher could just as easily begin with the third point about compassion, shift to the first related to the concept of neighborliness, and conclude with this elusive point about the incongruous divorcing of helping neighbors from religion. The points of this sermon—in whatever order they are arranged—invite the congregation to ignore the point of view of the one who has been robbed and beaten. In fact, the distance from the parable's world is stunning, especially when the congregation is invited to considerations of the incongruity of divorcing neighborliness from religion. On the other hand, the scandal of being unable to prevent compassionate help from a despised enemy is bypassed as well.[122] Put simply, the parable's narrative plot is irrelevant to the points of this sermon. Any sequential logic is simply ignored.

4 *The Preface, the Lectionary, and the Homily*—The Preface has as its companion "propers" several other variable-to-the-occasion elements within the Sunday service. These have included such liturgical components as the Introit (the opening fragment of a hymn or psalm within the Latin Mass and elsewhere),[123] the Collect (the opening prayer of the day), and the reading from Scripture (also specific to the day and occasion). The latter proper readings for the day, of course, have a direct and immediate relationship to the ministry of proclamation; the lectionary is a compilation of lections for every Sunday and festival within the church year. Within ecclesial traditions in which a lectionary is mandated or commended as determining the Scriptures for the liturgical

occasion—thus becoming one of the propers of that day—the preacher is provided with the texts from which or through which the sermon is to proceed.[124]

Since the various Western Church ecclesial communities vary widely on the use of a formal lectionary, and therefore to what extent if any the sermon should be based on such propers, it is essential that we turn to consider the origins and development of this proper and the contemporary issues regarding its use. Simply put, the question we now address has a two-fold structure: How did we come to have this three-year lectionary (whether the Roman Catholic Lectionary or the Revised Common Lectionary) and what are the compelling issues at stake in its use or disuse? An investigation regarding the origins of the lectionary seems warranted.

In synagogue worship of the Post-Exilic period, the Jewish practices regarding the selection of Scriptures varied according to three systems. These included, Marion Hatchett notes: "(1) the synagogue ruler's discretion; (2) 'in-course' readings (*lectio continua*); or (3) a fixed lectionary."[125] Within the New Testament, evidence is abundant that all three of these systems remained in use in early Christian worship. Lessons from the Hebrew Scriptures (though, in fact, the Greek Scriptures of the Septuagint) were derived by way of one of the same practices in usage in Post-Exilic Judaism. A reading or singing of a psalm may have followed the first lesson and further readings were selected from early Christian writings. Hatchett now makes a striking conclusion with regard to these early Christian writings: "Those lections which found regular place in liturgical usage eventually became the New Testament Canon."[126]

Here, a remarkable reversal is asserted to that more conventional assumption as to the relationship between the Canon and ordered liturgical practice of scripture usage. Conventional "wisdom" is that after the Canon was closed, the post-New Testament church began its alignment of particular lessons to specific occasions resulting eventually in some lectionary scheme or other. Hatchett turns this prevalent viewpoint on its head, proposing instead that the New Testament churches were already in the business of selecting liturgical occasions for particular texts from the early Christian writings. The Canon, from this point of view is derivative in part from the ordering of these writings within the communities constituting early Christianity!

The ordering of the New Testament writings according to occasions and days, however, did not end with the close of the Canon. Once again, an interplay seems to have obtained between text and liturgical occasion. So it is no surprise, for example, that as St. Augustine chose lections for various occasions within the church year, the texts were those that were actually generative of those liturgical days. We are not surprised, then, to find Augustine preaching on texts that gave birth to the liturgical event in the first place. So, the Christmas narrative in Luke 2 was his reading for, of all things, Christmas Day, while Matthew 28 was the Gospel lesson for the Easter Vigil, and Acts 2 was the epistle lesson for Pentecost.[127]

The interaction between text and occasion is dynamic. On one hand, the lection points the church to the day and focus of its observance. On the other hand, the text then becomes the obvious lesson for the occasion. Given this interplay between text and liturgical context, the outcome is the emergence of the church year itself as well as the arrangement of biblical texts that will become a fully developed lectionary. In the course of this complex development, the New Testament texts first generated the occasions within the Paschal cycle of the year (what we would later term the Lent-Easter cycle). For example, the lections for the Great Fifty Days—the Season of Easter—were among the earliest to be fixed, including the church's decision to focus on readings from the Acts of the Apostles during this Season.[128] The last of the Sundays to be given a specific lection were those following Pentecost, the long series of Sundays now included in Ordinary Time.

The first complete lectionaries date from the seventh century[129] although those of the eighth century are more prevalent and determinative for the future. Various regions followed their own distinctive arrangements—for example, the Gallican eighth century Lectionary of Luxeuil. By contrast, the lectionary of the Roman Rite during this same era was distinctive in two respects—the lections "were shorter than those typical of other rites" and there existed "a particular dearth of Old Testament readings."[130] The latter distinctive characteristic was to have grave consequences for the Western Church until the reforms of the Second Vatican Council (1963-65). Once the Old Testament lesson was largely deleted from the readings for Sundays and festivals, the psalm which functioned as a response to that reading was also lost.

With the triumph of the Roman Rite in the West by the eleventh century (excepting a few local rites of particular distinctiveness), the Western Church would limp through the next nine hundred years with a lectionary composed on most occasions of an epistle lesson and a gospel. Moreover, the lectionary of the Roman Rite, adopted with minor variations after the Reformation by Lutheran and Anglican communions, provided only for a one-year sequence of these lections.[131] Not only was the church deprived of the Old Testament in its Sunday worship, the churches retaining this lectionary suffered an inadequate diet of New Testament readings as well. The sea change came in 1963 with the first decree approved by the Second Vatican Council, "The Constitution on the Sacred Liturgy." Here, a principle was announced that from a later perspective was a reform badly needed by most every tradition within Western Christianity: "The Scriptures are to be opened more lavishly to the people."[132]

The Roman Catholic Lectionary for Mass that resulted from this reforming action of the Council was promulgated in 1969. It was organized around a three-year sequence and the Gospel lessons for each year focused on each of the Synoptic Gospels respectively. Hence, Year A belonged mostly to the Gospel of Matthew, Year B to Mark, and Year C to Luke. The Gospel of John was featured in the seasons of Lent and Easter during every year and in Year B—St. Mark being the shortest Gospel—the Bread of Life Discourse of John 6 was intercalated into the Markan sequence during Ordinary Time. The First Lesson for each season, Sunday, or other occasion was derived from the Old Testament except during the Season of Easter when, in accordance with ancient practice, readings from the Acts of the Apostles became the First Lesson. In addition, a Psalter selection responded to the First Lesson and an Epistle reading completed the offerings. The First Lessons were selected with regard to some connective logic to the Gospel Lesson, whether by way of thematic congruence, a promise and fulfillment motif, or typological connection.

During the next decade, various Protestant denominations along with the Episcopal Church adopted the RCL, though in every instance, modifications were made either by way of shortening or lengthening the verses in a given lection or, in a number of cases especially related to the selections from the Acts of the Apostles, replacing texts from the RCL with others. (The latter dynamic, it was discovered involved the replacement of the community-building pericopes of Acts in the RCL with other texts embodying kerygmatic proclamations of the New Testament church.) However, by the latter years of the 1970s, it was becoming clear that the initial motivations for an ecumenical consensus with regard to the readings within a new three-year lectionary were being threatened by denominational and Protestant-Catholic centrifugal forces. Two denominations—the three Lutheran synods about to merge into the Evangelical Lutheran Church of America (ELCA) along with the Episcopal Church—published official resources that already canonized their own variants of the lectionary. Other denominations were at least potentially heading in the same direction. Therefore, The Consultation on Common Texts convened a conference on calendar and lectionary in late March of 1978 and thirteen denominations participated in the discussions. Given the evidence of a potential squandering of the gift of unity promised in the advent of the three-year lectionary, the CCT established the North American Committee on Calendar and Lectionary (NACCL) with a charge to attempt a Common Lectionary. A Common Lectionary was achieved by NACCL and several years later some further revisions produced the Revised Common Lectionary which has persisted as the alternative to the Roman Catholic Lectionary.[133]

The two primary purposes of a lectionary, as noted in *Fulfilled in Your Hearing*, are to establish appropriate Scripture lessons for the various days, festivals, and seasons of the liturgical year and "to provide for a comprehensive reading of the Scriptures."[134] The former purpose—establishing lessons appropriate for various occasions in the year of grace—needs to be nuanced with regard to the dynamics of the New Testament canon and the emergence of the two Christological cycles of Incarnation and the Paschal Mystery (Advent/Christmas and Lent/Easter). In a number of instances, by the fourth century, various "historic-feasts" are being established that have their origin in specific narratives within the New Testament. So, for example, the Christian festival of Pentecost is entirely dependent upon St. Luke's rendition of the Pentecost story in Acts 2. The same may be said with regard to the fourth century creations of Christmas in the West and Palm Sunday in the East. None of these festivals would have emerged in the early church except for the generative force of specific biblical narratives.

Thus, in these and other cases, a lectionary does not as much *establish* appropriate lessons as it *recalls* for the church the Scriptures that gave birth to the liturgical occasions in the first place. By way of drilling into these relationships between an ordered sequence of Scripture lections and the church year, one other purpose gains a central importance while a second fades to the margins of our considerations. The core purpose of the lectionary—whether the Roman Catholic or Revised Common Lectionary—is to shape a service of the Word so that the hearing and proclamation of these lessons forms a people such that they come to the Eucharist with faith, expectancy, and joy. Put simply, both versions of the three-year lectionary are Eucharistic projects with a sacramental lens governing the selection of texts and occasions.

In this we once more encounter the interplay between proclamation and Eucharist. The proper preface for the liturgy is grounded in the same biblical texts that will become the lessons through which the sermon is given birth. Given the rich sources for proper prefaces to the Great Thanksgiving, and even entire "proper" Eucharistic Prayers, during Ordinary Time the careful preacher in many traditions will find a mode of Eucharistic praying that resonates effectively with the lessons and the sermon.

There is one, somewhat questionable, rationale for the use of the lectionary that is voiced from time to time, especially by church judicatories and publishing houses. "The lectionary," these voices chime, "is a fine preaching plan for the Christian Year." The obvious sub-text of this persuasive argument is that a preacher may come up with any number of "preaching plans," but the abundance of lectionary-based preaching resources is a compelling rationale for using this particular plan. The problem here is not with the abundance of homiletical and liturgical resources based on the lectionary; rather, it is with the implication that the preacher and her or his choice of a preaching plan is the governing principle. Thus, we hear preachers announce that their sermon series for Easter, for example, will be based in the chapters of a new book on spiritual formation. (Such a series, of course, might be a gem of a project for an adult education class.) The issue here is not the relative merit of this or that author's book on spiritual formation. Rather, it is that of the source of our authority as those called to preach is the gospel.

A compelling question, then, is, must control over the choice of Scripture, themes, and topics for our preaching always remain with ourselves? Or, to the contrary, is the authority more grounded in the nature and work of Christ's church through the power of the Holy Spirit? Stanley Hauerwas is perhaps the most provocative spokesperson for the latter, ecclesial location of the preacher's authority as he argues:

For preaching to be a practice intrinsic to the worship of God requires that the preacher, as well as the congregation, stand under the authority of the Word. That is why preaching should rightly follow a lectionary. To preach from the lectionary makes clear that preaching is the work of the church and not some arbitrary decision by the minister to find a text to fit a peculiar theme that currently fits the preacher's subjectivity. Rather, the exercise of the ministry of proclamation requires the minister to make clear that the Word preached is as painful to him/her as it is to the congregation. Such an acknowledgement makes clear that preaching is not just another speech but rather the way this people here, including the preacher, is formed into the Word of God.[135]

The Ordo of the Eucharistic liturgy—the sequence of liturgical words and actions we are tracing in this homiletical mystagogy—is the work of the church and not an arbitrary decision of any minister at the Table. So, too, the proclamation of the ordered lessons of the Word are a gift and task to the one called to preach. The proper preface offers the variable themes, imagery, and narratives of the church year, various pastoral occasions, and local and global issues to qualify Eucharistic praying and to locate the assembly in some context or other. "Proper preaching" is grounded in the lections of the church year in order that vital enduring relationships obtain between the Service of the Word and the Service of the Table. Also, "proper preaching" safeguards the preacher from returning to favorite texts, themes, and issues in place of "the whole counsel of God"(Acts 20:27, NKJV).

Conclusion

The qualities of the proper preface—compact, succinct content; a changeable focus; and an inherent sequential logic—all inform the shape of the liturgical homily. These qualities, then, will also be embodied in "proper preaching." Among the complex elements of Eucharistic praying, perhaps no other words and actions have such immediate and direct relevance to the ministry of proclamation. But as we have seen, the Proper Preface also points the preacher toward the texts and rhythms and spirituality of the liturgical year. The context for preaching is indicated by these proper prefaces—it is the Year of Grace.

4

THE SANCTUS
AND
BENEDICTUS QUI VENIT

"Holy, Holy, Holy Lord" [136]

During the early days of introducing the "new" communion service (in the United Methodist Church), I still remember pondering the profoundly beautiful text of the Sanctus and Benedictus—Holy, Holy, Holy—as I drove along Interstate 40. How could our earthly song join that of the company of heaven, with a tune which would almost seem familiar and accessible to those who had never done this? It came to me rather suddenly and profoundly that creating a musical setting which traced the contours of the first hymn in the 1939 Methodist Hymnal *just might work; thus, the general shape of the NICAEA tune inspired my musical setting, first shared at Claremont in 1980 by my husband Richard Eslinger and Dr. Carlton Young. It became the primary setting for the Upper Room Academy for Spiritual Formation, and was subsequently chosen for the* UMH 1989. *It still is a wonder to me to hear it sung by heart and heartily in many contexts around the country . . . not attached to me, but as a simple gift of the Spirit which does help this essential song of the people continue to be heard on earth as in heaven.*[137]

Investigating the Rite

By the time of the immense flowering of Eucharistic liturgies during the Patristic era from the middle of the fourth century to the middle of the sixth, the Sanctus is in usage almost everywhere. While the liturgical location of the Sanctus varies—being found, for example, in a familiar location following the opening prayer of thanksgiving in Spain and Rome or, less familiarly, well into the thanksgiving and intercessions in Alexandria—the "Holy, Holy, Holy" is ubiquitous and of recognizable content. The matter of the origin of the anaphoral Sanctus, however, "remains something of a mystery."[138] Early Christian liturgical sources for the Lord's Day service persist in extending this mystery of the where and when of the origin of the use of the Sanctus in the Eucharistic Prayer.

1. An Argument for Nicene Origins—Louis Bouyer, for example, argues for evidence of quite early usage of the Sanctus to be found in sources that embody Jewish-Christian prayer types similar to those of the *Didache* (c. 100 CE). Specifically, Bouyer points to the 7th Book of the *Apostolic Constitutions* in which prayers are found "which give us not only primitive Christian material but also, undoubtedly, Jewish material used at a very early period by Christians."[139] Significant for his exploration of the Sanctus, the following text is found in the Eucharistic Prayer of the 7th Book of the *Apostolic Constitutions*:

> And the zealous Army of Angels, with the intelligible spirits, says: "One alone is holy . . . , and the holy six-winged Seraphim with the Cherubim, singing to you the hymn of victory, cry out with (their) voices that are never silent: Holy, holy, holy, the Lord Sabaoth; the heavens and the earth are full of your glory . . ."[140]

On the other hand, the *Apostolic Tradition* stubbornly begs to differ from this arguably ancient usage of the Sanctus. Indeed, Bard Thompson notes in his introduction to the Hippolytus liturgy for the ordination of a bishop, "there was no Sanctus, the dialogue led directly into the Eucharistic prayer."[141] The same observation obtains for the Paschal Eucharist in the *Apostolic Tradition*; there was no Sanctus.

We could extrapolate from the missing Sanctus in Hippolytus' rites that its introduction was one significant aspect of the Eucharistic ferment of the Nicene and immediately post-Nicene church. Such an argument, then, would go as follows: The *Apostolic Tradition* represents the earlier stage of the development of the Eucharistic Prayer in which the entirety of the prayer following the Dialogue was one contiguous narrative fabric. Later, then, in the famous words of Gregory Dix, the Sanctus becomes inserted as "a sort of liturgical cuckoo."[142] The origins of this liturgical cuckoo, however, may remain obscured by the paucity of historical evidence and the ambiguity of some of the sources that are in hand. One conclusion, then, could be that put forward by Maxwell Johnson: The when and where of the introduction of the Sanctus into the anaphora "has long been an unresolved issue in Eucharistic praying. . . ."[143]

2. *Arguments for Pre-Nicene Origins*—This is not to say that bits of evidence related to the Sanctus are absent from the pre-Nicene church, or that scholars have not connected the dots related to these sources leading to conflicting historiographical hypotheses. First, however, it may be best to gesture toward the most prominent "dots" that have been connected differently by various historians of the liturgy. We may, then, note several locales, and the resultant theories, in which the Isaiah hymn may be discerned, both in specifically liturgical settings as well as more general writings:

A. There is evidence of the Hymn of Isaiah 6 in the Jewish berakoth—the extended prayer of thanksgiving and intercession which followed Jewish meals. This meal prayer has been claimed as the precedent, both in structure and in theological content, for the early Christian Eucharistic prayers. So, famously, the *Didache*'s prayer at the Meal (whether an agape meal or the Eucharist) is dependent on Jewish prayer forms and style, especially as those aspects of Jewish prayer are embodied in the after-meal berakah.[144] There is, most would agree, this "close link we shall see to exist between these prayers of the *Didache* and the Jewish tradition of blessing for meals."[145] Moreover, these Jewish prayers frequently locate the Isaiah hymn as the climax of an opening sequence of the blessing of God.

The logic of such a location of the "Holy, holy, holy . . ." being, of course, that the local praise of God at this particular meal is joined with the eternal and heavenly praise offered by "the multitudes above."[146] The question of the liturgical trajectory from such Jewish blessings for meals and the anaphoras of the early Church as regards the Sanctus is, to be sure, compromised by the absence of the hymn in the prayers contained in the *Didache*. However, as we shall see, other Eucharistic prayers deemed quite early in their origin do, in fact, share both the structure of the berakah as well as the presence of the Eternal Song.

B. The Eternal Hymn of Isaiah 6:3 and Revelation 4:8 are both well-known and widely used by the Ante-Nicene writers outside of specifically liturgical references to the hymn. These writers include such luminaries as Clement of Alexandria (c. 96 CE), the anonymous author of "The

Passion of Perpetua and Felicitas" (c. 200 CE), Tertullian (c. 160- c. 225 CE), and Origen (c. 184/185- 253/254 CE).[147] So, for example, Origen employs, among other biblical texts, the vision of Isaiah to argue for the ultimately unknowable nature of God. The two wings of the Seraphim that cover the face of God stand to insure that no creature in heaven or on earth except the Son gain full knowledge of God.[148] In every case, some reference is made to the text of Isaiah 6:3 as each engages in biblical interpretation, apologetics, or constructive expansion of Trinitarian thought; and also in every case, some scholars have insisted that these references to Isaiah's vision imply the liturgical context of the anaphoral Sanctus. However, as has been discerned in Origen's writings, the Eternal Hymn is one of numerous Scriptures chosen to support his argument concerning the incorporeal and unknowable nature of God. No liturgical context is implied whatsoever.[149]

A dominant scholarly consensus, however, has accumulated that undercuts any such projection of these as sources of possible liturgical practice. For example, in 1 Clement 34:6 the Eternal Hymn is quoted, leading some commentators to propose the text's liturgical use in Rome in the 90's of the first century. However, a closer examination of the context of the Hymn in the Epistle points us in other directions. The Isaiah 6 text is carefully introduced by reference to the countless heavenly host "ever ready to minister to His will."[150]

Following the Hymn, Clement appeals to the Corinthians to join with those innumerable angels, singing "in harmony . . . as with one mouth."[151] Writing to the fractious church, as did the Apostle Paul, Clement is both critiquing their disunity and schisms, and encouraging a new unity in Christ. Clement appeals to them to join "in harmony" with the angelic host in singing the Hymn as one body. No liturgical use of the Hymn, then, can be discerned here; "Clement," one recent commentator concludes, "is simply quoting from scripture."[152] The same conclusion Unnik applied to I Clement 34—the simple quoting from Scripture—may equally be the best judgment with regard to the appearance of Isaiah 6:3 in other Ante-Nicene writing, including all but Origen.

C. As mentioned, a discussion of the importance of the Eternal Hymn in early Christian writings inevitably leads to the question, what can be deduced about the introduction of the Anaphoral Sanctus in those writings? When did it first come into use in early Christian communities, and which of those communities first adopted it? Several competing theories exist with regard to the "where and when" of the introduction of the Sanctus within the Eucharistic prayer in early Christianity, beginning with Origen's mention of the "Holy, holy, holy" in his writings. An impressive series of scholars have attempted the argument that Origen's mention of the text in *De Principis* discloses the earliest reference to an anaphoral Sanctus. According to these theorists, the use of the Eternal Song in Origen denotes not only the biblical texts but also the liturgy contemporary with the writer. Moreover, the theory holds that this Egyptian location is the sole generative source for the inclusion of the Sanctus within early church anaphoras. Gregory Dix, the most prominent champion of this theory, sums up the argument nicely by concluding that "the use of the preface and sanctus in the Eucharistic prayers began in the Alexandrian church at some time before A.D. 230, and from there spread first to other Egyptian churches, and ultimately all over Christendom."[153]

This "Egyptian Theory" is opposed by the so-called "Climax Theory,"[154] which proposes a very early Eucharistic tradition embedded within the text of the *Apostolic Constitutions*. Although the present text of the *Constitutions* dates from the mid-fourth century, Bouyer (and more recently Robert Taft) argues that the Sanctus in the anaphora of the *Apostolic Constitutions* harkens back to "the very origins of Christian Eucharistic praying."[155] Both theories remain in play in contemporary liturgical studies, though the Egyptian theory may have more supporters.

A third theory remains. This position concludes that both the Egyptian and the Climax theories are wrong; "it is only in the fourth century . . . that we know with certainty [of] the presence of the *Sanctus* within the anaphora."[156] Maxwell Johnson argues for this point of view from the emerging evidence of the liturgical Sanctus from the mid-fourth century onward (the initial appearance of the anaphoral Hymn being that of Sarapion of Thmuis in Egypt while abundant employment of the "Holy, Holy, Holy" is widely seen in both East and West by the end of the fourth and beginning of the fifth centuries). Upon reconsideration, this third theory may well be interpreted as a variant of the Egyptian theory, though with significantly later dating than Bouyer and others had in mind.

Within the fascinating literature analyzing the earliest evidence for the emergence of the anaphoral Sanctus, one other "when and where" proposal carries support equal to or even surpassing that of Origen and the Egyptian theory. The anaphora of Addai and Mari, of East Syrian derivation, is not only one of the earliest liturgical texts of Eucharistic praying (early third century origin), but remains in use today among Chaldean Christians. This rite, then "is the oldest Eucharistic prayer still in use today."[157]

The anaphora of Addai and Mari resonates both in structure and liturgical rhetoric with the Jewish berakoth. Evidence of the intimate relationship between the Jewish berakah and this East Syrian Eucharist includes a common share in such themes as the glorification of God and the meal as a memorial of God's gracious acts toward the covenant people. Also in common with Jewish berakoth, the Sanctus, standing alone without the Benedictus, is to be found in the most ancient texts of the East Syrian tradition. (On the other hand, those same ancient testimonies to this Syrian tradition lack the Words of Institution.)

As we have come to expect, however, historians of the liturgy have once again chosen to disagree about the status of the Sanctus in the Addai and Mari text. Such notables as Gregory Dix, Louis Bouyer, and E. C. Ratcliff insist that the Hymn was a later interpolation. On the other hand, more recent scholars, including

Bryan D. Spinks and Gabriele Winkler, have argued for the integrity of the Sanctus within the earliest strata of this tradition. Thus, Spinks insists, contrary to Dix and all:

> The sanctus, therefore, has as much claim to antiquity as any other part of the common material. If any of the common material can be given a third century date, then the same can be claimed for the section which contained the sanctus.[158]

The evidence now leans in opposition to the earlier consensus among scholars of the liturgy; the emerging consensus is that the anaphora of Addai and Mari has always contained the Sanctus.

Once the dots have been connected, then, we seem to be left with two ancient traditions in which the Eucharistic prayer contains a Sanctus, both pre-Nicene in origin. On one hand, the Egyptian theory, whether generated by Origen or reported by him, continues to have merit. On the other hand, the anaphora of Addai and Mari in East Syria appears to be of early third century origin as well: more recent scholarship argues that it contains from its inception the anaphoral Sanctus. Hence, the only theory not strongly supported, once the dots have been connected, is that no pre-fourth century anaphora contained a Sanctus.

The Sanctus in Fourth Century Catechesis

However scholars may connect the dots—or see no dots to connect—with regard to the Sanctus in the Pre-Nicene

Eucharist, by the later decades of the Fourth Century, bishops both in East and West were interpreting the sacramental mysteries to the newly baptized. Just as this current project attempts to interpret the sequence of liturgical acts within the Eucharist on behalf of the renewal of preaching, so the bishops in the post-Nicaea church sought to interpret those same liturgical components with regard to the formation and instruction of the newly baptized faithful. Within these catechetical homilies and lectures, the various bishops exercise a certain freedom to elicit certain aspects of the anaphora just experienced by the new Christians at the Easter Vigil. Some components of the anaphora are only mentioned in passing or, in some cases, simply not mentioned at all. Augustine of Hippo, for example, tends toward a minimalist position when explicating the dynamics and sequence of his Eucharistic Prayer. Perhaps, as William Harmless proposes,

> Augustine's silence about the Eucharistic Prayer stemmed from his assessment of the pedagogical needs of his hearers: that is, he spoke not so much about what *he* said or did during the Eucharist, but about what the *neophytes themselves* would be expected to say and do. Explaining their role as faithful must have seemed more urgent, from a pedagogical standpoint, than explaining his role as presider.[159]

Consistent with this summary, then, in several sermons Augustine turns the attention of the newly baptized to their liturgical words and actions in the Sursum Corda. The underlying reality was the grace of God; the giving of thanks in the Dialogue "meant that uplifted hearts were a gift of God, and not something ascribed 'to your own strength, your own merits, and your own labors.'"[160] An argument from silence, thusly, could be made that the Sanctus has not yet been introduced within the Eucharistic

Prayer at Hippo during Augustine's episcopate. Certainly the Sanctus would be one of those liturgical acts that relate to what the neophytes themselves say and do. In fact, Augustine proceeds over the entirety of the Eucharistic Prayer in order to pause and explore the Great Amen, the Lord's Prayer, and the Communion itself. Like mentee, like mentor as well.[161] In Ambrose of Milan's mystagogical homilies, there is no reference to the Sanctus as he interprets the Eucharist to the neophytes. "The anaphora began with praise and intercession,"[162] Ambrose then continues to track the sequence of prayers within the anaphora, but no reference is made to the Sanctus or Benedictus. It will be another generation before liturgical texts in Milan include the Eternal Song.

Given the possible origins of the anaphoral Sanctus in Egypt, with early rites in Syria also perhaps dependent upon that generative location, it is no surprise that we would find the Hymn present in the worship at Jerusalem. Within the catechetical lectures of Cyril of Jerusalem this bishop's survey of the sequence of the Eucharistic Prayer for the neophytes reviews the communal participation in the Sanctus as a matter of course. Cyril relates that the reason for this participation in the Sanctus "is this, that we may be partakers with the hosts of the world above in their Hymn of praise."[163] Cyril then proceeds to his interpretation of the epiclesis which follows after the assembly has been "sanctified . . . by these spiritual Hymns."[164] What we may surmise from these references by the bishop at Jerusalem in the late fourth century is that the anaphoral Sanctus is well in place in the Eucharistic practice of that liturgically influential episcopate. And as has been observed, the West may indeed wait another generation for this liturgical cuckoo to be introduced within its Eucharistic praying.

The Addition of the Benedictus to the Sanctus

The early evidence, both East and West, indicates that the assembly's eruption in the Eternal Song was limited to the text of Isaiah 6, the Sanctus. The East Syrian tradition, along with the Egyptian, contains the Sanctus, though without the Benedictus. Thus, once more the "where and when" issues arise, this time with regard to the second biblical song which begins, "Blessed is he who comes. . . ." Only in the sixth century was this second hymnic text, the Benedictus, added. This later hymnic addition, of course, is derived from Psalm 118 as well as the Triumphal Entry accounts in all four gospels.

As we have come to expect, an earlier consensus developed among liturgical scholars that the interpolation of the Benedictus was a rather late development in early Christianity. Reed, for example, states that it was added to the Sanctus first in Syria early in the fifth century.[165] The evidence, however, is context-specific to homilies delivered at Easter, and Spinks offers a promising theory that the Syrian use of the Benedictus was restricted to the Paschal festival.[166] By extension, a related liturgical context for the Benedictus may well be seen in Cyril's Jerusalem liturgies. Egeria reports that at the outset of "The Great Week," the bishop, the other clergy, and the laity all process from the heights of the Mount of Olives singing, "Blessed is he that cometh in the name of the Lord."[167] Thus, the liturgical use of the Benedictus on the Sunday of the Palms may then have migrated to the anaphora and become attached to the Sanctus.

More recent scholarship, however, has now explored Jewish sources (including the Ethiopian Book of Enoch, a pseudoepigraphical work dating to the early Common Era) that align the Sanctus with the abbreviated "Benedictus" of Ezekiel

3:12. This text, "Blessed be the name of the Lord," also appears in a Christian Ethiopic source, although separated from the Sanctus by the anamnesis and epiclesis.[168] Another theory of earlier origins focuses on the pseudoepigraphal source of the Ethiopian Book of Enoch and proposes a Jewish precedent for linking the Sanctus and Benedictus. A second cluster of theories serve to undergird the Syrian sixth century evidence: in both Syria and Jerusalem, some meager evidence suggests a possible introduction of the Benedictus within the anaphora during liturgically specific occasions in Holy Week.

We are therefore left with one matter of certainty and several companion theories. The certainty is that the Benedictus emerges within the church's Eucharistic celebrations in the East initially and by the beginning of the sixth century. In the West, the Roman rite settles on an enduring text for the diptych hymn:

Sanctus, sanctus, sanctus, Dominus Deus Sabaoth.
Pleni sunt caeli et terra Gloria tua. Hosanna in excelsis.

Benedictus qui venit in nomine Domini.
Hosanna in excelsis.[169]

Protestant Revisions of the Diptych Hymn

The protests of Martin Luther regarding his assessment of the abuses of the Mass were both intense and narrowly drawn. Central to his critique, Luther sought to rid the Mass of any hint of its character as a sacrifice. The offertory with its oblation and certain features of the Canon were suppressed. On the other hand, those elements of rite that did not participate in what Luther construed as the cultic abuses of *sacrificium* and that were deemed of ancient origin were to be retained. Hence, in his

Formula Missae of 1523, the Sanctus and Benedictus were not singled out for any invective nor, as he progressed through the revisions of the liturgy, even mentioned directly at all. A reader could conclude thereby that Luther intended that these hymns were to be deleted from the Mass. However, in this instance, an argument from silence would be in error.

What was altered, however, was the location of the Sanctus and Benedictus. Now, the Preface led directly to the Words of Institution and following the consecration, "the choir took up the Sanctus and the Benedictus, at which point the elevation occurred."[170] The revised location of the Sanctus led to the deletion of any mention of angels and archangels. Later in his commentary on the revisions within the *Formula Missae*, Luther turns to the reforms with reference to congregational vernacular song. Locations for congregational song in the vernacular, he notes, should immediately follow various traditional rites such as the Sanctus and Agnus Dei.[171] The more thoroughgoing vernacular revision of the Latin Mass was, of course, the *Deutsche Messe* of 1525. Once again, the Consecration proceeds directly to the Verba, the bread being distributed before the wine (with Luther appealing to Luke and Paul for this dual distribution). Luther adds that "During the distribution of the Bread the German Sanctus could be sung"[172] (or other vernacular hymns). The German Sanctus was now an extended vernacular hymn text and no longer led to the Benedictus, the latter being excised from the liturgy. By the adoption of the Lutheran *Common Service* in 1888, the Sanctus and Benedictus were restored in participating Lutheran churches to the Prayer of Consecration in their traditional location.

The sacramental reforms of John Calvin were of a more radical temper than those of Martin Luther, perhaps by virtue of his "Having had no priestly tenure. . . ."[173] In both his Strassburg and Geneva "Form of Church Prayer," a sequence of liturgical acts leading to Communion included an extended Exhortation, the Invitation, Self-examination, and Excommunication. Then, as this highly penitential sequence was completed, there followed the Confession and Assurance of Pardon. The Words of Institution immediately followed these discursive rites followed by the Reformed Susum Corda and Communion.

The Sanctus and Benedictus were entirely removed from the order of worship. (Interestingly, Calvin's interpretation of the sacramental nature of the Lord's Supper centers on the Spirit's work to bring the faithful to heaven where Christ reigns. One could assume that Calvin would find the Sanctus of particular importance in the Lord's Supper since the Eternal Song is the auditory sign of the lifting of the worshipers to heaven.[174]) Zwinglian and Anabaptist services of Holy Communion agreed with Calvin as to the essential nature of the Words of Institution but would not agree to be elevated with the faithful to a heavenly Communion. Here, too, the Sanctus and Benedictus were left behind.

The First and Second prayer books of the Anglican Reformation traced a pattern similar to that of Luther's two revisions of the Mass. The 1549 *Book of Common Prayer* retained both the Sanctus and Benedictus in their location immediately following the Preface. However, the force of Bucer's critique of various elements within the 1549 Prayer Book may have encouraged Archbishop Cranmer to delete the Benedictus from the Prayer of Consecration in the 1552, more Protestant, version of the *BCP*.[175] The Sanctus soldiered on alone within Anglican prayer books in general until the reforms following the Second Vatican Council of the Roman Catholic Church (1963-65). Only in the *Book of Common Prayer* of 1979 was the Benedictus restored to the anaphora among American

Episcopalians. Moreover, Methodists in America followed a similar path regarding the use of the stand-alone Sanctus. Receiving a modest revision of the 1662 *Book of Common Prayer* from John Wesley, American Methodists continued to omit the Benedictus through the *Book of Worship* of 1966.[176] Finally, in the various on-trial liturgies of the 1970's the Benedictus was restored within the United Methodist Church. Similar reforms also were engaged by other churches in the U.S. including the Presbyterian Church (U.S.A.), the United Church of Christ, and the Disciples of Christ.[177]

Theological Considerations

Underlying all of these questions of the origins of the anaphoral Sanctus in early Christianity, its eventual pairing with the Benedictus, and its fortunes among various Protestant traditions until the post-Concilior reforms, are the theological claims these anaphoral hymns bring to the assembly making Holy Eucharist. Once the Sanctus was interpolated into the anaphora in early Christianity, several claims were thereby made regarding the celebration of the Holy Meal. The first is immediately apparent: the faithful who gather at the breaking of the bread are joining with the communion of saints and "all the company of heaven" in this eternal song in praise of the glory of God.

More deeply, however, the assembly gathered at the Eucharistic celebration sings the Sanctus for the very same reason as the company of heaven—we, and they, come into the presence of the Holy One, the Lord. The Eucharist, then, is the Holy Mystery, and the Sanctus functions to make manifest "the very place where the glory and presence, the *Shekinah*, of God is revealed."[178] The two Scriptural sources of the Sanctus both speak to this mystery, as witnessed by Isaiah (Isa. 6:3) and John (Rev. 4:8b). We who gather at the Holy Meal are blessed to join in the eternal song in praise of the glory of our God. Moreover, it is of great significance that the Sanctus is sung by all the baptized during the Eucharist. What is firmly located here in the liturgical action of the congregation's share in the Eternal Song is the more general affirmation regarding the assembly's essential participation in the sacrament.

The Eucharist is the holy mystery in which Christ reconstitutes his one Body in the world, feeds its members with the Bread of Life, and strengthens the Body for its mission to the world. The assembly's worship can never be delegated solely to various leaders. Rather, the entire assembly shares in praise with the heavenly hosts, specifically at the Sanctus and, by extension, throughout the service of Word and sacrament. The United Methodist statement on the Eucharist emphasizes this core doctrine:

> The whole assembly actively celebrates Holy Communion. All who are baptized into the body of Christ become servants and ministers within that body, which is the church. The members are claimed by God as a royal priesthood, God's own people (1 Peter 2:9). The one Body, drawn together by the one Spirit, is fully realized when all its many parts eat together in love and offer their lives in service at the Table of the Lord.[179]

Given the inherently communal character of the faithful who celebrate the Eucharist, practices that revert to the dominant culture's individualism are aberrant and fail in the theological and pastoral task of "discerning the body" (1 Cor. 11:29). In particular, the practice of "cafeteria Communion" where the consecrated elements are left out for persons to commune as they drop by the church violates this essential communal identity of the assembly.[180]

Further theological claims were to be made once the Benedictus was joined with the already interpolated Sanctus. Modern assertions included the notion that the diptych hymns "span the Old and New Testaments."[181] A particularly romantic interpretation proposes a scenario in which Christ, on the Cross, is encompassed by all creation, the angels singing the Sanctus and the disciples chanting the Benedictus.[182] Another commentator sees the two hymns as proclaiming "the glory of God in the first paragraph and the praise of Christ as God in the second (see John 12:41)."[183] However, these claims err in assigning the Sanctus as an Old Testament text (referring to Isa. 6:2-3) and the Bendictus as the New Testament text (related to the Triumphal Entry narratives in the gospels). Actually, the two hymns do span the First and Second Testaments—both are in both! The assertion, then, has merit, especially when explored more in depth.

What the two hymns embody in their close alignment with each other is a profound metaphor at the heart of the faith of the church. The first pole of the metaphor involves the beatific vision of all the company of heaven singing praise in the presence of the unsearchable glory of God. Here is the song ceaselessly resounding in the presence of transcendent Deity. The other pole sings of a different vision—that of the Son of God riding upon a beast of burden along a path leading to the Holy City and a death of suffering and dishonor on a Cross outside the walls. The followers of Jesus intone their Hosannas as this tragic-comic procession wends its way into the city; "Benedictus," they continue, "Blessed is he who comes in the name of the Lord." The church sings both hymns as a profound metaphor of its faith.

Since the resurrection of Jesus Christ, Christians cannot remain solely at one pole or the other.

To attempt a relaxation of the tension held within this metaphor by focusing only on one pole or the other results in a distortion of the faith or outright heresy. For example, the suppression of the Benedictus may lead the church to a rather lopsided gospel in which all must be "glory Divine." Such a temptation is to be found in the excesses of nineteenth century Romanticism (see Karl Barth's critique of this liberal and romantic spirit in his seminal *The Epistle to the Romans*[184]) or in some excessively "happy-clappy" "contemporary worship." Ultimately, this abandonment of the metaphor leads to docetism.

If the latter pole is retained (the Benedictus) while the former is dismissed (the Sanctus), we may be left only with the life of a Palestinian peasant whose body becomes food for dogs after the crucifixion.[185] As the mystery of the Incarnation is dissipated, what remains may be a concern for justice and a resistance to the "isms" as social agendas. That resistance is ultimately wearing and even self-defeating; lacking the confidence in the redemption won by Christ in his death and glorious resurrection, waging the fight against the world's darkness leaves the church both disheartened and ironically focused inward on those who do not join in this perpetual resistance. The liberating joy of the Exultet sung at the Easter Vigil is lost:

> This is the night when the pillar of fire destroyed the darkness of sin. . . .
> This is the night when Christ broke the chains of death and rose triumphant from the grave.[186]

On the other hand, when the church makes bold to sing both the Sanctus and Benedictus, that essential tension-filled mystery of the Incarnation is proclaimed, as God's will for earth as in heaven is undergirded. As one of the most enduring hymns to the Incarnation chants, "Christ our God to earth descendeth, our full homage to demand."[187]

Homiletical Implications

If our preaching has as its listeners the baptized assembly who will, in the course of the ordo, be offering their gifts and making Eucharist, then we do well to take into account that this assembly will also soon join with all the company of heaven in singing "Holy, holy, holy. . . ." This trajectory from sermon to Sanctus/Benedictus informs the preacher in two important respects. On one hand, we who are called to preach will need to take seriously the identity, the traditions, the theological location, and the piety of this congregation of the faithful. (After all, this people is extended the honor of joining with all the company of heaven in singing praise to the glory of God.) The congregation, then, will be caringly exegeted in its particularity and in its catholicity in the normal course of sermon preparation. Leonora Tubbs Tisdale assembles perhaps the most compelling arguments for this ethnographical aspect of the ministry of proclamation. She summarizes,

> Pastors need explicit skills and training in "exegeting congregations and their subcultures—just as they need skills and training in exegeting the Scriptures. What is distinctive about a particular congregation's subcultural identity? How does one go about reading the signs and symbols of congregational life in order to discern congregational worldview, values, and ethos? Are there any paradigms by which a local pastor can distinguish between his or her own subcultural understandings and those of the congregation?[188]

Engaging with Tisdale in a homiletical grappling for answers to her questions is crucial for an effective preaching ministry and a broader pastoral ministry as well. However, the deepest explanation for the necessity of an engagement in these issues extends beyond pastoral effectiveness or even likeability. We develop skills in exegeting the congregation because they are a distinctive assembly of God's saints who are privileged at the sacrament to sing with all the saints. They are a particular people within the whole people of God on earth who join with all the company of heaven in singing "Holy, holy, holy. . . . "

There is a further dimension to this identity of the congregation as those privileged to join with all the saints in their eternal song.[189] The converse also obtains. If during Eucharistic praying the congregation makes bold to join with all the saints and company of heaven in the Sanctus, the preacher is offered the comforting presence of those saints in particular who are needed week in and week out. Perhaps some saints in glory also need to be present in the preacher's balcony as the sermon is prepared and then preached, a kind of "default list" of the heroes, saints, angels, and martyrs of the church! These perennial saints serve to encourage and to caution, to embolden and to succor. They also offer worthy ministries to imitate and make one's own.

Many of those called to preach have found themselves drawn to one of the gospel Evangelists or epistolary writers. For these preachers, as an example, the beloved St. Luke will always be one of the blessed auditors as the sermon is prepared and preached. Others who follow the three-year lectionary will thereby have a sort of "bullpen" of saints who will take their turn in the preacher's balcony on Sunday. So, in such cases, when in Year B of the three-year sequence of lections, the gospel texts from Mark shift over for some five weeks to attend to the sweep of the Bread of Life discourse in the sixth chapter of the Fourth Gospel. For those Sundays, St. Mark will quietly exit the preacher's balcony while St. John passes on the way in.

A converse strategy may also be helpful to congregation and preacher. If one biblical writer is particularly challenging or even distasteful to the preacher, then from time to time, it is important to put aside the dislikes and welcome that saint into the "balcony" of witnesses.[190] This practice of inviting the preacher's antithetical saints is important for several reasons. First, we are encouraged along our own saintly path as we invite into our worship those who do not have an affinity with our own theological and pietistic leanings. So, for example, if we find the Fourth Evangelist to be unduly mystical and ethereal for us, then St. John's presence in our homiletical balcony is important from time to time to further ratify our long-held convictions. Second, there is always the possibly that our maturing faith may stretch us beyond any previous ideological boundaries. (This encouragement of a more tensive and expansive faith becomes possible as we welcome such antithetical saints not only into the balcony, but into the pulpit with us!) Third, the importance of inviting the saints we do not naturally find congenial to us and our convictions has to do with fleshing out the Body of Christ beyond those who are "like us" and who, similarly, we like.

The analogy with the non-balcony congregation "downstairs" is obvious. Not every listener finds our approach to the interpretation of biblical texts and our contemporary ecclesial and cultural situation to be ideal. To the contrary, if we have by our own celebrity and rhetorical powers assembled a community that does, in fact, celebrate us, our convictions and vision of church and society, then we especially are in need of some "saints to the contrary" in our balcony to keep us humble and to remind us of the need for integrity. Put simply, the more unanimity within the congregation as to our popularity and success, the more our need for those "antithetical saints" witnessing our preaching in the homiletical balcony.

When the church began its interpolation of the Benedictus into its Eucharistic praying, it created a diptych set of hymns that proclaimed the central metaphor of Christian faith. The Sanctus and Benedictus become this metaphor by virtue of their inherent opposition along with their interconnectedness. On one hand, as has been noted, the Sanctus sings with heaven's company and all the saints of the unspeakable glory of the Godhead, a glory before which all mortal flesh otherwise keeps silent. In the words of the Nicene Creed, this utterly transcendent God is "maker of heaven and earth, of all that is, seen and unseen."

Held in metaphorical polarity is the Benedictus, the song of the disciples of Jesus, both men and women, as he leads a ragtag procession into the Holy City and ultimately to the cross. The song, this acclamation beginning "Blessed is he who comes . . . ," is one of Incarnation, of the One who, again in the words of the Creed, "came down from heaven" and through the power of the Holy Spirit "became incarnate from the Virgin Mary, and was made man." The Word made flesh also "suffered death and was buried." Now, when the church makes Eucharist, it sings both hymns; they bond together the mysteries of the transcendent holiness of God and the immanent glory of the Father's only begotten Son.

And, in spite of that anomaly within Anglican and Methodist liturgical practice when, for a season, the Benedictus was suppressed and, therefore, the metaphor at the heart of Christian faith was obscured, this marriage of the two hymns is enduring and essential. Preachers will adopt a "one hymn" stance at their own peril and in violation of the command to preach "the full counsel of God." Thus, we can hear preaching that specializes solely in the glory of God afar while others preach a very human, and typically tragic, version of the "Jesus of history." However, "serious distortions of the gospel result when the metaphor of faith is relaxed and collapsed into a pious casserole of self-help encouragements and prosperity gospel promotions. Beyond these all too familiar sermonic varieties, moreover, the collapse of the tensions held within the Sanctus/Benedictus metaphor has led to seriously "Bad Religion"[191]—some version or other of docetism. Several especially toxic homiletical distortions may be spotted with ease:

1. *Preaching the Prosperity Gospel*—It will only take a few minutes of channel-surfing to come upon some TV preacher or other, beaming out at the viewers, and enthusing about the prosperity God intends for those who believe, and, not parenthetically, "support this ministry." On one hand, the high-rating preachers of the prosperity gospel, along with their acolytes, appear to remain mostly on a distorted version of the Sanctus side of the metaphor of Christian faith. Even when their preaching does come down to earth, it is incarnate mostly within visions of glory promised in this world to those who truly believe. On the other hand, the preaching of a prosperity gospel could be misperceived as some kind of aberrant version of the Benedictus, in which the things of earth may become transfigured into a glory once only reserved for the Parousia.

   What has happened instead is that the tensions inherent within the metaphor of the Two Hymns have been collapsed into a squishy gospel of personal and material aggrandizement. While those preaching the prosperity gospel display little interest in the Parousia in particular, or eschatology in general, a dualism exists between what is earthly (always cast in the negative) and what is heavenly (the this-worldly blessings showered upon believers). Of course, this dualism is a crude parody of the earthly and heavenly dichotomy in the Fourth Gospel. Still, the "heaven on earth" promise to the faithful stands in bold contrast to the "hell on earth" lives of the mediocre and the disbelieving.

One prosperity preacher illustrated this dualism by way of his visit to an underdeveloped country. He explained in his sermon how vast was the poverty in this country and how "sorry" the housing conditions of most of the citizens. Then the preacher related how he turned and lifted his eyes to a majestic mansion upon the hilltop nearby. The beauty of the building was depicted in detail, including the high wall that separated it from all the sorry conditions that surrounded it. He asked his interpreter who lived in the mansion. The reply: "The ambassador lives there." The preacher then concluded by proclaiming that God considered his children as ambassadors, as deserving of the mansion on the hill, if only they had faith in the promises of the Divine. The message of the illustration was striking. The world was composed of the sorry folks living in sorry conditions and the ambassadors who claimed these this-worldly blessings of God. Further reflection will conclude that for this preacher, the reason for the sorry state of the poor was their mediocrity and faithlessness.

This conclusion was inescapable even though it was morally obscene and biblically untrue. That Jesus would be down among the sorry folks, serving them, suffering with them, and feeding them was completely outside the homiletical purview of this prosperity preacher. Ross Douthat comments regarding this "gospel,"

> If you fail to master everyday events, and fall into struggles and suffering, it's a sign that you just haven't prayed hard enough, or trusted faithfully enough, or thought big enough, or otherwise behaved the way a child of God really should.[192]

The other side of the coin is equally apparent. If you pray hard, trust faithfully, and act the way a child of God ought, blessings are forthcoming that provide a heaven on earth. If the followers of the Lord do sing "Blessed is he who comes . . . ," they chime in on the way to Nieman-Marcus and not to Calvary.

    This absence of eschatological promise is intrinsic to a gospel of prosperity. The future hope for such prosperity preachers as Joel Osteen, for example, is not a proclamation of the Good News that God will make all things right in the fullness of time. Rather, the message "is firmly on personal progress in the present tense."[193] The polarities here are not between memory and hope or the already and the not yet. Rather, the duality is that of a state of non-blessing (created by sloth, mediocrity, and faithlessness) and heavenly blessing on earth now (obtained by excellence and trust). "Your Best Self Now" displaces the heavenly Jerusalem come down from heaven.

2. *Preaching and the God Within*—The Sanctus and the Benedictus sing of the true God who is the creator of all things and who is "high and lifted up," residing in glory, and yet has come to dwell in our midst in the Incarnation of Jesus Christ. The metaphor is freighted with mystery: The triune God is at once acclaimed as Lord, worshipped by all creation, and acknowledged as Father everlasting, and incarnate to set us

free, humbly accepting the Virgin's womb, "the eternal Son of the Father."[194] Whether described as mystery, scandal, or dilemma, orthodox Christianity, as Ross Douthat notes, leaves this tension between the transcendence and immanence of God unresolved. Further, Douthat highlights the contrast between the orthodox decision to abide with this "dilemma" and the "God Within" theology. The appeal of the latter "rests in the way it addresses a more ancient dilemma: the problem of how to reconcile God's immanence with His transcendence."[195] Interestingly, one of the outcomes of this abolition of the tension between the theological witness of the Sanctus and that of the Bendictus is a largely unnoticed depersonalization of God. The God Within is "so absolute that He's immanent, so beyond space and time that He's available to everyone at every moment, so universal that He's in you as you."[196]

Perhaps the contrast between the God of Christian orthodoxy and the God Within is best grasped from the perspective of the implications for praxis and life together. Here, too, the Sanctus and Benedictus provide guidance to preachers. The Sanctus, we are reminded is the song of the heavenly host—those cherubim and seraphim—heard by Isaiah at his vision in the Temple. Immediately, in response to the sight and sound, the prophet cries out, "Woe is me! I am lost, for I am a man of unclean lips and live among a people of unclean lips; yet my eyes have seen the King, the Lord of hosts" (6:5). And after being cleansed of that sin—the live coal from the altar touched to his mouth—Isaiah responds to the Lord's call, "Here am I; send me!"(6:8) Isaiah is now a prophet of the holy and righteous God of Israel.

Moreover, the Benedictus, as well, has its own trajectory between doxology and praxis. In the Fourth

Gospel's rendition of the Benedictus, the Evangelist immediately reflects that the Scripture is being fulfilled, quoting Zephaniah: "Do not be afraid, daughter of Zion. Look, your king is coming, sitting on a donkey colt" (John 12:15). A glance at the context of that Scriptural text being fulfilled reveals that the entire sequence is about covenant and praxis. "The Word being fulfilled promises that God's people will "seek refuge in the name of the Lord—the remnant of Israel." Then Zephaniah adds,

> They shall do no wrong and utter no lies, nor shall a deceitful tongue be found in their mouths. Then they will pasture and lie down, and no one shall make them afraid. (Zeph. 3:13)

Because the Benedictus depicts the coming of the humble king upon a donkey as the inauguration of his reign, a time when truth will abound and all falsehood be abolished the Scriptural context for the Hymn is at once eschatological and ethical—two issues that the God Within theology regards as fully dispensable.[197]

While the God Within theology yields little or no emphasis on matters of ethical or eschatological import, its core convictions are readily identifiable. They present a coherent, if heterodox world view. Douthat lists these tenets as follows:

A. "(A)ll organized religions offer only partial glimpses of the God or light or Being that all of them pursue, . . ."[198] hence, "the true spiritual adept must seek to experience God through feeling rather than reason, experience rather than dogma, a direct encounter rather than a hand-me-down revelation." The essence of what Eckhart Tolle labels "ancient religions" has been over-crusted with later teachings and practices to the degree that the earlier and deeper meaning is no longer discernible. The "transformative power" has been lost.[199]

B. "God is everywhere and within everything, but the best way to encounter the divine is through the God within, the divinity that resides inside your very self and soul."[200] Thus, the way to God is through the process of enlightenment, a journey in which the matters of the mind are left behind and one's true self is attained. That place, that state, is one of bliss, joy, and love. "When you return there," Deepak Chopra says, "you will experience yourself as one with God."[201]

C. "God's all-encompassing nature means that sin and death and evil—or what seem like sin and death and evil—will ultimately be reconciled rather than defeated."[202] Words and actions that injure others or the planet derive from persons who are alienated from their true selves and its being, love, and peace. Since enlightenment, deeply achieved, is the state of selflessness, evil or sin are absent from this place of unity. Anger, rage, and resentment are emotions symptomatic of an estrangement from the state of enlightenment. Even those whose rage is a revulsion against the world's evil need to learn that "moral outrage is still rage." Chopra does allow for combat against the injustice in the world, but only when not motivated by anger and rage.[203]

D. (B)eatitude is constantly available . . . eternity can be entered at any moment, by any person who understands how to let go, let God, and let themselves be washed away in love."[204] To dwell in the past or long for a future fulfillment is fruitless. As Deepak Chopra insists, "The present moment is the only time that is eternal."[205] Given this prescription for happiness, therefore, the young Isaiah should have sought to remain in the Temple and in this mystic harmony with the Divine. His "fault," of course, was in his delusion that the Holy One was sending him on a prophetic mission that would be anything but happy! In like manner, the procession into the Holy City on Palm Sunday could have been toward the Temple and a beatific Oneness; certainly not a journey toward the Cross. Chopra would correct Jesus' mistaken commitment which has led to this "Triumphal Entry" and its Benedictus. "How could discovering your true self," he asks, "possibly be a form of sacrifice?"[206]

In addition to these four tenets of the God Within theology, two other qualities of its advocates need further treatment, especially in juxtaposition to the Two Hymns of the Great Thanksgiving. On one hand, in contrast to the inherently communal and covenantal expression of the Sanctus and Benedictus, the God Within theology is at its core profoundly individualistic. Alyce McKenzie notes a deep contradiction in the God Within emphasis on the restoration of the self, community and world on one hand and the focus on only attainments of the self on the other. McKenzie adds,

> Ironically, this emphasis on the oneness of all things does not always translate into a focus on the present-day local community. Much New Age self-help writing focuses on the individual's attainment of desired goals. It tends to view [the] God as immanent and at the service of our heart's desire.[207]

This is not to say that any vision of a world in harmony is inherently flawed. Rather, the ways and means of opposing evil—by combating it, individually and collectively—will typically result in only more dysfunction and alienation from enlightenment. Preaching, therefore, that encourages resistance[208] and moral outrage is ironically flawed, contributing to further evil and violence. The ultimate liberation is profoundly personal; in the midst of the world's dysfunctions and one's own, a path exists toward true liberation. "The good news," Tolle asserts, "is that you *can* free yourself from your mind."[209] Notice the symmetry: only the self can free the self from its delusions and negative emotions. "Self-help" is not only a section on the eBook web site directory; it is the only real path to love, peace, and unity.

The other side of this coin is that of the impossibility of any transformation beyond the individual's own self-healing and enlightenment. Put simply, what can the person becoming enlightened do to ease the evil and injustice in the world? Here, the God Within theology proposes several alternative responses to this question, though the primary answer is "Simply be about your own enlightenment." However, the most pervasive response that comes closest to any moral or ethical position is one of a kind of benign contagion. The logic of this response is as follows: First, since there is a continuum between the Being one discovers within oneself and within the cosmos, discovering the eternal Now within also offers a oneness with the entirety of Being. Second, the alternate path of mindfully strategizing against evil, as has been seen, is a self-defeating option. This path leads only to more anger and to negative self-righteous actions. However, those few who are attaining enlightenment will serve as benign contagions for peace and love. Tolle therefore addresses the dynamic from this "contagious" perspective:

Are you polluting the world or cleaning up the mess? You are responsible for your inner space; nobody else is, just as you are responsible for the planet. As within, so without: If humans clear inner pollution, then they will also cease to create outer pollution.[210]

The "as within, so without" principle, preachers should note, is remarkably similar to that employed by the more conservative revivalism. In this latter example, however, the "as within" dynamic sought is not personal enlightenment, but the salvation of one's soul. The response to the social evils of the world becomes a variant on the "so without" reasoning of the God Within theology. Enough saved souls, revivalists argue, and the evils of the world will wither away and die off. Both positions assume a kind of individualism as the launching pad for any societal transformation.

Given the interest in personal spiritual formation within the church, especially in the retrieval of Eastern and Western Church traditions of spiritual practice, the question naturally arises regarding any critique of the "God Within" movement. After all, are not Tolle and Chopra fundamentally after the same goals as Keating, Pennington, and other advocates, for example, of Centering Prayer? Do not both appear concerned for the individual's healing and wholeness? The two movements even sound quite similar, sharing a vocabulary of words in common including numerous references to "consciousness," the "false self," and even celebrations of "God." However, a more considered analysis of Christian spirituality will lead to an awareness of the profound gulf between the "God Within" acolytes and interpreters of Christian spirituality. Among the numerous emphases that distinguish Christian spiritual formation are five core convictions that are distinctly not shared by God Within advocates. These include:

A. While God Within spokespersons will sometimes quote texts from such "teachers" as Jesus, the entirety of Christian spiritual tradition is rooted in the Scriptures. Thus, in the course of advocating the spiritual discipline of *Lectio Divina*, M. Basil Pennington reasserts this canonical ground for the practice: "The choice source for this lectio always was, and always will be the Sacred Texts."[211] There is, to be sure, what Pennington terms "the larger book of revelation: the whole of the work of the Creator, his wonderful creation."[212] But the grounding of the larger book of revelation is in the particularity of the revelation in Holy Scripture.

B. There is a covenantal context for Christian spiritual formation. Divine grace is prevenient to an individual's journey toward authentic being. "In Christianity redemption from the false self is understood as a gift of God's grace."[213] The sacramental gift of covenant and the subsequent promise of participation in the Divine, of course, is that of Holy Baptism. "We have been baptized into the very life and love of the Son," Pennington states. Our disciplines of spiritual formation derive from the originating grace of our baptism and are toward a share in the life and love of the Triune God.

C. The contemplative life, then, has a deeper goal than some turn from the false self toward authentic existence. The goal is both deeper and more extensive than that offered by the God Within teachers. As we are incorporated by baptism into the Body of Christ we are relocated to a life-in-community and within that community we are invited to enter more deeply into the mystery of God. The disciplines of spiritual formation offer us the avenues available for a journey both intensely personal and abidingly communal. Moreover, as we take up the discipline of contemplative prayer, for example, the goal is to be refashioned in the image of Christ, to encounter the mystery of the Holy Trinity, "the unfathomable source of our very existence."[214]

D. The God Within program for personal spiritual transformation and enlightenment, as noted above, remains that of individuals on a solitary quest. However, within Christian spiritual formation, the various personal and communal disciplines become one centering point around which Christian life orbits. The other point—both forming an ellipse—is that of the liturgy and the sacramental life. Thomas Keating therefore adds,

> Contemplative prayer is the ideal preparation for the liturgy. Liturgy, in turn, when properly executed, fosters contemplative prayer. Together they further the ongoing process of conversion to which the Gospel calls us.[215]

For the liturgy to fulfill its purposes of praise, proclamation, petition, and Holy Communion with Christ, there is a need for the assembly to be about the disciplines of spiritual formation. Conversely, Christian spiritual formation prepares and undergirds the faithful for their liturgical and sacramental activity.

E. The God Within movement assumes that social and political change and care for the creation are the by-products of the individual's journey toward self-transformation and enlightenment. The definitive goal of Christian spiritual formation, however, is an ever deeper participation in the *missio Dei*. Pennington, therefore, notes as the outcome of the contemplative life,

> We become compassionate persons who feel with, are with, in a sensitive and sensing presence—with reality,

with God, with his creation, with other persons, with our own true selves.[216]

That all Christians are not far along this journey toward the compassionate life is sadly all too evident. However, the mission of God is founded upon gratuitous love for the creation, the human family, Christ's church, and every baptized member. Those who encourage the disciplines of spiritual formation, therefore, have their vision fixed on the biblical vision of a time when there will be a new heaven and a new earth. The journey toward that Day tracks our growth in compassion as we grow into Christ.

While it may be argued that the God Within advocates and those committed to such contemplative disciplines as centering prayer do share some common terminology and evidence a concern for healing and wholeness, it is equally true that their methods and goals are widely divergent. When all is said and done, the differences distill down to one core question: are the dynamics of such healing and wholeness the outcome of human technique and personal enlightenment or, in the case of Christian spiritual formation, grounded in the grace of God, especially manifest in the sacramental life? The answer to the question is obvious and compelling, and leads to a specific conclusion; perhaps one of the most ironic celebrations of the Eucharist would be at a local church where preacher and people share a God Within theological perspective. The Sanctus and Benedictus would either need to be deleted from the anaphora or, more likely, simply ignored or interpreted at a more "spiritual" level.[217]

3. *The Two Hymns and the Gnostic Impulse*—Whether the "bad religion" is inherent in the promises of the prosperity gospel or the lures of the God Within theology, the result is a

distorted form of Christian faith, one aptly described as the "gnostic impulse." In contrast, as the early church came to shape that "liturgical cuckoo"—the Sanctus and the Benedictus—an orthodox expression of biblical faith was sung by the assembly. The former, the contemporary versions of the gnostic impulse, offer a salvation by gnosis, a belief, in the words of Thomas Long, that "human beings, given the proper knowledge, given illumination, can learn their way to wholeness." Long continues,

> The gnostic impulse does not imagine humanity captive to sin and needing divine rescue. In fact, the idea of a sinful humanity is minimized, even repudiated. . . . (T)he human problem is not sin but ignorance, and the ethical implication is that people, when they are fully enlightened, will choose the good.[218]

As a correlate, there emerges an aversion to the material world, to the flesh, and, therefore, to the Incarnation.

In a perfect expression of Gnosticism, Eckhart Tolle teaches that "underneath the level of physical appearances and separate forms, you are one with all that is."[219] Orthodoxy, however, proclaims that "the Word became flesh" and that through the power of the Holy Spirit, God in Christ continues to care about and abide in this world. The faith of the church, Thomas Long summarizes, "sees human flesh and history as a place that God has chosen to dwell, a place thus made sacred."[220] The metaphor of orthodox faith holds in tension the glory of the transcendent and the immanence of the Incarnation.

Two other aspects of the Gnostic impulse are highlighted by Thomas Long. This impulse represents a turn toward the God Within. Christian orthodoxy, then, is regarded not as an ally by those championing this inward search for deity but as an institution consciously attempting to prevent the quest for enlightenment. Burdened by an overlay of fossilized doctrine and liturgy, and complicit in an ages-long conspiracy of silence, the institutional church stands in the way of authentic spiritual life. Those who take the turn inward do so in spite of the organized church. In addition, as has been explored above, the Gnostic impulse emphasizes "present spiritual reality rather than eschatological hope" and focuses on "the God of timeless truth rather than the God who will bring history to consummation."[221] Memory and hope both corrupt the seeker of enlightenment; the longing looks back and ahead create a temporal consciousness. This fabrication, called time, is a symptom of consciousness in need of liberation. And, as Tolle reminds, "There is no salvation in time."[222] Asserting the claim of orthodox faith, to the contrary, Don Saliers insists that "every act of Christian prayer and worship is always eschatological in the sense that it is an act of hope based on the promises of God."[223]

Conclusion

Whatever else, the Sanctus and Benedictus offer the congregation songs whose depth of imagery and meaning reverberate at each Eucharistic celebration. Both songs are derived from the Hebrew Scriptures and given further overlays of significance within their New Testament contexts. Then, church tradition aligned the hymns within the Great Thanksgiving and the assembly joins with the entire company of heaven and the followers of Jesus in singing "Holy, holy, holy . . ." and "Blessed is he who comes. . . ." The two hymns belong conjoined in Eucharistic praying because they hold together the mystery of the transcendent holiness of the Godself and the Incarnate Word, Jesus Christ.

In preaching, then, the Two Hymns point the preacher toward the polarities of the mystery of God's transcendence and immanence, and invite those called to preach to range across this Divine expansiveness. But the Sanctus and Benedictus also set boundaries for orthodox proclamation. Preaching that speaks only of blessing, prosperity, and glory attempts to defeat the juxtaposition of the Two Hymns—the One preexistent with God took the form of a slave and became obedient even to death on a cross. By contrast, preaching that names the this-worldly expressions of the principalities and powers, but stops short of announcing the redemption that has been won by him who was exalted and given the name above every name is also sadly deficient. Perhaps in the Two Hymns, the church has set the mysteries around which faithful Christian preaching will orbit, an ellipse of Divine glory disclosed as the assembly sings with the hosts of heaven and with those who follow Jesus into the Holy City.

5

THE POST-SANCTUS NARRATIVE

*"You are holy, O God of majesty,
and blessed is Jesus Christ, your Son, our Lord."* [224]

There is an uneasiness that permeates some congregations after the Sanctus has been sung—after joining with the song of angels and archangels. Will the minister at the Table now move on into the wonders of the Narrative following the Sanctus or will that member of the clergy set aside the ordo and substitute talk about God in place of direct address to the Holy One? If a substitution occurs, the congregation may hear a summary of the topics addressed in the sermon (once again) or a third person discourse on the meaning of the sacrament of the Lord's Supper. But in any case, the biblical grammar of giving thanks is set aside on behalf of some other thematic or narrative. What has been supplanted is the narration of the One who is the blessed Son, Jesus Christ our Lord.

Investigating the Rite

If the broad consensus is assumed, that "The Eucharistic Prayer is (probably) *derived* in form and structure from the normal Jewish grace after meals,"[225] then it would be expected that the Post-Sanctus would take up the liturgical action of giving thanks. That is, we will be especially alert to the early Christian Eucharistic praying that picks up, and even extends, the address to God in thanksgiving of the Jewish berakah,

> We give you thanks, Lord our God, for giving us as our heritage a desirable, good and ample land, the covenant, and the Torah, life and food.[226]

As with the thanksgiving psalms of the Hebrew Scriptures and the prayers of thanksgiving in both Testaments (see, for example, 1 Chronicles 29:10-19), the grammar of this form of address to God has a deep narrative structure. Simply put, the biblical people give thanks to the God of covenant by reciting the miraculous deeds and gracious acts by which this people have been called out, delivered, led, and given provision. This continuity of narrative thanksgiving from the Jewish prayers after meals to early Christian anaphoras is especially evident in the Egyptian Eucharistic tradition of St. Mark. One liturgical text shaping this tradition—which in turn may well have been one of the formative roots of the Roman Canon—opens its second strophe with the words, "We give thanks." This opening parallels the structure of the Birkat ha-Mazon (a significant text of the berakah) as well as the late first century church order document, the Didache.[227]

In spite of this proposed liturgical continuity, however, the Post-Sanctus does, in fact, begin to display alternative modes of prayer in East and West. The former, as seen most typically in the Liturgy of St. Basil, has an extended narrative Post-Sanctus in which thanks is offered to God for the history of salvation and the mighty acts of God. The narrative spans from Eden to the prophets to the Incarnation (Jesus as the New Adam) and the gift of a redeemed holy people and royal priesthood. The narrative continues its thanksgiving by reciting Christ's passion, death, resurrection, and ascension.[228] Later Eucharistic Prayers of the Eastern Church continue this Post-Sanctus narrative of thanksgiving.

In the West, by contrast, the Post-Sanctus prior to the Words of Institution takes a differing approach that sets aside a narrative rhetoric. The Roman Canon moves to its distinctive Preliminary Epiclesis and then to the Intercession of the Saints accompanied by a more condensed and discursive statement of dogma. Eucharistic praying in the West, therefore, makes a rather abrupt shift from language that calls down and makes intercession to that of the narrative of the Institution. In the East, however, the Institution continues a rhetoric of prayer begun immediately after the Sanctus; the warp of prayer remains that of narrative and thanks.

The Sixteenth Century reformers either eliminated this portion of the Eucharistic Prayer entirely (recalling that Luther transposed his "German Sanctus" to the Communion itself, there now being no Post-Sanctus) or, in the case of the Anglican tradition, continued the Western practice of dense, discursive theological language. Moreover, the 1552 *Book of Common Prayer* interpolated the Prayer of Humble Access following the Sanctus (without Benedictus) and prior to the Consecration. Thus, in place of a continuity of narrative thanksgiving, the Anglican Post-Sanctus opened with communal penitence before shifting to a discursive consecratory prayer that continued to focus on the unworthiness of the people and the atoning work of Christ for their salvation. The only narrative fragments remaining were the Words of Institution themselves. Thanksgiving had been washed away in the West—both Roman and Anglican—by this later rhetoric of penance and atonement.

Following the liturgical reforms of the Second Vatican Council, the newly revised Eucharistic liturgies of the Roman Rite, as well as major Protestant traditions, tended to return to a more ancient and more Eastern approach to the Post-Sanctus. The former, the Roman Catholic revisions of the Mass, still retained the Rite's particular practice of a Preliminary Epiclesis and, in the first of the four anaphoras now offered, also continued the early intercessions of the saints. Within the Protestant communions that also turned to revisions of their liturgies following the Council, the Post-Sanctus narrative was restored in most versions.

The United Methodist Post-Sanctus, for example, opens with a common lead-in to the narrative, "Holy are You and blessed is your Son Jesus Christ." The narrative then varied according to season and day while centering its thanksgiving on the Spirit-anointed baptism and ministry of Jesus Christ, his baptism of suffering and death, his resurrection, ascension, and promise to be with us always "in the power of your Word and Holy Spirit."[229] The "Holy Eucharist II" of the 1979 *Book of Common Prayer* of the Episcopal Church provides a less expansive and therefore less fully narrative Post-Sanctus, serving as a more condensed version of the United Methodist text. Again, the focus is primarily Christological:

> . . . you, in your mercy, sent Jesus
> Christ, your only and eternal Son, to share our human
> nature, to live and die as one of us, to reconcile us to you,
> the God and Father of all.[230]

The Presbyterian Church, U.S.A. recently published a new hymnal and worship book, *Glory to God*, in which a revised Eucharist is also provided ("The Service for the Lord's Day").[231] The Post-Sanctus will be provided in full form for ministers of the Table in separate publications, but the rubrics indicate that its narrative and Eucharistic qualities are being fully restored:

> *The prayer continues, thankfully remembering:*

> *the Word made flesh;*
> *Jesus' life and ministry;*
> *his death and resurrection;*
> *the promised coming of his reign;*
> *and the gift of the sacrament:*[232]

Nicely, the new Presbyterian text continues the giving of thanks with a trajectory from the Incarnation to the grace of the sacrament.

The Roman Catholic Church's Missal of 2011 evoked considerable controversy with regard to the shift away from the ecumenical texts of the liturgy at certain points. However, the revisions of Eucharistic Prayer IV may well enhance the narrative thanksgiving of the Post-Sanctus. Based on Eastern sources, including the Liturgy of St. Basil, Eucharistic Prayer IV is distinctive among the four anaphora of the 2011 Missal. Especially effective is the Christological centerpiece of this Post-Sanctus:

> And you so loved the world, Father most holy, that in the fullness of time you sent your Only Begotten Son to be our Savior. Made incarnate by the Holy Spirit and born of the Virgin Mary, he shared our human nature in all things but sin. To the poor he proclaimed the good news of salvation, to prisoners, freedom, and to the sorrowful of heart, joy.[233]

Homiletical Implications

The character of liturgical rhetoric ranges from the highly imaged and symbolic to the densely discursive and dogmatic, and then on to the narration of a biblical event or events. A Eucharistic Prayer drawing on early church forms and shaped with contemporary pastoral and theological care brings these rhetorical loci together with complexity and yet with graceful flow. Moreover, the shifts within the Prayer may be sudden and unannounced. These shifts include not only rhetorical form but voice. The presiding minister at the Table addresses the Prayer on behalf of the people to the Father and then shifts and engages the assembly in dialogue. The congregation responds to the presiding minister with one voice, yet at another occasion joins its voice with "angels and archangels and all the company of heaven." Eucharistic praying is a complex rhetorical event.

For our interests in the Post-Sanctus narrative, it will need saying that the particular events of Holy Scripture that are narrated are not done so in full "storytelling" mode. Rather, the Prayer will refer to incidents within the Incarnation, baptism, ministry, passion, death, resurrection, and ascension of Jesus by way of terse phrases and image-laden expressions. So, in the United Methodist Post-Sanctus narration, the minister at the Table recites the Christological material including, "He healed the sick, fed the hungry, and ate with sinners." Each of these phrases is heavy with a depth of multiple stories in the gospels. Each of the three is presented in various renditions according to the theological interests of each Evangelist. Moreover, the three categories of Dominical ministry evoke other narratives from the Hebrew Scriptures and, as well, point toward the fulfillment of all things when all shall be healed, fed, and gathered into one flock. Memory and hope are latent within the narrative recital of the Post-Sanctus prayer.

This quality of Eucharistic praying—its complexity, mobility, and shifts in voice and rhetorical form—places several responsibilities on the preacher if, as advocated by the Constitution on the Sacred Liturgy, the laity's involvement is to be that of "active participation."[234] All the more, the narrativity of the Post-Sanctus (and of the Words of Institution) calls preachers to disciplines of preaching related to homiletical method and pastoral care. Shaping persons within the community of faith to fully and faithfully enter into the Eucharistic celebration is a serious responsibility and high honor for those called to preach. The process formally began during the catechumenate, but continues week in and week out as the Word is proclaimed at the Eucharist on the Lord's Day. Since the Eucharistic Prayer provides only a terse summarizing statement of the narratives during the Post-Sanctus, these referential images will need to connect with the assembly's familiarity of the biblical stories themselves.

Apart from the ongoing discussion as to the place of narrative preaching with regard to seekers, introduction to and invitation within the world of the biblical narratives is essential for maturing a community of disciples.[235] Inviting the baptized into the world of their Scripture's narratives, then, is a vital ministry on behalf of their maturing discipleship, mission, and sacramental life. The world of the biblical narratives awaits the new Christian and longs to begin the journey of personal and communal formation. By way of a *via negativa,* we will first consider those homiletical practices and assumptions that provide serious obstacles to the critical work of delivering the Scriptures to a maturing people of God. These barriers—seen and heard in countless attempts at "saying something on Sunday"—are the pitfalls into which the preacher may all too easily fall.

Pitfalls in Narrative Preaching

1. *The Homiletics of Distillation*—It was David Buttrick[236] who led the assault against the version of biblical interpretation that regards stories, according to Buttrick, as ornamental baubles swirling around the Bible's great religious and moral themes. Whether these are the parables of Jesus, the extended narratives of the Hebrew Scriptures, or perhaps, a Johannine sign, Buttrick descried the hermeneutical assumptions of this rationalistic methodology.

   Despite the fact that each of these stories shows significant narrative characteristics, the prevailing hermeneutic does not take the narrative as a whole seriously. One example of the development of a plot in scripture can be noted in "The Parable of the Good Samaritan" (Luke 10:29-37); it certainly displays a plot, a movement through time involving various characters, their actions and thoughts and words. In some cases, the characters may be well-rounded, fleshed-out as it were, such as the Samaritan, in others, "flat," stock characters (such as the thieves and the innkeeper) are employed. In the case of our parable, the setting provides some sense of tone—it is a dangerous place for the man going down from Jerusalem to Jericho. Sure enough, the plot thickens, he is robbed and beaten, left half dead in a ditch along the road. But the plot continues by delivering various potential helpers along the road to the "accident scene." Two just pass on by, but a Samaritan stops and goes out of his way (literally!) to provide help. End of parable.

   Now the way liberal interpreters have sought the meaning of the story—ever since Adolf Jülicher in 1899[237]—is through an attempt to discover the "kernel" of meaning under the "shell" of the story. In fact, Jülicher and his liberal main-idea followers do find that kernel: a truth about the moral high ground in life of helping other persons. But this German interpreter of Scripture insists that there is one and only one idea buried within any given parable. Once that main idea—in this case a moral lesson about social helpfulness—is teased out, the story itself is entirely disposable. The "shell" has served its function as a temporary host body for the kernel's main idea.

As this main idea hermeneutic of parable interpretation proceeded along its way during the last century and an eighth, an interesting phenomenon occurred. Interpreters from differing theological and ecclesial traditions, all assuming the same main idea hermeneutic, approached the parables in quest of their kernel meaning. What transpired is fascinating to observe. Orthodox Lutheran interpreters found orthodox Lutheran kernels, charismatic preachers found charismatic main ideas, and liberation theologians found liberation theology main ideas![238] More recently, it is popular for evangelical preachers patterning their preaching after some celebrity or other to search the parable for its "big idea," that pragmatic, life-skills-building insight buried down within the story told by Jesus. In every case, what the "one and only one" main idea interpreters failed to discern was that each preacher found a kernel very much like his or her own concern. To shift metaphors, when main idea parable interpreters looked in the pool of the story, they came away seeing their own reflection. The one constant was that the story itself—those items related to plot, character, narration, setting, etc., were all deemed dispensable once the story's idea was ascertained.

Since at least the early years of the 1970's, members of the Parables Seminar of the Society of Biblical Literature (SBL) have been training preachers to consider parables as narrative metaphors, stories inviting us within their worlds in order that they may perform some needed reconstruction of our overly hardened personal, social, and ecclesial worlds. According to this, more comprehensive hermeneutical view of scriptural story, one might think of the parables of Jesus more as "shaped-charged" stories deployed to break apart our well-defended story worlds on behalf of the kingdom of God. So, the terror of the Good Samaritan story is that it always takes the privileged world of the hearer, roughs it up considerably, deprives us of being in control (a perennial reality of those suddenly lying half-dead in a ditch), and then delivers as our helper our most hated enemy! The parable always reverses, never vindicates our hardened world with its securities and certainties as to who is "good" and who is "enemy." Rather than coming away from a sermon on the Parable of the Good Samaritan with a surety that we are doing good along with some encouragements to do better, a more faithful response to this Word might be "Dear God, why did you have that happen to me!"

2. *Generic Narratives*—A further obstacle to the congregation's literacy about and formation within biblical narratives is that of assuming that a generic sermon will suffice when dealing with pericopes with multiple attestations. That is, if a text from Matthew presents itself that also has parallels in Mark and Luke, the temptation is to think, "I have a sermon on that." The sermon in mind may have been from one of the other Synoptics or, much worse, already fashioned with some thematic assumed to be found in every version of the story. So if the preacher is anticipating the Sunday of the Transfiguration in the liturgical year,[239] and if it is Year A in the lectionary, the assumption may come to mind that "one size fits all" when it comes to these multiple attestation stories.

Two major issues emerge if the preacher succumbs to the temptation to preach that generic sermon. On one hand, the preacher is settling for way less than what the homiletic calling entails. In his discussion of the African American homiletic tradition, Warren H. Stewart, Jr. points to what should be a common assumption in all preaching traditions, "the preacher will become intimate with the particular scriptural passage that he or she seeks to interpret."[240] That is, before inviting the congregation to journey along through the text's terrors (and glories), the preacher will first have waded out deep in those waters.

The worst violation of this sacred trust and responsibility, of course, would be for the preacher to simply "borrow" a sermon and, without acknowledgement, preach it as her or his own. But only moderately better is the attitude that a sermon can be recycled without significant revision if a text presents itself that has parallels in other gospels. The preacher is denying him or herself the growth in wisdom and pastoral effectiveness that comes with a deep engagement with the lesson at hand. Moreover, since the work of interpretation begins in prayer, using generic sermons robs the preacher of the spiritual discipline of *lectio divina*, a holy reading of the text.[241]

On the other hand, yielding to the temptation of preaching a generic sermon on a multiply attested text impoverishes the congregation. One of the joys of deepening discipleship for faithful members of Christ's church is to discover that they resonate with the spirituality and theological perspective of a particular Gospel Evangelist or, perhaps, the Apostle Paul. Generic preaching defeats this joy-filled journey of Christ's people when they discover, for example, that the world of St. Luke, with its many stories of the women followers of the Lord is *their* gospel.

Another aspect of discipleship formation that may also be prevented extends more deeply. Maturing Christians come to discover that holding in tension the differing nuances and details of these multiply occurring stories produces a faith-enhancing tension. Persons growing in discipleship are not weakened by the variation and even disagreements between texts; they are strengthened and encouraged by living in this biblical world with its rich diversity of interpretations. Thus, preaching a generic sermon in place of proclaiming the distinctive witness of the lesson at hand becomes a serious barrier to the congregation's maturity as a community of disciples. In this default to a generic sermon, everyone loses.

3. *Stories All Our Own*—Perhaps spurred by the internet sermon web sites, and spread exponentially by forwarded e-mail, a certain elephantitis of story has increasingly infected American preaching. Huge, often sentimentalized, stories are being deployed and function, in many cases, as a substitute for the hard work of diagnosis.[242] These mega-stories often extend to fill one-third to one-half of the time of the sermon. Moreover, they create a narrative world that is itself a displacement of the world of the biblical text. Often, their theological claims and ethical formation are in direct opposition to that of the narratives of Scripture.

Their usual qualities? They tend to portray males as exhibiting agency or emerging as the heroic figures. They also lean toward an unbiblical and individualistic gospel; the communal expressions of faith are often missing. These mega-stories also veer toward works rather than grace. The gravest issue resulting from the use of one of these huge stories is that as they become the "world" of the sermon; they move to become a kind of quasi-scripture. That is, the extra-narrative portions of the sermon are typically devoted to an elaboration of the meanings of the mega-story itself. The actual Scripture reading that had been selected as the "text" of the sermon was displaced by the new "text," a vast mega-story imported by the preacher. Listeners will be hard-pressed to even recall the Scriptural text for the sermon; the mega-story, though, will be remembered. Because such vast stories typically provide some sentimental and individualistic narrative environment, they are likely, above all else, to be alien to the gospel. Thomas Long comments,

> Because pulpit storytelling is a dress rehearsal for the living of the Christian life, this means that it is ethically irresponsible to tell the canned and simplistic preacher stories that drain away the moral and theological ambiguities inherent in real life. Preacher stories that always yield the right moral lesson or end up in triumph without struggle are a damned lie about human life and Christian faith.[243]

Another expression of "stories all our own," is to be found in the chronic dependence on first person illustrations by the preacher. Apparently the lived experience of the members of the congregation fails to measure the rich significance of most every experience of the preacher. So the congregation comes to expect that the preacher will introduce this Sunday's sermon (again) with a personal anecdote ("When I was a kid growing up in Kentucky . . ."). Significant incidents from the preacher's life and that of the parsonage family become the illustrative fare for most of the issues developed through the course of the sermon. Thus, the Christmas traditions of the preacher's family are presented as the warmest ways of observing the holiday. The congregation hears that the parsonage family donates to the Heifer Project instead of lavishing presents upon each other, certainly a more excellent way. The preacher's call to ministry serves as the sole expression of response to the gospel within the congregation. The list goes on.

Consequences of this habit of drawing largely on stories of the preacher him or herself include a series of homiletical pitfalls. First, the listeners will grow restive and even resentful of the steady diet of first-person stories dealt out in most every sermon. Although it would come as a real surprise to the preacher, many in the congregation are really hearing the message from the pulpit that "my life and my family's experiences are better than anyone else's." While a quick survey would discover that most every adult in the parish was a child who grew up somewhere, went off to school for the first time, and experienced times of joy or sorrow, the message is given in the sermon that these little narratives are not worthy of mention, only those of the preacher.[244] However, a problem abides here that is even graver than the congregation's resentment of a perceived primacy of the preacher's experiences over their own. The first-person stories related by the preacher present for the most part analogies to suffering and success that shrivel the gospel to a mundane vestige of itself.

What the Apostle Paul was saying about love in 1 Corinthians 13 cannot be adequately expressed by the preacher's slightly cute story of his infatuation with a certain girl in his seventh grade class. When that same Apostle spoke of the thorn in his flesh, its analogy is not fully provided by the preacher's self-deprecating remarks about his male-pattern baldness. (The modest chuckling of members of the congregation may serve to convince the preacher of his wit and homiletical skills, but if our analogical references to Paul's "thorn in the flesh" evokes chuckles, we have failed.) David Buttrick warns of an inescapable outcome of any and all such first-person references: These stories will wind up illustrating the preacher rather than the sermon. Thus, "congregations will *always* remember the illustration as a disclosure of the *preacher's* character."[245] And as with the effects of the mega-stories already explored, first-person pulpit references will serve to erase other homiletical material within range. What will be recalled, for better and for worse, are the first-person stories. But since the surrounding material may be completely lost, the significance of the "stories all our own" will be now assigned by the listeners.

Strategies for Narrative Preaching

The terse references to biblical narratives contained in many Post-Sanctus sections of the Eucharistic Prayer invite the preacher to explore in depth the narratives of Scripture as they present themselves through the course of the liturgical year. Through the course of the Year of Grace, there will be ample opportunities to invite the listeners within the many stories whose shorthand designation in the Post-Sanctus is that "To the poor he proclaimed the good news of salvation, to prisoners, freedom, and to the sorrowful of heart, joy."[246] Viewed from this perspective, one goal of the preacher is to faithfully build up the storehouse of biblical narratives becoming the "world" of the parishioners such that their formative work is bearing fruit in their lives and life together. The perspective also functions in reverse: as the presiding minister at the Holy Meal offers such a narrative Post-Sanctus statement of thanksgiving, various narratives within the accumulating storehouse of the assembly will resonate and be evoked as the terse naming proceeds.

Fortunately, those called to preach today are not living out ministry in a season when one dominant method—for example, the three-point sermon—reigns supreme; there simply is no one strategy for preaching the narratives of Scripture that covers every pericope and each liturgical and pastoral occasion. Rather, the preacher is graced with a suite of available methods as she or he approaches the lections for the Lord's Day or festival occasion.

Among the available suite of options, several homiletical methods are trustworthy means to shape any narrative sermon, recalling that such sermons will be characterized by mobility, an episodic movement, and a performative intention (that "so what?" issue). In all instances, the dictum applies that the best way to preach a biblical narrative is by way of some narrative strategy or other. Among the suite of narrative homiletic methods are the following:

1. *"Running the Story"*[247]—The basic principle here is that the narrative plot of the passage of Scripture becomes the entire plotted movement of the sermon. That is, if the story of Naaman the Leper is the text at hand (2 Kings 5:1-14), the sermon's introduction is the same as that of the pericope—Naaman's stature and favor as commander of the army in Aram along with the information that he has the dreaded disease of leprosy. By way of contemporizing the biblical story, thereby inviting the listeners and their world into the narrative, this introduction can be addressed in several ways, but one approach is to evaluate the various locations in the story where some issue is at stake or some question begs an answer. These *"topoi,"* these places of weight all present

themselves as occasions to pause the running of the story and to open up the place to our contemporary situation.

Clearly, in the case of our example story of Naaman the Leper, there will be more such topoi than the preacher will want to explore in any given sermon. Upon a return to this text in a later sermon, some of the same topoi may be selected or, in most cases, some previously used may be set aside in favor of others not explored in the prior homily. The context and the situation for the sermon will determine the most appropriate topoi to center on in each homiletical visit to the narrative.[248] The context and situation will also inform the preacher's decision as to the specific ways in which to image each excursus taken at the respective topoi in the sermon.

So, again remaining with Naaman, the first such possible location for expansion into the listener's world is that of the young Hebrew girl taken captive from her home during one of the Aramean raids, now serving as a servant to the commander's wife. The image is powerful and this girl's words set the entire narrative in motion: "If only my lord were with the prophet who is in Samaria" (5:3). The excursus could be developed with regard to her surprising compassion given her captivity. Jesus taught such compassion. Then, too, she courageously speaks up to point to the true Source of all healing and liberation, the God of Israel. She is a saintly evangelist for the God of the covenant. Notice that the specific direction of the excursus is determined by the context and situation; again, we will not preach generic sermons! After the excursus is appropriately developed, the preacher returns to the biblical narrative and continues to run the story until the arrival at the issue-laden place for a further exploration of its contemporary implications and analogies.

2. *"The Lowry Loop"*[249]—The distinctive characteristic of a narrative sermon, Eugene Lowry argues, is its sequence, the shaping of a plot that first invites the congregation to engage in some felt discrepancy, some bind, problem, or "itch." Some trained in an older approach to preaching would nod and smile at this sermonic starting point, for they were taught that once the problem was adequately identified for the congregation, the solution was then to be applied from the gospel. However, Lowry insists that this "problem-solution" sermonic vehicle is deficient in several key areas. First, it becomes predictable, moving rapidly from any felt discrepancy toward resolution. Second, this well-seasoned approach lacks the capacity to bring the congregation along on any sort of journey of exploration. Once the problem is identified, the solution is, well, Jesus. End of story. However, what the problem-solutional form missed was that the sermon is a narrative art form and, as such, involves an intentional extension of the ambiguity of the opening issue and a correlate "strategic delay"[250] in resolution. Therefore, the preacher's task, once some opening issue or conflict is discerned and adequately explored, is not to immediately jump to some fit-it solution.

The hard work of analysis is now the preacher's task; the opening issue may become redefined as we explore it more deeply, but if the sermon is to follow a narrative plot, the problem will become more complicated, not less so. Lowry observes, then, that for a narrative sermon, "once conflict happens, things always get worse—and in such diverse ways."[251] Rather than rapid resolution, this stage of complication in the sermon "must be movement toward the actually irresolute, the truly dilemmic, the really bound."[252] The analysis that drives the initial issue, question, or bind to this kind of complication provides the opportunity for deeper challenges to emerge and be confronted.

This same tough work of analysis also extends the stage of complication and thereby strategically delays the resolution—an essential factor in any good narrative plot. At some point, though, it is time for a sudden shift, that turn toward the good news marked by its surprising advent and a clear sense that neither the preacher nor the congregation can return to the status quo ante. The gospel is the torque that provides the turn in the sermonic plot from stymied complication to surprising resolution. This irrevocable turn, the "sudden shift," Lowry argues, will only be deployed toward the latter third of the sermon, the prior stages being devoted to the presenting conflict and the extended complication. Finally, Lowry sees the occasion for the narrative sermon's sense of an ending, its "unfolding."

> It could be called "settling in to tomorrow." The focus here is anticipated genesis, imagined effect, gracious inducement, surprising releasing, unexpected blossoming—indeed unfolding. The most likely temptation for the preacher here is the temptation to say *too* much about this result of the gospel's intersection with human life.[253]

The narrative homiletical plot, then, will move from an opening problem or conflict through an extended, deeper engagement with issue that leads to further complication. Then, there is a sudden turn, a "torque" provided by the gospel that brings new possibility not foreseen in the earlier stages and which finally leads to an evocative yet brief unfolding of the implications of this new life.

3. *The Mode of Immediacy*[254]—For David Buttrick, a sermon is comprised of a sequence of modules of communal language, each attending to one single meaning. Buttrick labels this unit of oral, communal language a "move." Implied thereby is his

notion of a homiletical plot in which the preacher has assembled a series of moves intending to form within the consciousness of the listeners. As opposed to the old homiletics points (which could be renumbered and shifted without any significant confusion), the sermon's moves will be shaped into a plot that will have a theological intention about it. Moreover, the moves will follow easily one after the other, inviting faith consciousness to be formed within the listeners. Within each move, the rhetorical specifications needed for that single meaning to form in a communal hearing call for a homiletical discipline absent in more "casual" approaches to pulpit talk.

At the same time that rhetorical disciplines are being addressed, the preacher is also called to be about an exercise of imagination—each move will be imaged concretely out of the lived experience of the congregation.[255] The suite of lived experience available to the preacher within any given move includes the following:

A. One illustration, which is a story brought into the congregation's lived experience from elsewhere. Illustrations are "imports," not familiar nuggets of the congregation's homiletical storehouse. Furthermore, since any story imports a narrative world into consciousness, the rule—never to be violated—is that only one illustration per move may be deployed. Two illustrations attempting to attend to the same single meaning will compete for attention, a collision of worlds that will confuse the listeners.

B. One or more examples may be derived from the lived experience of the listeners. Since an example does not need elaboration into a full story, there is no potential clash of narrative worlds. Therefore, examples may be provided either in the singular or plural within a given move. An additional qualification of this variety of concrete language was not discussed in Buttrick's *Homiletic* in 1987: our increasingly imagistic culture now calls for some bit of perceptual imagery to be built into the example. Labels alone no longer function (such as "human trafficking" in a move dealing with the world's darkness). The congregation will need to be provided with a brief experience of the category in order for the example to function as the catalyst for the move's conceptual language.

C. Imagery has the capacity to evoke reflection and affective response as well, whether evoked in the personal, ecclesial, or societal experience of the faithful. Imagery abides in personal and communal consciousness, providing lenses through which a "world" is envisioned; persons can act with ethical consequences only within this world that by way of imagery is envisioned.[256] However, Buttrick notes that any image in consciousness comes with some built in point of view or other. "The fallacy in our homiletical thinking," Buttrick argues, "has been to suppose that point of view is only an occasional device, a rhetorical gambit used to relieve what is otherwise third-person objective discourse."[257] He adds that "we must understand that point-of-view is *always* in language and, therefore, must be integral to sermon design and development."[258] Lacking such an intrinsic point of view, the congregation may not have the time or skill to create the perspective intended by the preacher. The result can be a rather garbled hearing of the move if not the entire sermon.

Given a biblical narrative for homiletical consideration, a careful analysis of the story will notice that a number of scenes comprise the surface structure. Again, narratives are graced with mobility, a sequential (scenic) plot, and some sense of intention. In the mode of immediacy, then, the preacher will engage in this work of uncovering the narrative pericope's inherent scene and engage in the engrossing work of teasing out their meanings and locating possible imagery. Retaining an immediate relationship with the plotted movement and logic of the biblical text, the preacher may now shape a series of moves that follow a similar trajectory. Preaching a biblical narrative in the mode of immediacy, then, is to preach a narrative sermon. So, for example, the Parable of the Barren Fig Tree" in Luke 13:6-9 may inform the following series of moves:

- o We live in a world that calculates gains and losses. Investments are supposed to produce results.
- o So when the owner of this vineyard comes out and sees the fig tree, still as barren as ever, he declares to the servant, "Cut it down!" We look at barrenness and join with him to say, "Cut it down!"
- o But the gardener replies with surprising force: "No sir. Leave it stand!"
- o Now is the season of caring and feeding, of digging around the fig tree and spreading on of manure. Now is the season of mercy and tender compassion and care.
- o Still, there is that "after a year" end of the story as one possibility. But the intended finale is a glorious fig tree there in the midst of the Lord's vineyard bursting with luscious big fruit. Just as God intended in the first place!

The sequence of moves, we note, follows along with the scenes in sequences in the parable. Since the outcomes of the gardener's efforts are left up in the air at the end of the Lord's parable, the sermon will keep a similar ambiguous sense of an ending. But, the congregation will have been invited to turn and nurture their places or barrenness and work and pray for fruitfulness.

Conclusion

In the course of this survey of narrative preaching methods, along with an investigation of some of the aberrations of so-called narrative preaching, we are tracing for the sermon the implications of the Post-Sanctus Narrative within the Eucharistic Prayer. Preaching toward this aspect of Eucharistic praying invites the homilist to shape more narrative homiletical plots, ones that are mobile, episodic, and intentional.

The key term is "plot." Just as the Narrative Post-Sanctus embodies movement, an episodic quality of scenes that invite the listener to move along in the prayer, and a sense of an ending, so too the shape of the sermon embodies the movement of a plot. Some of the less appropriate approaches to narrative interpretation and illustration have been identified. However, these excesses and misuses do not argue for another eclipse of biblical narrative, nor a shyness concerning narrative homiletic methods. The Post-Sanctus Narrative teaches us this much: the Great Thanksgiving is impoverished when these stories have been dropped in favor of discursive doctrinal speech. A similar dynamic obtains within faithful preaching; we preach the story and invite the assembly to enter fully into its world.

6

THE INSTITUTION NARRATIVE

"On the night he was handed over to suffering and death, our Lord Jesus Christ took bread; ..." [259]

On a pilgrimage to the Holy Land, while in Jerusalem our group was invited to celebrate the Eucharist at the Church of St. Anne— a Crusader-era Catholic Church just by the Stephen Gate. On the way from our hotel outside the old walls of the city, we passed through one of those ancient gates, now the site of a pita bread bakery in the Muslim quarter. Then, we moved on to St. Anne where we were welcomed with abundant and gracious hospitality. At the Institution Narrative during the Great Thanksgiving, there were smiles of recognition as the Muslim-baked bread was lifted at the altar and the Words of solemn joy were spoken: *"This is my body, broken for you. ..."*

Investigating the Rite

Commonly known in some traditions as the "Words of Institution," or even more simply as the "Verba," the narrative of the Lord's words and actions at the Upper Room meal have long stood as the core of the Service of the Table. Whatever else may come and go in the revisions of the Eucharistic Prayer, the Words of Institution would seem an abiding central feature. No matter how truncated some consecratory remarks may be, these words will be spoken. This enduring legacy of the "Moment of Consecration" debates, [260] then, permeates the Western Church; whether they are experienced in a hospital room setting with a

Protestant minister presiding, or at Mass downstairs in the hospital chapel as the Sanctus bells are rung thrice, few Western Christians will understand that they have had "Communion" without hearing these words.

Early Usage

It may come as a surprise, therefore, to discover that the practices and theology in the early church do not share this consensus as to the required place and meaning of the Institution Narrative within the Eucharistic Prayer. On one hand, historians of the liturgy have noted that a number of the most ancient anaphoras simply do not contain the Words of Institution—from the Didache (late first century) to the East Syrian tradition of Addai and Mari (c. third century).[261] Scholars are increasingly convinced that other early traditions which do contain a recognizable institution narrative, such as the *Apostolic Tradition*, have had the Verba interpolated into the Eucharistic Prayer at a later time. "There is a growing consensus among liturgical scholars," Paul Bradshaw concludes, "that in other extant early Eucharistic prayers both the Sanctus and also the institution narrative were usually fourth-century additions to an older core. . . ."[262] This is not to conclude, however, that some version of the Dominical words were not used in other liturgical locations when the early church broke bread. However, the institution narrative would not have accrued to itself the weight of being the major, if not only, necessary component of a prayer of consecration.

Making matters even more complex, scholars of the ancient liturgies also note that the formulae related to what later becomes known as the Verba are neither directly derived from the Synoptic Gospels, nor from Paul's Corinthian correspondence. The texts related to the bread and the cup seem to reflect a different and earlier tradition, perhaps dating back to the New Testament church's own liturgical practices. In other words, the liturgical and sacramental practices of the New Testament churches were significant contexts for shaping and transmitting early traditions about the Lord. Bradshaw adds that "it would appear that it was not until the third century that the New Testament texts came to dominate what was said by Christians about the institution of the Eucharist."[263] Noteworthy as well, is the focus of these pre-third century texts prior to the dominance of the canonical words. The sacrificial and Paschal context, so important to Paul and the Synoptic Evangelists, is mostly absent in pre-fourth century Eucharistic narratives of institution. Just as can be seen in the catacombs, references to eating and drinking with Jesus refer more to the stories of the miraculous feedings and the resurrection meals with the Lord than any other parts of the Gospel narrative. The theological emphasis is much more centered on a spiritual feeding on the presence of Jesus, than on a focus on his sacrificial death.

The Post-Nicene church (325 C.E. forward), however, moves toward a common understanding of the necessity of the Institution Narrative in Eucharistic praying, along with the adoption of language more reflective of the Synoptic and Pauline traditions. At the same time, it should be noted, a number of episcopal leaders across the church advocate for a specific operative place within the anaphora when consecration takes place. Such diverse theologian-bishops as Ambrose of Milan, Chrysostom at Constantinople, and Gregory of Nyssa in Asia Minor advocate for this consecratory agency of the Institution Narrative.[264] As will be developed later, the situation settles out eventually with the West locating the Moment of Consecration at the Verba while the Eastern Church comes to insist (in most instances) on the operative power of the Holy Spirit at the

Epiclesis. Meanwhile, in the West, from about the sixth century onwards, the priest increasingly spoke the Post-Sanctus prayer in an inaudible or completely silent voice, this "silent canon"[265] was broken only with the words of consecration: *"Hoc est enim corpus meum"* ("For this is my body") and the corresponding words over the cup. By the medieval era, the choir was engaged in its own series of chants during the entirety of the "silent canon," interrupted only when the bells rang three times at the Verba and the priest turned and showed the Host to the assembly. In the West, ratified by such theologians as St. Thomas Aquinas, the Moment of Consecration is firmly fixed at the Institution Narrative.[266]

Protestants Re-set the Words of Institution

The opening salvos of the sixteenth century reformers against the Roman canon were directed primarily toward what was perceived to be unbiblical theologies of sacrifice, of the priestly office, and abuses in liturgical practice such as the withholding of the cup from the laity. In 1520, Martin Luther penned *The Babylonian Captivity of the Church*, specifically advocating Communion in both kinds (bread and wine) while attacking the church's dogma of transubstantiation and the teaching that the Mass is "a good work and a sacrifice."[267] Luther regarded the entire Canon as participating in this third and "most wicked" abuse of the Mass. Consequently, he rejected the Canon in its entirety, leaving only the Words of Institution along with the Lord's Prayer. (Luther also insisted that the Verba be chanted aloud in order to correct the "silent canon" practice of the late-medieval era.)

In his treatise, *The Babylonian Captivity of the Church*, Luther interpreted the Verba as a testament by which Christ, knowing of his impending death, bequeaths to his followers the gift of forgiveness of sins and the status of heirs. The only appropriate response to this word of promise by the Christian is, of course, faith. "From this you will see that nothing else is needed for a worthy holding of mass than a faith that relies confidently on this promise, believes Christ to be true in these words of his, and does not doubt that these infinite blessings have been bestowed upon it."[268]

Ironically, it may be argued, Luther persisted in the view that at the Verba there occurred a Moment of Consecration, a view now intensified more than in the Roman Rite because of the deletion of almost every other aspect of the Canon. Consequently, the "Protestant" Eucharist of Martin Luther focused even more narrowly on the sacrificial work of Christ on the Cross while excising any references to the Incarnation, resurrection, and ascension of the Lord. The Sacrament of the Altar remains a sacrament; Christ's testament is surely fulfilled at the Table. The liturgical rite securing these promises is that given by the Lord Jesus in his last will and testament. This testament is renewed as the Dominical Words are spoken and heard by faithful believers.

According to a number of liturgical scholars, several unfortunate outcomes resulted from Luther's attempts at reform of the sacrament, as Luther Reed noted:

> His amputation of all prayer forms—good as well as bad—surrounding the Words of Institution robbed the liturgy of its historical and ecumenical character and fastened a strange and unique use upon subsequent Lutheran history. Overwhelmed at the moment by his realization of the supreme importance of the Word of God, he discarded all other considerations and made the Sacrament at this point illustrate his own powerful

concentration upon a single idea, the thought that here and now we must do away with all "words of men and angels" and listen only to the words of Christ as they reveal the heart of the gospel message.[269]

Reed adds that while dismissing the doctrine of transsubstantiation, Martin Luther actually "intensified the medieval conception of consecration by a fixed formula, and in a single moment of time. . . ."[270] Frank C. Senn concurs with this assessment, referring to Luther's "truncating" of the Canon as "the most serious defect of Luther's eucharistic revision."[271] Continuing to agree with Reed, Senn labels Luther's revisions by deletion as being "primarily medieval defects."[272] The outcome, such commentators would agree, is the intensification of the moment of consecration doctrine derived from the theology and practices of the Middle Ages.

More recently, Robin Leaver, among other scholars, has challenged this interpretation of the intent and consequences of Luther's "truncating" of the Roman Canon. Leaver argues that both the epiclesis and the anamnesis of the Eucharistic Prayer were not deleted, but rather relocated within the German Mass and given as chant or song, to the people. The former, the epiclesis, was brought forward to replace the *Graduale* between the lessons and became a hymn ("Now Let Us Pray to the Holy Spirit") sung by the congregation.[273]

In addition, according to Leaver, the anamnesis was also not eliminated entirely; it was moved to a later location as the congregation communed. Such songs, which were now congregational in Luther's mass, as the Agnus Dei, therefore fulfilled the role of the anamnesis. The argument, then, concludes that both of these elements of Eucharistic praying remained in the German Mass, although both are moved from the Canon to elsewhere in the service. Both, Leaver insists, had for Luther "musical dimensions, as did the proclamation of the Gospel, which is fundamental in his eucharistic theology and practice."

That this crucial emphasis of Martin Luther regarding his revisions of the Roman Canon were misunderstood by so many scholars, Leaver contends, is, in large part, due to the practice of later editors of the German Mass to print only the liturgical texts themselves, devoid of their musical settings. So, for example, Bard Thompson provides Luther's written directions for tone settings and hymn suggestions (or directives) within his text of the *Deutsche Messe* along with Luther's Preface;[274] however, what Thompson and other such editors and historians of the liturgy tend to omit, Leaver notes, is the incredibly detailed attention Martin Luther devotes to the musical context of the German Mass.

The import of Luther's approach to the liturgy is evident in the *Deutsche Messe* (1526) where, "27 of its 49 pages were filled with musical notation, and the remaining 22 pages contain frequent references to the musical aspects of the liturgy."[275] Liturgical music, then, leads the congregation to the Words of Christ at the Institution Narrative and from this apex guides the faithful to the act of Communion itself. In fact, there are two summits within the German Mass, both constituting the Dominical Words—first at the Gospel Lesson and then at the Verba. Both, Luther adds, should be chanted in the most joyful and sublime of musical tones, the fifth Mode.

Even while acknowledging the strength of Leaver's arguments, it is not inaccurate to point out the severe diminishment of the text itself in Luther's setting of the Mass. So, while the Sunday service of John Calvin would not as severely "amputate" the Canon, what stands in place of the Preface in his Strasbourg "Form of Church Prayers" is a "Prayer of Humble

Access" followed then by the Words of Institution. The minister, however, continues "in a loud voice" by way of warning the congregation of unworthy reception of the "holy food" and reminding them of the medicinal benefits available to those whose worthiness consists solely in an awareness of their sins and the desire "to find all our pleasure, joy, and satisfaction in Him alone."[276] The Roman Canon, consequently, was utterly suppressed in Geneva and Strasbourg.

The opposite obtained with regard to the first *Book of Common Prayer* of the Anglican Reformation (1549). Here, Archbishop Cranmer undertook a skillful revision of the medieval Eucharistic Prayer, retaining an extensive sequence of Post-Sanctus prayers "for the whole state of Christes churche"[277] followed by the Verba. The latter are introduced by a version the *Quam oblationem* of the Latin Mass in which the prayer now asks that the bread and wine "maie be unto us the bodye and bloude of . . . Jesus Christe." The subtle change from the Latin text serves to dispel "any exact definition of consecration."[278] An extended, yet carefully revised prayer of oblation follows the Verba. The 1549 *Book of Common Prayer* was followed by a much more Protestant version in 1552, evoked in large degree by the publication of Martin Bucer's *Censura* in 1550.[279]

In the 1552 version of the *Prayer Book*, the Post-Sanctus moved directly to the Prayer of Humble Access and then on to the introductory material affirming the "one oblation of himself once offered" and the Words of Institution. The Canon came to an immediate end upon the speaking of the Verba and Communion followed. The epiclesis of 1549 was deleted entirely, serving to reify even more intensely a "moment of consecration" located at the Words of Institution. Later versions of the *Book of Common Prayer*, however, did not continue with the abrupt ending of the Prayer of Consecration of 1552. So, as can be discerned in the 1928 *BCP* of the Protestant Episcopal Church of the U.S.A., the Canon has been extended once more to include the Oblation and Epiclesis from the original version of 1549.

The more radical, memorialist, wing of the Reformation was led by Ulrich Zwingli who revised the Mass for the churches in Zurich in 1525. All "ceremony and churchly custom," according to Zwingli, was to be removed from Sunday service excepting that plainly "instituted by Christ."[280] Zwingli also created a separate preaching service distinct from the Eucharist, the latter being observed four times a year. The sequence related to the Supper proceeded through various acts of worship—including the Gloria and the Creed—and then the congregation was admonished concerning unworthy communing before joining in the Lord's Prayer. What then followed was a further prayer best described as one of humble access and, following that, the Verba themselves. Immediately the bread and wine were distributed to the seated congregation on wooden boards, each worshipper serving him or herself or being served by the member of the congregation who carried the bread.

At the heart of the Zwinglian reforms, however, was the interpretation of the meaning of this communion. Any implication of a sacramental presence of Christ in and through the gifts was suppressed by Zwingli. Rather, "the Supper remained to him a vivid spiritual exercise in which the elements of bread and wine were but reminders, not vehicles, of grace."[281] The ubiquity of the Words of Institution in the Lord's Supper practice of churches in the Zwinglian tradition, then, did not relate to a "Moment of Consecration," as was the case for the children of Luther, Calvin, or Cranmer. Rather, the Verba were solemnly announced in a loud voice as a clear command of the Lord Jesus. "Do this in remembrance of me," he directed.

In Baptist, and other memorialist, traditions, then, the Words of Institution are essential at the observance of the Lord's Supper both by Dominical command and in order that the sacrifice of Christ be devoutly recalled. One summary of the Supper succinctly states this position: "The Lord's Supper is a symbolic act of obedience whereby members of the church, through partaking of the bread and the fruit of the vine, memorialize the death of the Redeemer and anticipate His second coming."[282] The Words of Institution represent and call to mind the death of Christ and anticipate his glorious return. In summary, William Kervin asserts, "For all its advances in the cause of faithfulness and integrity, the legacy of the Reformation with respect to the Words of Institution was largely reductionistic, didactic and penitential—a spirit which continues to haunt Eucharistic theology and practice in the Reformed traditions to this day."[283]

Post-Vatican Two Reforms

The reforms of the liturgy following the Second Vatican Council did not so much affect the text of the Institution Narrative as make revision to its context in the anaphora. A number of church bodies broke with their immediate liturgical tradition and practice and turned to patterns derived from "The Springtime of the Liturgy."[284] So, for example, the United Methodist "A Service of Word and Table," broke with the Anglican legacy of the *Book of Common Prayer* and offered the denomination a new Eucharistic Prayer patterned upon early Christian and Eastern church models.[285] The Words of Institution now followed upon the Post-Sanctus narrative and led on to the sequence of anamnesis-oblation-epiclesis. "Holy Eucharist II" of the 1979 *Book of Common Prayer*[286] follows a similar pattern, as does the "Left Column" Post-Sanctus of the *Lutheran Book of Worship*, 1978[287] and *Evangelical Lutheran Worship*, 2006.[288]

Revisions in the Roman Missal of 2011, however, do not alter the structural patterns of the four authorized Eucharistic Prayers for Mass. The first Canon (Post-Sanctus Prayer) follows the *Quam oblationem* ("Be pleased, O God . . .") while in the remaining three texts, the Verba follow the Preliminary Epiclesis. What has changed, following the Missal's intention to disclose more fully the underlying Latin Rite, is the replacement of the word "cup" by "chalice." Therefore, Canon I now reads "when supper was ended, he took this precious chalice . . ." and later reads, "for this is the chalice of my blood . . . ."[289] The decision for "chalice" in place of cup, of course, relates to the Latin text in which "*calix*" translates the New Testament Greek "*potērion*." The revision has met with some controversy, as have other textual changes of the new Missal.[290]

First among these, has been a move away from a broad ecumenical consensus on the texts of the sacrament—such as the Gloria, the Creed (Nicene), and the Verba. Concern has also been raised as to the adequacy, in English-speaking communities, of the word "chalice" to evoke a sense of anything other than dusty and outdated, even romantic, churchly speech. Scholars also raise the question of the ability of "chalice" to convey the metaphoric meanings of "cup" in the New Testament and in contemporary English (as when Jesus prays in Luke 22:42, "Father, if you are willing, remove this cup from me;" a metaphor still in use). At any rate, the Verba in the Missal of 2011 now have replaced "cup" with "chalice;" the structure and location of the Institution Narrative remaining unchanged.

Homiletical Implications

Eucharistic praying involves considerations of both words and actions. Initially, the four-fold action of the Eucharistic liturgy has been noted, action derived from the Institution Narrative and related meal traditions in the gospels such as the Miraculous Feedings. The actions that broadly shape the anaphora then—the "taking," "giving thanks," "breaking," and "giving" of the bread—are now heard in their most particular form in the Verba. One Eucharistic Prayer is especially carefully to emphasize the Dominical actions at the Table:

> . . . when they were at table, Jesus took bread, blessed it, broke it and gave it to his disciples, saying: "Take, eat, this is my body given for you and for many. Do this for my remembrance."[291]

This Institution Narrative highlights the actions of the Supper, actions which are both concentrated here in the Verba and witnessed more broadly in the shape of the Eucharistic liturgy. Preachers alert to the homiletical sources within the Holy Mystery, then, will do well to consider the ways in which the actions of the liturgy offer examples and images for the sermon and for Eucharistic living.

What the presiding minister and the assembly do in the Service of Holy Communion is as important as what they say; those things which constitute the dramatic actions of the sacrament are as significant as its texts. At best, the texts and the actions will weave together in a coherent, poetic (and sung!) entirety. All a worshipper needs in order to be reminded of this ideal is to witness the all-too-frequent dissonance between words and actions in Eucharistic praying. For example, we may watch a presiding minister invite the congregation to give thanks while that same presider is clasping a worship book with both hands, eyes downcast, reading the Sursum Corda (all too often in less than a thankful voice).[292] Another example is the selection of the most individualistic and sorrowful songs for the Communion at the "Eucharist." At its best, however, the sequence of liturgical actions and words will be woven of one cloth and thereby offer the preacher a rich resource for proclamation.

The initial task, when assessing the sacramental words and actions for preaching, is to explore, perhaps once more, the dynamics of such homiletical strategies for concretion as examples and images. Actions, especially those of a ritual, and therefore holy and recurring, sort, fall within the general protocols for the sermonic use of examples and imagery in preaching. Such concrete "lived experience," is necessary to shape a communal language that will form in the hearing of the congregation as well as to locate the gospel within its life together and mission in the world. The homiletics of David Buttrick, along with insights of other hermeneuts, poets, and music composers provide the foundation for the use of imagistic acts in preaching.[293] Put simply, we now turn to explore the dynamics of liturgical actions with reference to their use in preaching.

For the sake of this particular analysis, these explorations will be limited to the four actions that comprise the shape of the liturgy in general and the Institution Narrative in particular. The resource of sacramental actions for preaching is grounded in the ways in which analogy is not only enriching to the sermon, but essential to it. "Therefore," Buttrick cautions, "preaching must resort to analogy, saying, 'God is like . . .'"[294] But analogy is not limited to talk about God—as limitless as such holy speech may be! Rather, we employ analogy also to speak of ourselves, both communally and individually, saying "The church is like . . ." and "We are like. . . ." The dynamics of analogy for preaching are more complex and interesting than this, that is there are numerous approaches one might take toward the use of analogy, but this list, of course, begins with the most basic expression of analogy and moves from there.

1. *"Is like" analogies*—As Gregory Dix proposed, the four-fold shape of the Eucharistic liturgy is derived from the Dominical actions embedded in the Institution Narrative itself. Jesus "took," "gave thanks," broke," and "gave." It has been noted that each of these actions have served to shape the four-fold structure of the Holy Meal, resulting in the sequence of Offertory, the Great Thanksgiving, the Fraction, and Communion itself. Each of the four-fold actions of the Eucharistic liturgy as a whole, as well as the Institution Narrative specifically, may be developed with regard to analogies of self, church, and world.

    Analogous actions may be identified that will be enriched and deepened when aligned with the appropriate liturgical action. The rite that initiates the anaphora, the offertory, is a resource-laden series of actions which offer the preacher opportunities for analogy. If the sermon, for example, is exploring the eschatological Parable of the Sheep and the Goats (Matt. 25:31-46), a positive move could depict the youth of the congregation in procession at the offertory bringing the bread and wine for the Holy Meal and, by analogy, image them feeding the homeless during the parish's hosting of these beloved strangers. (It would be even more apt an analogy if the youth could bake the Eucharistic bread at the same time they were building homemade pizzas for the homeless meal!)

    Turning to the liturgical action of making Eucharist, a sermon for the Second Sunday of Advent, Year B, could offer an image for the Zephaniah 3:14-20 text, along with the First Song of Isaiah canticle (Isa. 12:2-6), as the promise of emancipation portrayed by a particular piece of art. One might say, "A huge mural on the wall at the Law School of the University of Wisconsin portrays the emancipation of the slaves. At the center of the painting, a group of freed slaves stand, 'making eucharist,' their arms extended to heaven, as a host of others journey from the backdrop of storm clouds into the light."[295]

The action of Breaking the Bread offers numerous "is like" analogies including the powerful act of literally "breaking bread" at the grace prayed at mealtime in some Christian homes. A more intimate glance at the mystery by analogy could be: "The aide at the nursing home bends near Mr. Stafford after she serves him the tray. She removes the warming lid from the plate and with care breaks the slice of bread in half for him. 'Thank you,' Mr. Stafford says. 'Amen,' she adds."

The Communion itself will need to be imaged, in most instances, as a communal analogy. One film, "Babette's Feast,"[296] can become the illustration of the Messianic Banquet. The 1987 film narrates the exile of a French refugee (Babette) from the turmoil of the descent of France from the Second Empire (1852-70) into a season of riots, firing squads, and social chaos. Babette seeks refuge far from home in an alien place—the bleak seacoast of Jutland—where a tiny Lutheran sect lives out its days and its piety. This refugee, who can never return home, brings the most sublime artistry of her home to this place of exile—her genius as a chef. Having won a French lottery, she spends all she has on a feast in memory of the sect's founder. Her offering is initially resisted by the twelve who gather to dine, but in the end, they discover

145

themselves much less at a last supper than a resurrection feast. And, as a feast, it is "all about public participation,"[297] a dance between the chef and those at the table. Here, the analogy works in both directions. On one hand, the Eucharist is the ground motif for the meaning of Babette's Feast. On the other hand, Babette's careful preparation, and the abundance of the meal are images that can expand the assembly's vision of Christ's Holy Meal.

It is important to note, however, that when shaping analogies in preaching in which one term is a sacramental action, a state of asymmetry between the two polarities always exists. That is, we do not mean by any of the above "is like" analogies that, for example, every family meal is also a sacrament nor that Babette's feast conforms to the full meanings of the Eucharistic feast. Listeners in the congregation should be able to discern the asymmetry in these "is like" homiletical analogies without the need for the preacher to emphasize the disproportionate aspects of the relationship. The latter emphases, however, are at the heart of the next type of analogy.

2. *"How Much More" Analogies*—We employ analogy when the presence of literal equivalence is not available. That is, our deployment of something that "is like" the other implies that the two entities are not exactly identical. If we deal with identical items, we do not use analogy, but turn to markers as we count them off (counting sheep on a sleepless night comes to mind). Our resort to analogy, to the contrary, assumes some distinction between the two terms—whether concepts, images, or concrete artifacts. When two terms are related by way of analogy—when they are coupled by "is like"—the relationship will typically involve a greater as well as a lesser entity.

Moreover, not only can we shape analogies that deal in the great/lesser relationship, we may also turn the equation on its head and speak of one term that "is not like" the other. David Buttrick, therefore, speaks of, "The language of amplification and the dialectical language of denial."[298] With regard to the former, the analogy by amplification, the asymmetry between the terms is intensified because one term in the relationship is significantly more expansive than the other. These analogies might be understood to be shaped by denial, but may be better understood as shaped by qualification. We may find these analogies developed in the sermon with the latter, the more expansive term, introduced by, "How much more . . ." or some equivalent phrase. It is not as much denial that deemphasizes the former term; rather, it is seen as a lesser expression of what is at stake in the analogy.

"We magnify," Buttrick notes, "in order to establish a realm distinction between the human and the divine."[299] Still, qualification is at work here, but mainly with regards to issues of scale. The "how much more" analogy is developed by way of an emphasis on the quality of the divine that is being juxtaposed to a related quality with regard to the human. So we may depict the grieving and sorrow of an entire nation as children are brutally murdered while in elementary school in Connecticut. Then the analogy is deployed: *"How much more does our Savior weep and grieve with us. He longs to gather us under his wings as a mother hen her chicks."* (Matt. 23:27). The analogy is rendered asymmetrical by an expansion of the quality of the divine in relation to the human expression of that same quality.

While David Buttrick's description of the "how much more" version of analogy is clear and consistent, preachers may be inadequate to its performance precisely when attempting to achieve an asymmetry by virtue of expansion. That is, the achievement of a "how much more" analogy depends both on a careful depicting of the human issue at stake, as well as an amplification of the divine side of the relationship. The issue is our capacity to provide precisely this amplification; that is, to "name grace."[300] When preachers turn to "naming grace," the listeners soon discern that the sermonic language tends to lose its specificity and shifts to generalization. Whereas the human situation is often described with large pathos-ridden illustration, the "God-side" of the analogy is left weakly imaged or not imaged at all.

This dynamic is especially evident in the language of qualification that weakens these "how much more" attempts at analogy. Mary Catherine Hilkert suggests that one contributing factor to this over-functioning in naming human situations while "vagueing out" concerning Divine grace, is our impoverished "sacramental imagination."[301] She reflects on this issue:

> In the story of Jesus, Christians discover that in its depths, and even in radical suffering, humanity has been united with God. The word that Jesus preached, the word that Jesus is, discloses both the mystery of human existence and the mystery of God. Thus when preachers listen to human experience they are listening from a perspective; they are listening for an echo of the gospel. To tell the story of Jesus is to tell the final truth about the human story, and to tell the human story in its depth, as Jesus did, is to point to the mystery of God at the heart of human existence, to "name grace."[302]

A language of qualification in our analogies is always implicit when one point of reference is our human condition and the other is the Holy Three, Holy One and the sacrament of the

Holy Meal. However, to develop such asymmetrical analogies in preaching will need even more attentiveness—and amplification—to the echoes and trumpet sounds of the gospel.[303]

3. *Analogy by Denial*—Homiletical analogies, Buttrick advises, may also be shaped by way of a language of denial by which he means both the qualification of analogy, as well as the framing of analogy thereby producing paradox.[304] So any analogy expressing human love will need to be qualified with reference to the love of God by denial—our love is finite, incomplete, sporadic, even self-serving—while the love of God is absent these denials. Once again, the distinction is one of scale; analogy by denial will focus more intently on the diminution of the human side of the analogy rather than an amplification of the divine. For example, we could shape an analogy with reference to the four-fold actions of the Eucharistic Prayer and the Verba as we preach on the Miraculous Feeding in Mark 6:30-44: "So 'all ate and were filled,' St. Mark tells us. But you have to wonder if St. Mark would say the same words about our meager feeding of the hungry here in our parish."

Still, the emphasis may need to be placed on the "How much more . . ." side of the analogy, especially since we know full well about our own capacity (sometimes more accurately, our incapacity) in the area of loving. In fact, if there is a problem in much of contemporary preaching, it is that we are expert in imaging the darkness, evil, and suffering of the human condition, imaging it concretely and extensively. However, what distinguishes this version of homiletical analogy by denial is its intentional focus on our own failure to live up to our identity as "children of God." Thus, the same issue obtains here as with the "how much more" version of analogy. If we do not name grace concretely and effectively, the congregation will remain focused solely on the bad news with its well-imaged darkness. Of course, the outcome of this dissipation of the good news is that the attempted analogy also dissipates. The assembly is left with only bad news being heard and retained.

4. *Analogy by Opposition*—It therefore seems best to redefine Buttrick's proposal to "frame analogy by paradox"[305] with the label of "analogy by opposition." Here, the juxtaposition between the two terms of the analogy is solely that they share a common category of evaluation. That is, if the common category is providential provision, we could align our Lord's feeding of his flock with his body and blood at the Holy Meal, with our disinterest in feeding the world's hungry. Or, since analogies with these sacramental actions may be related to self, church, or world, we could align the gracious provision of God in Christ with a society that is ever more divided between rich and poor.

God's provision at Communion—the gift of the presence of Christ in the bread and wine and in the assembly—could be aligned with our individual tendency to think ourselves undeserving of such grace. Here, the opposition is developed between the God who invites us to the Banquet and our own reluctance to trust such sure provision.[306] In every case, as David Buttrick notes, the interplay within the two terms of the analogy "is paradoxical because it conjoins . . . analogy with denial. . . ."[307] Preachers will need caution as they shape analogies by opposition when the sacramental actions of the liturgy are lifted up to serve as the positive side of the juxtaposition.

Preachers will need caution, however, when shaping most any analogy, particularly of opposition between the gift of the presence of Christ in the Holy Meal and the "simul justus et peccator"[308] state of the baptized. On one hand, we do not want to create a chasm ("so that those who might want to pass from here to you cannot do so" [Luke 16:26]) between the assembly and the Eucharist that heightens a sense of unworthiness to levels that cause the faithful to refrain from joining in Communion. Therefore, the mandate within Roman Catholic, Episcopal, Lutheran, Presbyterian, and United Methodist Eucharistic practice that a Prayer of Confession along with Absolution remain an abiding component within the liturgy is an important pastoral consideration. This principle within United Methodist Eucharistic practice states:

> When Holy Communion is celebrated, it is important to always begin with the words of Invitation, including Confession and Pardon. If these are omitted, all those present may not understand either the openness of the Table of the Lord or the expectation of repentance, forgiveness, healing, and entrance into new life in Christ.[309]

Still, it is a recurring experience of pastors serving congregations in denominations where weekly Communion is avoided in favor of less frequent observance (whether quarterly or monthly) that they will discover a member or members who stay away on the Sunday when the Eucharist is celebrated. When a conversation eventually takes place with these non-communicants, the typical interpretation given recalls some preacher in the past who convinced them of their unworthiness to receive Holy Communion. The other side of this coin relates to those who pastor in contexts of infrequent

Communion and in their preaching so trivializes the sacrament that a different type of chasm is built—one of indifference.

On the other hand, a tension does remain between the sacramental Meal and the baptized. (Otherwise, why do all these communions deem a penitential rite to be an essential activity as the assembly journeys toward the Table?) This tension is also acknowledged in the various expressions of our own unworthiness and the invitation is heard to join in the Holy Meal. Therefore, many traditions provide some sort of "Prayer of Humble Access," a prayer by the congregation acknowledging unworthiness yet trusting in the grace of Jesus Christ.

The "Prayer of Humble Access" was first written for the Book of Common Prayer, 1549, where it followed the Prayers of Confession and Pardon and then led immediately to Communion. In the 1552 BCP, the Prayer of Humble Access (PHA) was awkwardly relocated to a place immediately following the Sanctus (with the Benedictus deleted). Methodist practice continued to include the PHA located just prior to Communion within a succession of Ritual revisions, all derived essentially from the BCP.[310] However, with the reforms of the liturgy, the new Service of Word and Table deleted any Prayer of Humble Access while retaining a prescribed Confession and Pardon.

The Roman Catholic Missal of 2011 revised its "humble access" prayer while retaining its basis in Luke 7:6-7. Previously, the assembly prayed "Lord, I am not worthy to receive you, but only say the word and I shall be healed." The new Missal now revises the prayer to read "Lord, I am not worthy that you enter under my roof, but only say the word and my soul shall be healed."[311] The liturgical and pastoral issue here is that when establishing analogies of opposition between the words or actions of the Eucharist and the condition of the congregation, individually and communally, the various prayers of humble access (by whatever name) help retain a tension rather than a gulf between the assembly and their faithful participation in the Holy Meal. Given the avoidance of exceptional loads of guilt, carefully designed analogies of opposition may well encourage the baptized toward more frequent and more joyful Communion.

Conclusion

Having undertaken to explore the core liturgical question of the Verba, its placement and its importance in the liturgy, it is evident that Christianity in the West remains afflicted by a Moment of Consecration perspective on the sacrament of the Table. It is echoed in the teaching of the Roman Catholic Church—the Institution Narrative is the rite "by which, by means of the words and actions of Christ, that Sacrifice is effected. . . ."[312] The actions of the presiding priest or bishop coincide with the church's teaching regarding the consecratory words—there is a solemn genuflection honoring each of the Eucharistic Gifts in turn, following the respective Verba, and the Gifts are elevated in turn for the assembly to see and honor as well.[313]

However, such Moment of Consecration practice—if without the theological underpinning—is **also** on display on "Communion Sunday" in many Protestant churches. When the elements are solemnly uncovered, usually already placed on the Altar Table, the Institution Narrative by itself is spoken by the presiding minister and heard by the congregation. Nothing more is needed or desired. (An alternative practice involves the distribution of the bread and the cup in separate acts to the seated congregation, with the words spoken over each respectively.)

A variation on the Protestant "Words of Institution only" approach to consecration is on display more widely it would seem. In this variant practice, the preacher/presiding minister prefaces the Institution Narrative with some further remarks derived from the sermon. These "edifying comments" take the form of a summary of the sermon's thematics or bring to the Table some further remarks about the salient illustration. Here is an odd distortion of Luther's interest in holding in liturgical prominence both the hearing of the Gospel Lesson and the Institution Narrative. But in place of a practice designed to honor the words of Christ in their two honored locations in the service, the shift now focuses on privileging the words of the preacher, both in the sermon itself and in the remarks serving as the Verba's preamble! The outcome elevates the works of the preacher rather than the sacramental work of God.

7

ANAMNESIS/OBLATION/EPICLESIS

"And so in remembrance of these your mighty acts in Jesus Christ we offer ourselves . . . Pour out Your Holy Spirit on us gathered here and on these gifts of bread and wine . . ." [314]

When the newly merged United Methodists began work on a new Sunday Service that would embody the reforms of the liturgy since the second Vatican Council (1963-1965), one challenge was how to translate anamnesis into liturgical English while avoiding the use of the word "remembrance" with its more Zwinglian connotations. How could this "re-presenting" of the mysteries of the sacrament be expressed for United Methodists? The answer was to draw deeply on the well of Methodist piety and use the phrase, "experience anew." (Of course, few Lutherans or Roman Catholics would resonate with such a phrase, but it would be welcomed by clergy and laity within the United Methodist Church.) Therefore, the first publication of a reformed Sunday Service, "A Service of World and Table, 1972," states anamnesis this way: "When we eat this bread and drink this cup, we experience anew the presence of the Lord Jesus Christ and look forward to his coming in final victory." As revised and published in, "Supplemental Worship Resources, 10" in 1980, the phrase doubled in frequency; twice, the minister at the Table prayed that, "we experience anew." This phrase, so attuned to United Methodist liturgical piety, however, did not make the final version of the Sunday Service of Word and Table as published in the 1989 Hymnal *and 1992* Book of Worship— *now remembrance was back.*

Investigating the Rite

By the time the churches in East and West had settled down into their major liturgical traditions—from the end of the fourth century through the sixth—the sequence within Eucharistic praying following the Institution Narrative was established and commonly shared. The sequence began with the anamnesis, the recalling and making present of the past saving events; this leading to the oblation, an offering of the Meal and the community to the Father; and the epiclesis, that invocation of the Holy Spirit upon the celebration, the Gifts, and the assembly. This sequence is familiar to many of us in the Western church; it is the pattern that was retrieved by those communions engaged in the reforms of the liturgy following the Second Vatican Council. Then as now, however, each of the three acts of this sequence came to have differing emphases and embodied varying theological convictions.

Still, this sequence, representing the triumph of the Antiochene rite, is widely shared; Eucharistic celebrations in many traditions today are recognizable by members of others. There may well be more that binds us together in these rites than separates! However, it is important to explore the grounding sequence of anamnesis, oblation, and epiclesis, first by examining the origins of these distinctive sacramental acts and then by noting their subsequent formation, deformation, and reform. Of course, our interest here is not limited to euchology; we will proceed by way of exploring the implications of this sequence for proclamation at the Eucharistic feast.

Anamnesis

An enduring theory, stated most directly by Louis Bouyer, argues that the anamnesis has its roots in Jewish prayers in which a memorial is declared that forever renews God's saving actions. Especially on days of Jewish festival, the interpolations within the prayers after the meal, the *berakah,* intensify a sacrificial sense of making memorial. Bouyer notes that on these festival occasions the after-meal prayers "multiply the use of this word *zikkaron*, 'memorial,' with certainly the meaning we have just mentioned . . . its sacrificial character."[315] Making memorial is a communal, recurring action, by which God's people remember, make present, proclaim, and share in the salvific actions of their covenant God. Therefore, it is not surprising that when the Apostle Paul relates the tradition he had received, he taught that the Lord Jesus added a memorial statement to the reinterpretation of each element: "Do this in remembrance of me" and "Do this, as often as you drink it, in remembrance of me" (1 Cor. 11:24b, 25b).

Then, the further aspects of making memorial are heard as Paul conveys the Lord's concluding words: "For as often as you eat this bread and drink the cup, you proclaim the Lord's death until he comes" (11:26). The fullness of making memorial is conveyed in the Greek term used by St. Paul: "This do for my *anamnesis*." Notice, however, that the term as employed in the Pauline tradition, has what Ray Carlton Jones, Jr. describes as three temporal aspects: "(1) the saving act of the past: the death and resurrection of Jesus; (2) the present remembrance and praise; and (3) the future return of Jesus (only the resurrected Lord can return)."[316] "Remembrance" in its Scriptural sense is not centered in a present-tense individual act of mental recall. The salvific efficacy of the past act of God is represented by the present action of God, and thereby illuminates the future when God will set all things right.

The prayer of thanksgiving (*eucharistia*) found in the Didache conforms in its basic pattern to the Jewish *berakah*, a three-fold movement from the blessing of God to giving thanks for "Jesus your servant (or 'child')"[317] to finally offering intercessions for the unity and peace of the church and the coming in glory of Christ ("Maranatha!"). No specific memorial is present in these liturgical texts. Could it be, Willy Rordorf asks, that this is because they are "simply prayers spoken at table in connection with ordinary meals of the community?"[318] This proposal remains a matter of considerable debate among historians of the early liturgy.

By the time we reach the early third century, however, the anamnesis as well as the oblation, is clearly evident. The anamnesis in the Apostolic Tradition (AT) is as follows:

> Doing therefore the "anamnesis" of His death and resurrection we offer to Thee the bread and the cup making eucharist to Thee because Thou hast bidden us (or, *found us worthy*) to stand before Thee and minister as priests to Thee.[319]

Further along in the development of early Eucharistic praying, we find the "memorial" intercessions of the Didache paired with an anamnesis recalling the sacrifice of Christ in a mid-fourth century Egyptian rite, "The Euchology of Serapion of Thmuis:

> For this reason, we too celebrating the memorial of his death, have offered this bread and pray: through this sacrifice, reconcile us all to thyself, be favourable to us, O God of truth. For just as this bread, once scattered upon

the hills, has been joined together to become but one, so, too, deign to reunite thy holy church from every people. . .[320]

One further Eucharistic Prayer is worthy of note before arriving at the mid-fourth through mid-sixth century developments. The Apostolic Constitutions (AC) represents a vast collection of liturgical material and church order documents from across the span of the post-New Testament age, including material drawn from sources as early as the Didache.[321] It represents a significant stage in the development of the influential Antiochene liturgical tradition. The collection was clearly of late fourth century compilation even though some of its liturgical texts harken back to more ancient traditions (Christmas is mentioned in the AC and, while invented in Rome in 336 C.E., it was finding its way into the churches of the East later in the fourth century.)

In the so-called "Clementine Anaphora"[322] in Book VIII of the AC, an anaphora is provided along with other material drawn from the election and ordination of a bishop in the Apostolic Tradition of Hippolytus. However, the liturgical texts have been significantly up-dated, revised, and extended. This Clementine Eucharistic Prayer extends more than ten times the length of that provided by Hippolytus. Indeed, as Marcel Metzger notes, "no other known anaphora has anything comparable for sheer length."[323] And here, in Book VIII of the AC, within an amazingly extended anaphora, the anamnesis assumes record-setting proportions. Recalling that the Hippolytus Canon involves just one extended statement focusing on an anamnesis of Christ's death and resurrection, the Clementine anamnesis is a continuation of the narrative preface which itself spans from the glory of the Godhead before creation through an extended hymn to creation, proceeding then to salvation history from Eden through the deliverance of the covenant people across the Jordan and their possession of the Promised Land. Only then do we arrive at the Sanctus!

The anamnesis is a continuation of the narrative, now making anamnesis for the Incarnation of Jesus Christ and particularly for his Institution of the Holy Meal. In fact, the Clementine Book VIII anaphora may be said to constitute one extended anamnesis spanning from before time through the remembrance of the most recent saints and martyrs. The Verba are included within the narrative and the oblation and epiclesis are woven seamlessly into the completion of the anamnesis. (The anaphora is estimated to take over fifteen minutes to offer at a Eucharist!)

By contrast, the terse rhetoric of the Roman Canon devotes two entire sentences to the anamnesis, trimmed even further at the Council of Trent. Following immediately upon the Verba, the early form of the Roman anaphora reads as follows:

> Wherefore, Lord, we your servants and also your holy people, recall the blessed passion of the same Christ, your Son, our Lord. We remember his resurrection from the dead and his glorious ascension.[324]

In the Tridentine Mass, the brief anamnesis (*"Unde et memores . . ."*) functions as an introduction to the oblation while at the same time, recalling Christ's death, resurrection, and ascension.

In the revisions of the Mass orchestrated by the continental reformers of the sixteenth century, the diminished state of the Roman Canon as compared to the Eastern Church in general and the Clementine anamnesis in particular, now reached its "null point." For Luther, Calvin, and Zwingli, the anamnesis is simply deleted from the prayers over the gifts. We recall with Luther Reed that, "Luther's elimination, in his liturgical orders, of all surrounding prayer forms left the Verba standing alone in stark, if strong, simplicity."[325] In "The Form of Church Prayers" for both Strasbourg and Geneva, John Calvin appends an extensive amount of liturgical material following the Verba—almost Clementine in length! However, no anamnesis is to be found. Rather, the post-Institution Narrative material is a lengthy discourse on the unworthiness of the worshippers and the saving benefits of the worthy gift of Jesus Christ. Ulrich Zwingli, in his Zurich Liturgy, follows the Verba immediately with the Communion. Even the Lord's Prayer precedes the Institution Narrative.

The Anglican Reformation, however, was not so quick to simply drop the anamnesis from the Prayer of Consecration. In the *Book of Common Prayer* of 1549, the anamnesis opens with words that serve to remind the worshippers that the Son of God has willed them to make with the holy gifts, "the memoryall" that is commended.[326] The prayer continues with a modestly revised version of the Roman Canon's anamnesis of Christ's passion, death, and resurrection. The *Second Prayer Book* of Edward VI dropped the anamnesis in favor of a prayer petitioning God to accept this sacrifice of praise and thanksgiving. The 1552 *BCP* moves directly from the revised version of the oblation to the Verba (the Institution Narrative, therefore, retaining the only reference to "remembrance").

By the 1662 *Book of Common Prayer*, a stable anamnesis was in place that remained, in the United States, through the 1928 *Book of Common Prayer*. In these texts, the anamnesis consisted of "a perpetual memory of that his precious the death"[327] (the 1928 Prayer Book extended the anamnesis by adding "and sacrifice"). The revisions of the Anglican Rite of Holy

Communion in The Methodist Church, however, did not attend to the anamnesis through the 1939 Ritual; the anamnesis continued to refer solely to "this memorial of His precious death."[328]

The publication of the *Book of Worship* and *Hymnal* of the Methodist Church in 1964/1965 represented some modest reforms in the Anglican Holy Communion tradition. For example, the anamnesis in the 1964/65 Ritual of the Methodist Church refers to the "remembrance of his passion, death, and resurrection."[329] These Methodist revisions were soon of little consequence as they were being rendered obsolete by the publication of the much more radical reforms mandated in the Constitution on the Sacred Liturgy of the Second Vatican Council. Following the Second Vatican Council, the Roman Catholic Missals of 1969 and 2011 provided four primary rites of the Eucharistic Prayer, the first continuing closely to the Roman Canon while the fourth is a collation of Eastern sources largely derived from St. Basil.[330]

The four anamnetic statements within the Eucharistic Prayers of the Missal of 2011 are as follows:

> EP 1 – ". . .we celebrate the memorial of the blessed Passion, the Resurrection from the dead, and the glorious Ascension into heaven of Christ. . . ."
>
> EP 2 – ". . .we celebrate the memorial of his Death and Resurrection. . . ."
>
> EP 3 – ". . .we celebrate the memorial of the saving Passion of your Son, his wondrous Resurrection and Ascension into heaven, and as we look forward to his second coming. . . ."
>
> EP 4 – ". . .we now celebrate the memorial of our redemption, we remember Christ's death and his descent to the realm of the dead; we proclaim his Resurrection and his Ascension to your right hand; and as we await his coming in glory. . . ."[331]

The fullest expression of the Paschal Mystery is obvious at first glance; the Eastern Church, and St. Basil in particular, bless us in the Western Church with a rich and expansive anamnesis.

Major Protestant reforms of Eucharistic praying, following the Second Vatican Council, as regards the anamnesis, vary from versions of the three-fold aspects of the Paschal Mystery which the Roman Canon provides, to more expansive, and even more vague, expressions. The anamnesis in the *Book of Common Prayer*, 1979 represents the former, more common approach, "Recalling his death, resurrection, and ascension. . . ."[332] A richly expansive anamnesis is provided by the Evangelical Lutheran Church in American in "Setting One" of *Evangelical Lutheran Worship*:

> Remembering, therefore, his salutary command, his life-giving passion and death, his glorious resurrection and ascension and the promise of his coming again. . . .[333]

Another rendition of the anamnesis that is similarly rich and expansive is found in "Great Thanksgiving Three" of the Order of Saint Luke's resource, *The Book of Offices and Services*. Here, the anamnesis and oblation are inverted, thereby allowing the Acclamation to extend the remembrance of the Paschal Mystery:

> Remembering all that has been revealed to the world we proclaim the mystery of faith:
> Dying you destroyed our death.
> Rising you restored our life.
> Come Lord Jesus, come in resurrection glory![334]

The United Methodist Great Thanksgiving attempts such an expansive expression of anamnetic prayer with the phrase, "in remembrance of these your mighty acts in Jesus Christ;"[335]

however, by not becoming specific regarding any of these "mighty acts," the worshippers may not be provided with images of the Paschal Mystery sufficient to evoke robust experiencing anew.

Oblation

As we have come to expect, the anaphora prayers of the pre-Nicene church vary considerably as regards each of the three post-Verba elements—the anamnesis, the oblation, and the epiclesis. Turning to the oblation, it is striking that the Apostolic Tradition of Hippolytus lacks any such liturgical statement (the reference in its epiclesis to the Spirit being sent upon "the offering of thy holy church"[336] is probably a later interpolation, as well as more an extension of the epiclesis). In the Clementine anaphora in the Apostolic Constitutions, a "Prayer of Offering" follows that incredibly extended anamnesis with a simple sacrificial formula: "In accordance with Christ's disposition, we offer you, king and God, this bread and this cup."[337]

With regard to the Roman Canon, both in the early sacramentaries (seventh and eighth centuries) and the Tridentine Mass, the oblation precedes the Verba, the latter leading on to the anamnesis and a second series of intercessions for the saints. The oblation—object of vigorous scorn by the Protestant reformers—is for Bouyer "properly the presentation of the Eucharistic sacrifice to God for his acceptance."[338] It translates as follows:

> We pray thee, God, be pleased to make this offering wholly blessed, a thing consecrated and approved, worthy of the human spirit and of thy acceptance, so that it may become for us the Body and Blood of thy dearly beloved Son, our Lord Jesus Christ.[339]

The translation of *"rationabilem"* as "approved" is misleading, however. The term more accurately echoes a theology of the Word in earlier traditions; our "rational worship" is that shaped by the Word.

Once again, there is no need to explore revisions to the Roman oblation with regard to the Continental reformers. The oblation was readily and vigorously excised from those liturgies, whether at Wittenburg, Geneva, Strasbourg, or Zurich. Also, once more, the Prayer Books of the Church of England did not adopt the Continental move of deletion, but rather of significant revision. In 1549, Cranmer revised the Roman oblation by shifting that which is offered from the one sacrifice of Christ to that of ourselves, "oure soules, and bodies, to be a reasonable, holy, and li[v]ely sacrifice unto thee. . . ."[340] The 1552 Prayer of Consecration simply shifts the same wording to a location within a prayer immediately following upon Communion itself. That location along with the revised wording of the oblation—"we offer and present unto thee, O Lord, our souls and bodies"—also continued in the Ritual of the Methodist Church through the *Hymnal* and *Book of Worship* of 1966.

The traditional language of Holy Eucharist Rite I of the 1979 Book of Common Prayer also retained the words of the revised oblation. It relocated that text, however, within the Great Thanksgiving. The contemporary language of Rite Two varies among the alternative Great Thanksgivings as to the oblation. Prayer A is oddly terse, stating only "we offer you these gifts" while Prayer B (noted as "Alternative Forms of the Great Thanksgiving") nicely elaborates this sense of offering the eucharistic gifts to God. Oblation is difficult to identify in Alternate Prayer C while in Prayer D the familiar expression of oblation as an offering of the Eucharistic Gifts again is evident.

The oblation, then, as found in the *Book of Common Prayer*, 1979, expresses two differing theologies of offering. On one hand, the Eucharistic Rite One with its traditional language continues the Prayer Book practice of oblation as an offering of "ourselves. . . ." On the other hand, three out of the four Great Thanksgivings in the contemporary language Rite Two shift the theology of offering to that of the Eucharistic Gifts. It is almost inevitable that this latter expression of oblation connotes a sense of Eucharistic sacrifice. However, that term is not employed in any of the Rite Two oblation texts. Surprisingly, the 1979 BCP would seem to embody two alternative theologies of Eucharistic offering. The first—the "ourselves, our souls and bodies . . ." dates from the earliest Prayer Book usage—expressing the self-giving and adoration of the worshippers. The second is a much older, even ancient, theology of sacrifice and necessarily involves an oblation of a meal.[341] It will be of great interest to observe how various churches of the Anglican Communion negotiate between these alternative theologies of oblation.

The United Methodist Great Thanksgiving which was shaped after the reforms of the liturgy (1989) contains an oblation that embodies a dual, if uneven, set of oblationary theory. The dominant expression of this offering is that received through the Anglican *Book of Common Prayer* tradition dating back to 1549. The United Methodist version of the oblation updated from the Edwardian language of the Prayer Book states, "we offer ourselves in praise and thanksgiving as a holy and living sacrifice. . . ." Here, the "reasonable," "rational" element of the ancient Eucharist is left behind in favor of an emphasis on our "living" sacrifice. (Perhaps the decision by Archbishop Cranmer to translate *"rationabilem"* as "reasonable" so distanced the meaning of the terms that the latter became orphaned and, in time, quite dispensable.) However, the United Methodist oblation does not conclude solely with this expression of the spiritual sacrifice of the worshipping community. Rather, the prayer adds, "in union with Christ's offering for us." This concluding phrase certainly has no other reference than Christ's self-offering in his sacrifice on Calvary. "This Holy Mystery," the United Methodist statement on the sacrament comments,

> Holy Communion is a type of sacrifice. It is a re-presentation, not a repetition, of the sacrifice of Christ.[342]

To be sure, the United Methodist epiclesis expresses a "soft" version of Eucharistic sacrifice as compared to the "strong" version in the Offertory of the Tridentine Mass. Still, the ecumenical question may be raised whether some modest consensus may be achieved between Roman Catholic, Anglican, United Methodist, and other traditions at this point. Can we agree that the Eucharist brings together three primary aspects of oblation, including the spiritual sacrifice of the assembly ("ourselves, our souls and bodies"), the sacrifice of the meal ("offering to you, . . . this bread and this cup"), as well as the sacramental sacrifice ("once and for all") of Christ? Such a modest agreement would provide a common foundation regarding Eucharistic sacrifice while, at the same time, providing the various traditions with the occasion to deepen and expand various of the three facets of oblation. For United Methodists, it would seem that a possible next consideration relates to the inclusion of meal-sacrifice references within the Great Thanksgiving itself.

Epiclesis

Perhaps one fruitful approach to questions of the origin and development of the epiclesis within Eucharistic praying is to adopt the logic (the "*rationabilem*") of the collect prayer form. The collect is addressed to God, but the divine quality is specified from the outset ("Almighty God, to you all hearts are open, all desires known, and from you no secrets are hidden").[343] Following the opening attribution of the Divine quality, a petition is made ("cleanse the thoughts of our hearts by the inspiration of your Holy Spirit") which then, in many instances, is followed by a desired outcome ("that we may perfectly love you, and worthily magnify your holy name").[344] Given the logic of this prayer form, we may ask regarding the various ancient, medieval, Reformation and modern liturgical traditions as to the identity of that aspect of the Divine which is "called down," the agency sought, and the benefits anticipated upon this gift. Put simply: 1) Who or what is called down?; 2) What is asked?; and (3) For what end?

Once more we are cautioned by a number of historians of the earliest liturgies; we should not expect to find an explicit epiclesis anywhere much before the period following the Council of Nicaea (325 C.E.). Thus, Paul Bradshaw concludes that:

> The earliest known examples of prayers from the anaphora that ask God to actually send the Holy Spirit and specify what the Spirit is expected to do in relation to the Eucharistic elements date from the last quarter of the fourth century. . . .[345]

The one possible exception to Bradshaw's assertion may be the epiclesis in The Apostolic Tradition in which the Spirit is invoked to fill the assembly "unto the strengthening of the faith in truth."[346]

The earliest example of possible Eucharistic praying that "calls down" (the Didache) is addressed to the First Person of the Trinity and the request is for the blessing and unity of the church. Then, too, the pre-Nicene Egyptian tradition of Sarapion calls down the Logos upon the bread and the cup.[347] Other allusions to the Spirit's work at the epiclesis also predate Nicaea. In these examples—from Hippolytus in the West and, among others, Addai and Mari in the East, the Spirit is called down upon the Eucharistic elements or upon the assembly. The Spirit is petitioned in some rites to "come" while in others, the Father is asked to "send" the Spirit.

While no moment of consecration is evident in the early development of the epiclesis, nevertheless the Spirit is sought so that the gifts and/or the people may be sanctified, blessed, and made holy.[348] An intermediate stage in the development of the epiclesis is displayed in several fourth century compilations of earlier texts including the Eastern anaphora of St. Basil and the above-noted "Clementine Anaphora" of the Apostolic Constitutions. In both rites, the Holy Spirit is asked to "present" (St. Basil) or "manifest" (CA) to the assembly the body and blood of the Lord. In keeping with the abiding duality of Eastern Eucharistic praying, the St. Basil epiclesis also asks the gift of the Spirit so that "all of us who partake of the one bread and the one cup" will be united with each other "in the fellowship in the one Spirit."[349] Remaining with the Eastern tradition, the anaphora of Chrysostom marks a shift from the nuances of "present" or "show" the elements as the Body and Blood of Christ to more direct schema:

> God the Father is asked (1) to *send* down his Holy Spirit on "us" and the gifts and (2) to *make* bread and wine the Body and Blood, converting them with his Holy Spirit,

(3) so *that they would be to the benefit* of the communicants.[350]

Once again, we note the dual epiclesis in Eastern anaphoretic practice; the Spirit is invoked upon the gifts of bread and wine and upon the worshipping assembly.[351]

The Roman Canon presents challenges with regard to its distinctive bipartite epiclesis and the origins of the practice. Questions also have been raised as to the minimally explicit reference to the work of the Third Person of the Trinity in either the early or later epiclesis.[352] Both prayers express a petition to the Father that the sacrifice being offered is acceptable and be carried to the altar on high. The early epiclesis, it is proposed, may have originated as an intercession by the priest on behalf of his own unworthiness along with that of the people. Martin Luther's revisions of the medieval Roman Mass once again simply excised all material following the Institution Narrative, thereby eliminating any hint of an epiclesis.

John Calvin's sacramental theology as embodied in his two versions of "The Form of Church Prayers," has an interesting resonance with the dual epiclesis in the Roman Canon. First, neither the medieval Roman Canon nor Calvin's liturgical reform explicitly name the Holy Spirit. Moreover, both envision the worship to be brought up to heaven by the grace of God—the sacrifice offered here in the Mass and for Calvin is the congregation who may be lifted up to where Christ reigns in glory.

The *First Prayer Book* of Edward VI displays some important continuity with the Roman Canon with regard to the epiclesis. Cranmer retains two epicletic prayers, the first, preliminary petition asks the Father to "bless and sanctify these thy gifts" through the Word and Holy Spirit. In the *First Prayer Book*, moreover, the practice of the Roman Canon is retained with modest revision (the "*te igitur*,"[353] beseeching God to accept the "gifts" in the Roman Canon or "prayers" in the *BCP*)) and that prayer continues to avoid any explicit reference to the Holy Spirit. Cranmer is subtle and careful with regard to the ways in which the Eucharistic sacrifice is allowed to be mentioned. His strategy is to first state that we are unworthy ("through our manyfolde synnes") to offer any sacrifice, while adding, "Yet we beseche thee to accepte thys our bounden duetie and seruice, and commaunde these our prayers and supplications . . . to be brought up into thy holy Tabernacle. . . ." The implication here is that through the grace of God, the sacrifice of the people (a sacrifice of "prayers and supplications") will be welcomed into the heavenly and holy Tabernacle.

Opposing Cranmer's modest revisions with vigor, Martin Bucer attacks the first epiclesis in this manner:

> The prayer for such blessing and sanctification of the bread and wine on the Lord's table is not commanded by the Lord, and is twisted by Anti-Christs so as to conform and maintain some horrid impieties.[354]

The "horrid impieties" denounced by Bucer relate to what he describes as "the infinitely wicked and blasphemous dogma of the transubstantiation of the bread and wine into the body and blood of Christ."[355] (Bucer is apparently not aware that an epiclesis prayed over the gifts had been practiced in both the East and West centuries before the doctrine of transubstantiation was first proposed in the West.)

Likewise, Bucer argues that the second epiclesis—the words praying that the gifts be brought to the heavenly

Tabernacle—be entirely suppressed. He corrects Cranmer for misunderstanding that in the early church, such a prayer related solely to gifts set aside from the Table for distribution to the poor.[356] Bucer's critique of the 1549 *Book of Common Prayer* as it pertains to these two epicleses was completely successful. The 1552 *Prayer Book* has no reference to either of these prayers! (By the time of the 1928 *Book of Common Prayer*, the initial epiclesis of the 1549 rite with minor revisions was relocated in sequence following the oblation. Interestingly, the Service of Holy Communion of *The Methodist Hymnal*, 1939 displayed no such restoration; the epiclesis remained "missing in action.")

The liturgical reforms following the Second Vatican Council impacted a number of communions including, of course, those of the Roman Missal. The new Missal of 2011 continues to provide four alternate Eucharistic Prayers, although protocols are provided as to their appropriate use during the liturgical year. As has been the case, Eucharistic Prayer I is the modest revision and translation of the Roman Canon which agrees with the other three anaphora, and includes two distinct epiclesis prayers. In all four Eucharistic Prayer texts, the first epiclesis invites the Spirit's descent upon the Gifts to make them holy ("graciously sanctify," Eucharistic Prayer IV) "that they may become for us the Body and Blood of our Lord Jesus Christ."[357] The second epiclesis in these four Eucharistic Prayers follows the Verba and the anamnesis with Eucharistic Prayer I retaining the prayer for the ascent of the gifts to the "altar on high," while the remaining prayers center in a petition for the unity of the church.[358]

The new Eucharistic Prayer of the Evangelical Lutheran Church in America brings into one epiclesis the petition that "with your Word and Holy Spirit to bless us, your servants, and these your own gifts of bread and wine."[359] This epiclesis, then, invokes the Word and Spirit upon both the gifts and the worshipping community. A similar duality is found in The United Methodist Great Thanksgiving of 1989 which invokes the Spirit upon the Gifts and on the people:

> Pour out your Holy Spirit on us gathered here, and on these gifts of bread and wine. Make them be for us the body and blood of Christ, that we may be for the world the body of Christ redeemed by his blood.[360]

A further petition asks that the Spirit give unity to the assembly and empower its mission in the world. The Eucharistic Prayer of the Presbyterian Church (U.S.A.), published in 2013, provides both an initial set epiclesis and by way of a series of rubrics invites the presiding minister to add petitions so

> *that we may be made one with the risen Christ and with all God's people;*
> *that we may be faithful as Christ's body in ministry in the world;*
> *and that we may live in anticipation of the fullness of God's kingdom.*[361]

Similarly, the Episcopal *Book of Common Prayer*, 1979 prays for the Spirit to descend upon the community and upon the gifts, "sanctifying them and showing them to be holy gifts for your holy people, the bread of life and the cup of salvation, the Body and Blood of your Son Jesus Christ."[362]

To summarize, then, a strong ecumenical consensus exists within Western church traditions holding to an understanding of the Eucharist at this point. The epiclesis within contemporary Eucharistic praying spans across four related sacramental workings of the Holy Spirit. First, the Spirit is invoked that its work of making the bread and wine become for the assembly the Body and Blood of Christ. Whether reflected in the new Lutheran

Eucharistic Prayer, the Roman Mass of 2011, the Presbyterian anaphora of 2013, or the United Methodist Great Thanksgiving of 1989, all have at their epicletic core the petition that the Eucharistic elements become through the power of the Spirit the Body and Blood of Christ. The sacramental doctrine of the Real Presence of Christ in the Eucharistic Gifts is proclaimed across this wide span of Western Christianity. (We note, too, the extent to which the "*ut nobis*" ["for us"] phrasing of the earliest Roman Canon is now so widely employed across these same communions.)

A second common thread of these prayers is that the Spirit is invoked upon both the Gifts and the assembly. This is a remarkable achievement ecumenically. Many of us remember a time when the stereotype was widely held that "Catholics believe the Spirit does its work on the bread and wine while Protestants believe the Spirit is given to the community."

A third common feature of these prayers for the Holy Spirit now recovers one of the most ancient aspects of Eucharistic praying—the petition for the Spirit's work to grant that the assembly "may become one body, one spirit in Christ." Thus, the epiclesis in many contemporary epiclesis prayers echo the petition in the Didache:

> As this broken bread was scattered upon the tops of the mountains and being gathered became one, so gather Thy church from the ends of the earth into Thy kingdom. . .[363]

Finally, a majority of the epiclesis prayers surveyed manifest a relationship between the Eucharistic feast and the assembly's mission in the world. Even when not explicitly stated, the trajectory from the Holy Meal to the baptismal vocation of believers in the world is nuanced in these other prayers. (So, the epiclesis in the Roman Mass, 2011, Eucharistic Prayer IV concludes regarding the assembly, "that they may truly become a living sacrifice in Christ to the praise of your glory.")

Homiletical Implications

Anamnesis

If the proclamation of the Word at the sermon is to both prepare and invite the listeners to the Eucharistic Meal, then the homiletical work of preparation involves the formation of a people capable of making anamnesis. This most solemn responsibility, given to preachers in worship, that finds its summit at the Table and can be summarized in a question: "When the presiding minister at the Great Thanksgiving prays 'And so, in remembrance of these your mighty acts in Jesus Christ . . .' is the congregation's familiarity with, and understanding of, those *memorabilia Dei* sufficient to the prayer's intention?" Care must be taken here. It is not to be interpreted that the efficacy of the anamnesis is to be located within the assembly's mental storehouse of Bible stories. Such would be works righteousness of the lowest order!

On the other hand, the work of God in re-presenting those "mighty acts in Jesus Christ" does place a burden on the preacher to explore them in preaching, deepening the worshippers' pilgrimage into the depth of the atonement and, more expansively, the mystery of the Incarnation.[364] Put simply, "making anamnesis," means that the saving acts of God being re-presented, or "experienced anew," will resonate with the congregation's immersion in the biblical narratives. It is not that the efficacy of the anamnesis lies with our knowledge of the stories of Scripture, but remains with the God whose grace makes possible the thankful remembering of our salvation in Christ. And, because we have been so graced in this sacramental remembrance, it is our duty as preachers to proclaim these mighty acts just as they are proclaimed whenever we eat the bread and drink the cup "until he comes" (1 Cor. 11:26).

A narrow construal of this homiletical task and gift would be a decision to preach only on texts that do, indeed, "proclaim the Lord's death." In fact, some preaching at the occasion of the Lord's Supper does restrict itself to the most explicit Scriptures related to our Lord's passion and death. Here, making anamnesis of "His death and Passion" (the wording of the 1939 Methodist Service of Holy Communion which exactly repeats the 1552 *Book of Common Prayer*) could lead to a strict constructionist approach to preaching at the sacrament whereby we continually "bring the people to the Cross."[365] It is obvious that those wooden and stereotyped interpretations of the atonement do find their way into preaching; obvious, too, is the manner in which many critics of the church's historic doctrines related to the atonement assume only these same hardened and delimited views. So before extending the range of making anamnesis to the resurrection and beyond, it is salutary to explore the dynamics of interpretation that are available to the preacher while attending to this remembrance of Christ's "death and Passion." The insights of Peter Stevenson and Stephen Wright are rich resources in guiding this consideration. They include:

1. *A Fuller Doctrine*—The full doctrine of the atonement is not delimited to those specific pericopes in the gospels and in the Pauline Epistles and Hebrews that deal explicitly with the passion and crucifixion of Christ, whether in story, epistle, or homily. Moreover, as Stevenson and Wright insist, "Both

Testaments provide us with a range of stories and images that represent the truth, in partial but complementary ways."[366] To be sure, the specific biblical texts treating the atonement will be preached; guided by the lectionary, a conscientious preacher will pick up these lessons during Lent and Holy Week during all three years of the ordered readings. Additionally, a number of the Sundays after Pentecost in Year A have lessons from Romans (Propers 7-18), while Hebrews is featured in several Propers both in Year B and C, Sundays after Pentecost.

Opportunities for preaching aspects of the atonement, however, are not delimited to these lessons. In their book, *Preaching the Atonement*, Stevenson and Wright venture beyond these texts to explore, for example, Genesis 22:1-19 (The sacrifice of Isaac), Leviticus 16:15-22 ("Unholy fire" offered to the Lord), and Isaiah 52:13-53:12 (The suffering servant).[367] Both Testaments give witness to the atonement by means of narratives, epistolary, homilies (see Hebrews), and prophetic imagery.

2. *Connecting Explicit and Implicit Texts*—The connections between the texts most centrally focusing on the atonement and others within the canon are related more by "resonance" or "echo" than by specific points. So, Stevenson and Wright comment that,

> Without explicit quotation—maybe even without direct verbal parallels—themes, phrases, moods can suddenly or gradually strike a reader or hearer as uncannily similar, or in a way that can set off potent lines of interpretations.[368]

There is a mystery in such evocative intertextuality, usually not discernible through the familiar method of promise-fulfillment.

3. *The Lens of Tradition*—When preaching such a theme, doctrine, and image as the atonement, preachers will need to be alert to the ways in which the tradition has provided clear lenses through which to explore the biblical witness. On the other hand, the preacher's own church tradition may place blinders on the interpreter as well. These assets and liabilities of the preacher's own tradition include most emphatically the liturgical tradition that is brought into the contemporary ecclesial context.

Recalling that it was not until the publication of the *Methodist Book of Worship* and *Methodist Hymnal* in 1966 that these children of John Wesley were to be about an anamnesis that added "resurrection" to a remembrance of Christ's "passion and death," the long emphasis on unworthiness, sorrow, and penitence as dominant themes of hymns, prayers, and sermons suddenly becomes understandable. Moreover, when the Great Thanksgiving is shrunk down to some revisit of the sermon's theme or a reminiscence of the illustration that came to dominate the homily along with the Verba themselves, the result is a "Last Supper" reenactment.

In such a case, the rite is solely a remembrance of the "Passion and death." On the other hand, continuing with the Wesleyan tradition, it is in the Eucharistic hymns of Charles and John Wesley that themes in addition to atonement are sung. Holy Communion is precisely that for the Wesleys, a Communion with the overwhelming love of God; the sacrament "fills his faithful people's hearts with all the life of God."[369] Alert to the imagery and thematic depth that expand on this Anglican and Wesleyan core of atonement theology, preachers formed in this tradition have a much wider hermeneutic lens at hand than has been exploited in the past. But with the reforms of the liturgy, that which is recalled and re-presented at the Holy Meal is now a more ample feast than what most any in the Western church have previously experienced.

When the anamnesis expands from Christ's death and Passion to recall "his death, resurrection, and ascension," (*BCP*, 1979), the stories and images commended to the preacher expand exponentially. Directly at hand, of course, are the resurrection accounts of the gospels along with the ascension narrative with which Matthew and Luke close their Gospels and Luke opens the Acts of the Apostles. Again the same principle obtains here: as the sacrament recalls and proclaims these mighty acts of God, those of us called to preach have the joy and duty of proclaiming them also. Imagine the impoverishment and even confusion wrought within a congregation if, during the Eucharist, the ascension of the Lord is represented at the anamnesis, yet these rich narratives in Matthew, Luke, and Acts are never preached! Put simply, the richer fare[370] of the Eucharist calls forth a more lavish feast of the Word from the pulpit or ambo.

We do not, however, find ourselves constrained only to the explicit biblical texts which undergird a more expansive anamnesis. Rather, the savvy preacher will once again look for resonances, and listen for echoes of these narratives in other Scriptures. And once again, the ancient tradition of the church offers the preacher a wealth of Scriptural resonances as the assembly journeys through the Easter Vigil. "This is the night," resounds the *Exultet*, and after the holy light of the Paschal Candle is blessed, the congregation begins its vigil as Christ makes his Passover from death to eternal life. The stories of creation, of the Flood, the faithfulness of Abraham, the deliverance at the Red Sea, of Isaiah's invitation to come to the waters, Ezekiel's vision of the valley of the dry bones becoming alive—all of these lessons in the night speak of God's faithfulness in and through the waters of salvation.[371]

Then, the assembly attends to Paul's teaching that baptism is a dying and rising with the Lord. Only after this solemn vigil-keeping are the "alleluias" restored to the liturgy, and the community rises to hear the Easter Gospel. Notice that the church has collected these water narratives as a way of keeping vigil with Christ as he makes his exodus from death to new and risen life. By making anamnesis of Christ's resurrection along with his passion and death, it is now incumbent upon the preacher (along with cantors, media artists, and storytelling lectors) to "flesh out" and proclaim the stories the church has located on this most holy night. Of course, as we make anamnesis of Christ's resurrection we will also have responsibility for proclaiming the scriptures of Easter's Great Fifty Days through all three years of the lectionary. Now, we join with the Holy Spirit in the re-presentation of the stories of the Lord's appearance to Thomas, the Easter meal with Christ on the lakeshore, the walk to Emmaus, and many others. We will invite the congregation to "remember" the kerygma of the post-Pentecost church along with its growth in numbers and boldness; we will extend the invitation to the assembly to "live wet" by way of the baptismal witness of First Peter, and "live hopefully" as we preach the texts from the Book of Revelation. To make anamnesis of the death, resurrection, and ascension of the Lord is to be handed an entire corpus of Scriptures to proclaim and be fulfilled in the hearing of the assembly.

The scope of that over which God's people make anamnesis grows ever more expansive. To be sure, the remembrance of Christ's death and resurrection remains at the center of what is recalled. However, the anamnesis in the United Methodist Great Thanksgiving (1989) is a "remembrance of these your mighty acts in Jesus Christ." Therefore, the preacher's calling is to proclaim all these mighty acts witnessed in the Incarnation—from Gabriel's promise through resurrection and ascension, and beyond and before!

In their sequel to *Preaching the Atonement*, Peter Stevenson and Stephen Wright assemble a collection of essays and sermons on the Incarnation. The sermons focus on texts, again drawn from both Testaments, and include some predictable lessons (e.g., the kenosis of Christ in Philippians 2) to several surprising ones (e.g., the "Burning Bush" in Exodus 3). The authors introduce the interpretive and homiletical investigations by arguing, "If the central task of the preacher is to facilitate profound understanding of the claims and call of the gospel, then the task of 'preaching the incarnation' must assume a very prominent place within that."[372] Preaching the Incarnation, then, is at the heart of our call to proclaim the gospel. And the witness in Scripture to the Incarnation is extensive indeed.

As we have seen, however, the memory of the faithful that is exercised in some Eucharistic praying is marked by a "loquacity"[373] well beyond our usual experience. The so-called "Clementine Anaphora" (Book VIII of the Apostolic Constitutions) does not just contain a narrative thanksgiving, but is, more accurately, embraced by it. The Eucharistic narrative begins before time and extends through a vision of the end of earthly time. In between, events from Eden to Abraham, from the prophetic word to the annunciation to the Virgin are memorialized. Then, formally, the anamnesis in the Clementine liturgy includes the Institution Narrative itself and then projects forward to the passion and death of the Lord, his resurrection and ascension and "his future second advent."[374] This recalling even re-presents the coming again of Christ in glory! What if those of us called to preach become "Clementine Preachers"? That is, what disciplines would come into play if our canon is the Canon and our ordo is the Ordo? As Clementine Preachers, "Scripture remains the primary source and resource for preaching."[375] At the same time, the dynamics of Eucharistic praying in general and the anamnesis in particular guide us in the feast of the Word.

Oblation

With regard to the anamnesis and its implications for proclamation, our reflections followed the expansiveness of what is recalled, from the passion and death of the Lord to the addition of his resurrection and ascension (moving from the Atonement to Incarnation), and finally to the entirety of the Scriptural world and witness. Now taking up the question of the significance of the Eucharistic oblation for preaching, a related expansiveness is noted. We begin by considering the oblation as an offering of ourselves as a living sacrifice. Then, we expand our perspective on the oblation by raising the question of the meal sacrifice, the offering of the bread and the wine as a sacrifice before God. Finally, the once and for all sacrifice of Christ may have homiletical implications if an older Catholic-Protestant polemics can be set aside. Each facet of Eucharistic oblation will be interrogated for its significance for proclamation.

1. *"We offer ourselves . . . as a holy and living sacrifice."*—Immediately the question of the character of the preacher comes to the fore. If the entire congregation is offering itself as a holy and living sacrifice to God, so, too, the preacher and the offering of his or her sermon. Whatever else is implied within this initial aspect of oblation, then, at least this is clear: those of us called to preach offer ourselves and our proclamation, not someone else's. Unless otherwise informed—such as a notice that the homily for, say, the Easter Day Liturgy of Evening Prayer will be the Paschal Homily of St. Chrysostom—the congregation should safely expect that the proclaimed word is one that their preacher has created and not "borrowed." In the African American church, the saying is shared that "the preacher should be the first to ride the terror."[376] That is, the one who is called to preach the Word, first engages in its "terror" (and its glory), and first ventures to explore its meaning for the congregation and for the world.

Those of us called to preach will do no less if we live out of this calling; we will offer ourselves "as a holy and living sacrifice" in our sermon preparation and delivery. It will be our own sermon that we offer, not someone else's and it will be our self who preaches, not an imitation of some celebrity. This is not to say that from time to time a sermon shape derived from another colleague will not be used—but we will note something like "one preacher spoke of this holy Christmas Eve as being like the eye of a storm." Likewise, a brief notation can be made that attributes some insight or other within the homily—so we might begin a move within a sermon on Proverbs 31 by saying "Alyce McKenzie reflected on this 'wonder woman' and said. . . ."[377] These homiletical attributions do not need to conform to the latest edition of Kate Turabian's footnote protocols, but we do honor our colleagues and maintain our own integrity as we signal from time to time that our preaching is a communal enterprise. Nevertheless, our humble offering of ourselves in the ministry of proclamation gives substance to the quality of offering expected of all God's people who make bold to pray such a prayer and make such an oblation. It is a holy sacrifice we are about.

In the *First Prayer Book* of Edward VI, Archbishop Cranmer developed an oblation within the Prayer of Consecration that began with those familiar words, "And here wee offer and present unto thee (O Lorde) ourself, oure souls and bodies, to be a reasonable, holy, and lively sacrifice unto thee. . . ."[378] Thus, the homiletical implications of the sacramental oblation include this messy business of "bodies." In addition to reminding the preacher yet again of the dangers of docetism—of waxing too "spiritual" to the exclusion of embodied existence and, therefore, Incarnation—the matter becomes our embodied presence in ambo or pulpit[379] as we proclaim the Word.

Since we offer our souls and bodies when we preach, issues of embodiment bear directly on ethos of the on-going assessment by the listener as to the believability of the speaker's words. Because we bring our embodied selves to the event of proclamation, we can offer up too much of ourselves—downstage center on the "preaching stage"—or attempt to hide, even while coming before God's people with a word. The issue of ethos, the character of the preacher, has much to do with our embodiment. As a physician recently commented, the clergy used to be among the most well of occupations, but now they are among the unhealthiest. Obesity seems to be "the new normal" for preachers in some areas of the church and clergy health insurance costs outpace other groups in similar age cohorts.

If the message we proclaim is to have integrity, it will be coherent with the message we communicate with our bodies as well. So a preacher who preaches with fierce passion against the addiction of alcoholic drinks, but is morbidly obese (and therefore addicted to food) will not be heard. What is seen will trump what is being heard. On the other hand, a preacher with a handicapping condition may witness in a powerful way through her or his embodiment to the power of the gospel.[380] The message proclaimed through our body will be heard when we preach. Offering our souls and bodies in this holy sacrifice of proclaiming the good news is a true "living sacrifice."

2. *The Meal Offering*—The second meaning of Eucharistic oblation relates to the Meal Offering itself. We offer the bread and the wine as our grateful sacrifice. Founded upon the biblical metaphor of bread as wisdom, it seems appropriate to accept the analogy of the "meal" offered while proclaiming the Word as well as the Meal of the Eucharist. We are fed by the Word proclaimed in preaching, and by the Word of Life shared in the Holy Meal. Sergius Halvorsen, of the Orthodox Church in America, keenly discerns this interplay of the proclaimed Word and the sacramental Word: "The preaching within the eucharistic liturgy should be just as penetrating and sanctifying as the Eucharist itself."[381] Two excesses, though, must be avoided as we consider the offering of the bread of life in preaching along with the Meal at the altar. On one hand, no allegorization is acceptable; what is preached is not the Eucharist as a mystery play of Christ's passion and death (with the elevation as the lifting up of the Lord on the

cross).[382] On the other hand, a Protestant excess veers in the opposite direction, seeing in preaching the full and adequate sharing of the "bread of life." The nineteenth-century hymn by the name, "Break Thou the Bread of Life," is sung in Protestant piety with chiefly the preaching and hearing of the preached word in mind. It assumes the adequacy of the truncated Sunday service absent the Eucharist.

The Meal offering of the church is, indeed, a "double feast,"[383] and in the case of the first feast, the preacher—who him or herself continues to be nourished by the Word in Scripture and the Holy Meal of the Altar—needs to be fed before an offering can be given back to God. Conversely, the preacher who attempts to break the Bread of Life in preaching, but who abstains from a prayerful feeding on the Word and a joyful feeding on the Real Presence of Christ in the Eucharistic feast provides the congregation with only meager fare. So the oblation as Meal Offering has crucial implications for the spiritual disciplines of the preacher as well as the potency of that preacher's proclamation. Those called to preach are "under orders," are bound with a *sacramentum*, to feed the sheep of Christ's flock (John 21:15-17). And this offering of themselves, souls and bodies, cannot be made with full joy and faithfulness unless they first are fed by the bread of life, both within their personal and communal spiritual disciplines and in their Eucharistic practice.[384] Faithful preachers are first fed by the Word in the prayerful reading of Scripture and will come to the Holy Meal for the Bread of Life. They will not ignore either feast.

3. *". . .We have Such a High Priest . . ."* [385] The third meaning of oblation relates to the Eucharistic representation of the sacrifice of Christ. Whether in its "softer" United Methodist

expression or the more explicit oblation of the Roman Catholic Missal, it is clear that the sacramental Presence and sacrifice of Christ will be aligned with the holiness of the priestly office, and the consequent unworthiness of any given priest. Whether by way of the *"Suscipe, sancte Pater"*[386] of the Tridentine Mass, or the Prayer of Humble Access of the Anglican Prayer Book tradition, the re-presenting of Christ's offering calls the priest to a holiness that cannot be attained by human virtue. Hence, the call to priestly service is a call to a holy ministry within the holy church; it is a call that cannot be answered without the admission of unworthiness and the petition for Divine grace.

A holy priesthood, of course, is not some medieval accretion to the simplicity of leadership in the New Testament church. Nor is the holiness of priesthood even a dynamic invented in the post-Pentecost church. Rather, the holiness of biblical priesthood has its roots in the Mosaic tradition and its later interpretations. Interestingly, biblical scholar Thomas Dozeman notes that two dominant traditions regarding the Mosaic office may be discerned within the Hebrew Scriptures, "one prophetic and charismatic in nature and the other priestly and ritualistic."[387] The two foci of ordination—to Word and to sacrament—continue to be grounded in the dual functions and identities of the Mosaic office. Thus, those of us called to the ordained ministry move, mostly without self-reflection, between the two Mosaic roles as we preach and preside at the Sunday Eucharist.

When our ecclesial tradition privileges one of these Mosaic calls over the other, this selectivity "has been to emphasize one aspect of ordination over the other in the formation of distinct denominations and thus to weaken the power of holiness in the profession of ordination and in the life of the people of God."[388] On the other hand, if we fulfill our calling to faithfully proclaim the Word *and* administer the sacraments, our liturgical roles and ministerial identity will oscillate between the charismatic and prophetic, and the priestly dimensions of our office.

The proclamation of the Word has its own long history of interpretation with reference to the one called to bring the message, a tradition rooted in the prophets of Israel. And in a close alignment with the call to priesthood, the call to proclaim the Word of God also comes with a demand for holiness neither inherent within the preacher nor attainable apart from Divine agency. The familiar narrative of Isaiah's call to prophetic vocation reflects the impossibility of anyone to come before the presence of the Holy One and to "go for us" and preach the Word (Isa. 6:8). The beauty of the feet of those who bring good news (Isa. 52:7) is contingent upon divine grace—the forgiveness, call, and empowerment of the preacher.

In the New Testament, the Apostle Paul instructs the Romans that becoming right with God—by confessing aloud and believing in the heart—is the content of the message preached; it is also the precondition to service as a preacher. Paul intentionally quotes Isaiah's celebration of the beauty of the feet of those who bring good news. A more explicit connection between holiness and the preaching of the gospel is developed by Paul in 2 Timothy. Only following an extensive recital of a holiness code (2 Tim. 2:15-26) does the Apostle admonish Timothy to "Preach the Word of God" (2 Tim. 4:2). St. Dominic (1170-1221) expanded on this interplay of the personal and communal aspects of the vocation of proclaiming the Word. Dominic spoke of "the Holy Preaching," by which he meant the holiness of the preacher as well as the holiness of his community, the Order of Preachers. Paul Janowiak comments that for St. Dominic, "Every talent and gift, each act of service and prayer participated in 'The Preaching of Jesus Christ.'"[389] All of life in community will become Holy Preaching.

In spite of this persistent linkage of the office of the preacher with a vocation of holy living, there are numerous examples of a rupture in this bond in the contemporary church. Perhaps the worst violations of "the holy preaching," involving as it does the entirety of the preacher's life and life together, are the egregious acts of clergy sexual misconduct, up to and, including the abuse of children. Clergy may preach the "full counsels of God" from the pulpit or ambo, but if they are preying on the flock, their preaching is unholy. On another front, as noted above, the discovery by the parish of extensive pulpit plagiarism is also an assault on holy preaching, since one foundation of the relationship between preacher and people is a covenant that the homily will be a fresh Word from God. Of course, material from other preachers, both contemporary and within the tradition may be brought to bear, but their appearance in the homily will be noted with modesty and gratitude. Any unacknowledged 'borrowing' of other sermons or components of homilies is symptomatic of another violation of the holy preaching.

Perhaps an unexpected or unrecognized symptom of the distortion of holy preaching is the isolation, and even competition, evident between preachers. In order to renew preaching there must be a concomitant renewal of the college of preachers. St. Dominic's "The Preaching of Jesus Christ," was a prophetic and pastoral word to the Order of Preachers regarding their personal and communal holiness. Those of us called to preach are called as well to be in holy covenant with each other. A deep mutuality and trust among those called to proclaim the gospel is essential to the renewal of preaching.

Finally, there is this violation of holy preaching: a studied casualness and carelessness as to the preaching event. Thomas Long highlights one particularly grievous aspect of this too-lax approach to the task that stands in contrast to "the great peril of preaching."[390] Long relates tuning into "overly upbeat television preachers or, closer to home, run[ning] into the casual, chatty preachers of the relaxed suburban congregation, welcoming people with the perkiness of a TV weathercaster and running through the joys and concerns as if they were the recreational program directors of a cruise ship. . . ."[391] On the other hand, "the holy preaching" to which we are called has a terrible audacity about it; we are called to preach God's Word. Compare the liturgical warm up of the "TV weathercaster" preacher with that of the Armenian Rite. Instead of a vacant, if cheery, welcome to the scriptures, the ancient liturgy introduces the Gospel reading with the deacon inviting the people with the simple words, "Let us be attentive." The response of the people is, "God speaks."[392] God speaks and the one called to preach is always called to a holiness not her or his own. God brings the once for all sacrifice to the people and the one who presides is called to a holy priesthood not her or his own.

Epiclesis

It is the same Spirit that is invoked upon the gifts of bread and wine that is operative in faithful Christian preaching. Just as the epiclesis serves to invite the Spirit upon the Eucharistic Gifts and upon the assembly, that same Spirit is at work in multiple ways in the event of proclamation. John Calvin encompasses the work of the Holy Spirit in this way:

> For first, the Lord teaches and instructs us by his Word. Secondly, he confirms it by the sacraments. Finally, he illumines our minds by the light of his Holy Spirit and opens our hearts for the Word and sacraments to enter in, which would otherwise only strike our ears and appear before our eyes, but not at all effect us from within.[393]

Initially, then, our homiletical ruminations on the liturgical work of the Spirit will studiously avoid those divisive either-ors that have sought to locate the Holy Spirit only within one particular liturgical context or liturgical tradition. The Spirit, James Forbes reminds us, "has shepherded the word through compilation, translation, canonization, and transmission to the present time."[394]

Throughout the life of the church the Spirit has witnessed in many ways. The history of the interpretation of biblical texts is a witness to the Spirit's work both of the on-going diverse readings within catholic faith, and the perennial task of discernment by the church of readings that are antithetical to Trinitarian faith. The Holy Spirit "inspires the scripture lessons of the day,"[395] whether those lessons are derived from a lectionary the church has commended for the ordered reading, hearing, and proclaiming of Scripture, or by way of the prayerful discernment of the preacher with regard to a particular occasion. In addition to discerning the Spirit's activity in these ways, it is also necessary to consider the presence of the Spirit in the assembly for, "It is the task of the Spirit to convene the community of those who are being made ready."[396] The Holy Spirit, then, is that agency of

God through whom the chrismed community is called, gathered for Word and sacrament, and given ears to hear and eyes to see.

It is in the Reformed tradition that this more encompassing role of the Spirit's work in Scripture and its reception and proclamation is liturgically manifest. The Prayer for Illumination has its origin in John Calvin's insistence that the Word of God in Scripture also needs the Spirit's work in the act of proclamation and in the right and faithful hearing of the congregation. This Reformed emphasis rests on "the conviction that the words of Scripture themselves have no power apart from God's power."[397] A paradigmatic Prayer for Illumination is provided within the text of "The Service for the Lord's Day" in the most recent Presbyterian Church (U.S.A.) hymnal, *Glory to God,"* as well as the earlier published *United Methodist Hymnal:*

> Lord, open our hearts and mind
>   by the power of your Holy Spirit,
> that as the Scriptures are read and your Word proclaimed,
> we may hear with joy what you say to us today. **Amen.**[398]

The Spirit's work is ubiquitous across the span of Scripture's origins and writing, canonization, and liturgical presentation within the church year. That same ubiquity of the work of the Spirit also extends to its reading in corporate worship, the shaping of the sermon, and the faithful hearing of both text and homily by the congregation.

Further depth is explored within African American preaching as to the Spirit's work. Luke Powery focuses on the preacher's vulnerability while offering him or herself yet again to the preach God's Word. "Yielding to God is a sign that one desires the grace of God and reveals one's reliance on the presence of the Spirit."[399] Powery adds, "It is a step of faith to enter the pulpit to preach because only the grace of God can make preaching powerful."[400] Therefore, just as in the Reformed tradition, a Prayer for Illumination will precede the reading and proclaiming of the Word, so, too, in much African American preaching a prayer to God, or specifically the Holy Spirit, will be offered by the preacher. One such prayer may be heard:

> Lord Jesus Christ, fill us with your Holy Spirit, that we may be less of what we used to be and that we may become more of what you want us to be.[401]

Such prayers at the outset of preaching extend beyond the African American tradition and are now offered in white "mainline" church and evangelical settings as well as within Hispanic and other minority contexts. In every respect, as Luke Powery notes, such prayers suggest "the presence of the Holy Spirit at work in imperfect sermons."[402]

Ordained through the Spirit

The rootedness of both proclamation and the Eucharist in the Spirit is also revealed in most ecclesial traditions' theology and practice of ordination. Whether the same clergy are formally designated as the sole ministers of proclamation and Eucharist (as within the Roman Catholic Church) or in traditions where differing offices of liturgical leaders function at the pulpit and the Table (as within many churches of the Restorationist movement visible as the Church of Christ, Christian Church, and Disciples of Christ), those commissioned and/or ordained are recognized as called and empowered by the same Spirit.

In most churches, in continuity broadly with the tradition of the Western Church, ordination to the Order of Priest/Elder/Presbyter is to Word and sacrament and through the power of the

Holy Spirit. For example, in the current provisional ordinal of the United Methodist Church, the ordination to Word and sacrament is declared through words and liturgical actions:

> An elder
> is called to share in the ministry of Christ
> and of the whole church:
> to preach and teach the Word of God
>
> *Here a large Bible may be lifted by an assistant.*
>
> and faithfully administer
> the sacraments of Holy Baptism and Holy Communion;
>
> *Here a paten and chalice may be lifted.*[403]

Later in the Service of Ordination of an Elder, in words and actions the Spirit is invoked upon the "office and work" of the ordinand. Therefore, as we have seen, the anointing of the clergy in many Western traditions is for the ministries of both Word and sacrament. The anointing of the Holy Spirit is considered essential to the "office," implying a distinctive chrism for the ordained. Moreover, the "work" of that person is also raised in the epiclesis, implying the need for the Spirit's agency in the functions of the office.

> *The bishop lays both hands on the head of each candidate, praying:*
>
> Father Almighty (Almighty God), pour upon *Name* the Holy Spirit,
> for the office and work of an elder in Christ's holy church[404]

In a final acknowledgement of the work of the Spirit, a prayer is offered over the newly ordained that asks for the abiding presence and guidance of that same Spirit:

We rejoice that you have been called to serve among us, and pray that the Spirit of God may guide your ministry.[405]

Earlier in the Service of Ordination, the entire assembly has been asked to confirm the setting apart of the ordinands for the offices and ministries to which they have been called. The bishop asks the congregation, "Do you trust that they are worthy, by God's grace, to be ordained or recognized? The congregational response is: "We do! Thanks be to God!"[406] This affirmation—in its solemnity and joy—reflects a further pneumatological activity, pertaining to the Spirit-filled discernment of the entire assembly of the faithful.

Given the span of the work of the Holy Spirit as voiced and enacted within a contemporary service of ordination, we may now propose several theses that offer resolutions to misunderstandings that have beset Western Christians and served to divide their witness. These theses will allow us to honor the many traditions that have arisen in the West while confessing that a more thorough understanding of the work of the Holy Spirit must be embraced.

First, for any sermon, a scripture text which is prayerfully and faithfully chosen is a gift of the Holy Spirit. The Spirit works through both traditions holding to ordered readings of Scripture, and church communities in which the preacher chooses her or his texts independent of a formal lectionary. The use of the lectionary is no less a work of the Spirit than the weekly selection of biblical texts based on topical series or an interest in "relevance."

Another activity of the Spirit which is not bounded by a particular tradition, is the calling of certain persons to the ordained ministry. The Spirit's agency leads persons toward the vocations of ordained ministry and, in performing these works of ministry, the Spirit's anointing is essential to faithful preaching of the gospel and the right administration of the sacraments. The rites of ordination make clear that the Spirit's anointing is invoked upon the full work and offices of ministry.

Finally, the Spirit is present with any worship leader who works to understand the depths of a scripture passage in the preparation of a sermon. With regard to the ministry of proclamation, the Spirit anoints careful exegesis, prayerful consideration of Scripture (*lectio divina*), knowledgeable employment of homiletic method and a wide variety of written and oral styles of presentation. On the other hand, the Spirit anoints wonderfully extemporaneous moments of preaching where sermon text is laid aside (or never existed in the first place) and the preacher speaks words given from on high. Both of these alternatives, though, should be regarded as constructs. Authentic and anointed preaching may find both polarities come together in the homily.

Conclusion

The deeply traditional sequence in Eucharistic praying of anamnesis, oblation, and epiclesis provides the discerning preacher with further words and actions that accrue to her or his liturgical Bible. This ancient sequence in the Great Thanksgiving offers resources for the homily involving words and actions of both presiding minister and the assembly. So, for example, the more expansive expressions of the anamnesis ecumenically cue the preacher that there are sermons in which the appropriate location for the congregation is to be there, "When they crucified my Lord." Other Scriptures and congregational and societal contexts, however, will be led by the "experiencing anew" of the entire Incarnation which brings the hearers to a deeper remembrance of Christ's glorious resurrection, ascension, and coming again in glory.[407]

Analogous resources from the preacher's liturgical Bible include words and actions related to the oblation and the epiclesis. The aspect of Eucharistic oblation that includes the offering of the priest and priestly people as "living sacrifices" involving the souls and bodies of all who gather around the Table, gives the preacher important images for sermons focusing, for example, on disciplines of wellness, both individual and communal. Finally, the epiclesis "calls down" the Spirit in many sacramental traditions upon both the Eucharistic Gifts and the gathered assembly. Resources from the liturgical Bible here are clear and immediate in application. Wise preachers and pastors will see the numerous opportunities for members of the congregation to employ their baptismal gifts of the Spirit in a variety of liturgical expressions. The ministries of music and dance, of reading Scripture and offering intercessions, of presenting the Eucharistic Gifts to the Table along with gifts of tithes and offerings, and of serving Communion to the assembly—all of these and more are Spirit-inspired and Spirit equipped.[408]

Finally, it should be noted that the ethos of the preacher is latent in the homiletical implications of each of these three elements in Eucharistic praying. The investigations related to the preacher's critical role in grounding the anamnesis' reference to the "mighty acts of God" in specific pericopes within the biblical narrative have been noted at length. Consequently, a preacher who exercises personal selectivity—perhaps in service to sermon series or topical and ideological interests—impoverishes the congregation's capacity to envision, indeed, to live out those mighty acts of God that are remembered at the Great Thanksgiving. On the other hand, the more expansive anamnetic references to the entirety of the Incarnation, as well as Christ's ascension and coming again provide the alert preacher with a remarkably broad palette from which each sermon draws its focus and imagery.

The anamnesis calls the preacher and assembly to an always deepening engagement with the biblical witness. In the oblation, following in sequence in the Great Thanksgiving, the question of the preacher's ethos is unavoidable. The character and integrity of the preacher is perennially at stake as people and presiding minister offer their laud and praise as living sacrifices. Among numerous ethos issues, the homilist cannot offer that living sacrifice while living the falsehood as well that the preached word is authentically his or her own. "Borrowed sermons" (stolen, really) are not acceptable sacrifices of praise and thanksgiving except under very specific and limited circumstances.[409]

The sacramental invoking of the Holy Spirit during the Eucharistic Prayer provides rich imagery for the preacher as various lections and liturgical occasions are under consideration. For example, on "Palmarum" (the First Sunday of Advent) the First Lesson from Isaiah opens with the cry, "O that you would tear open the heavens and come down . . ."(Isa. 64:1). This end time descent of the Spirit is anticipated in the Spirit's coming down upon the Eucharistic Gifts and upon the faithful in the assembly. And in this coming down of the Spirit there is a "tearing" of any curtain that would keep separate the holiness of God and the worship of God's people.

8

DOXOLOGY AND AMEN

*"Through your Son Jesus Christ,
with the Holy Spirit in your holy Church,
all honor and glory is yours, almighty Father,
now and forever.
Amen."* [410]

St. Jerome remarked that the people's "Amen" at the conclusion of the Eucharistic Prayer "thundered" through the churches of Rome. Most assemblies that simply speak the Amen in these days, however, could not be described as thundering the great "So Be It." It is the gift of liturgical musicians rather, who are providing settings that invite the Great Amen "to flow from the community as a glorious and majestic acclamation." [411]

Investigating the Rite

Development of a Trinitarian Doxology

At the culmination of Eucharistic praying in the early church, a gradual shift may be discerned from Jewish patterns as seen in the berakah to a more explicitly Trinitarian formula found most everywhere by the end of the fourth century. In all instances, however, we may speak of these terminus statements of blessing as doxologies. Nonetheless, the shift is clear: the typical ancient berakah concludes with a blessing of God, an action continued in the Didache ("Hosanna to the God of

David").[412] The East Syrian rite of Addai and Mari concludes its anaphora with these words:

> And for all this great and marvelous dispensation towards us we give thee thanks and praise thee without ceasing in thy church redeemed by the precious blood of thy Christ, with unclosed mouths and open faces, lifting up praise and confession and worship to thy living and holy and lifegiving name now and ever and world without end.[413]

The transition toward a more formal Trinitarian doxology is evident in this text. While the "living and holy and lifegiving name" clearly refers to the First Person of the Trinity, now the Christ of God is also given praise and worship. An explicit reference to the Spirit is absent from this doxology though it follows immediately upon an extensive epiclesis.

In the West, from the time of the Apostolic Tradition forward, we see the more familiar Trinitarian doxology deployed at the conclusion of the anaphora, just prior to the people's assent of "Amen." Thus, the doxology concluding the presiding minister's text in The Apostolic Constitutions (from the late fourth century West) names Father, Son, and Holy Spirit who are offered "all glory, worship, thanksgiving, honour, and adoration. . . ."[414] Some version of the Trinitarian doxology would remain present in both East and West until the sixteenth century Reformation in the West when Luther, having retained only "those things which are pure and holy,"[415] moved directly from the Institution Narrative to the Communion in both the *Formula Missae* and the *Deutsche Messe*, thereby excising the doxology and Great Amen. John Calvin appends to the Institution Narrative an extended discourse on the unworthiness of the congregation (their state of "much frailty and misery").[416] The doxology, however, was transferred from its historic location to serve as the conclusion of the prayer after Communion.

Once more opting for the Western liturgical tradition rather than the more extensive revisions of the Continental reformers, Cranmer offers a nearly direct translation of the Latin for his doxology in the Prayer of Consecration of 1549. In the more Protestant 1552 version of the *Book of Common Prayer*, the consecratory prayer took on a Lutheran coloration, ending with the Words of Institution. Then, as with Calvin, the doxology is transferred to the end of the post-Communion prayer (although, oddly, with any reference to the Holy Spirit now deleted). Later expressions of Lutheran, Reformed, and Anglican euchology all have a Trinitarian doxology restored to its typical location, as do the major Catholic and Protestant traditions following the reforms of the Second Vatican Council.

A Note of Ecclesiology

From at least the traditions of Addai and Mari in the East, and the Apostolic Tradition in the West, an ecclesial note is occasionally woven into the closing doxology of the Eucharistic Prayer. The latter, for example, offers praise to "your Child Jesus Christ" and continues "through whom, be to you glory and honor with the Holy Spirit *in the Holy Church*. . . ."[417] One possible explanation for this ecclesial reference is that in several pre-Nicene examples of Eucharistic praying, the liturgical act immediately preceding the doxology is a series of commemorations of the saints. One anaphoric fragment, for example, follows these intercessions with an intercession for those who have died in the Lord: "Number them among your holy Powers." Then the intercessions add a thanksgiving for the people "who have gathered and who have brought the oblations and the eucharists."[418] The prayer then turns to the doxology and once more prays for the faithful who glorify the Holy Trinity. The reference to "in the holy church," then, may well be an artifact of this close linkage between the Eucharistic intercessions and the doxology.

It then disappears from Western Church usage for about a millennium; during this time there is no ecclesial reference in either the Roman Canon or the Reformation doxological rites. The "in the Holy Church" was not to resurface in the reforms of the Mass following the Council and, again, did not reappear in the revisions of the Lutheran (2006 Holy Eucharist),[419] Episcopal (1979 *BCP*), or Presbyterian ("Glory to God Liturgy") Great Thanksgivings. All of these retain a Christological, but not an ecclesiological formula. They follow the Roman Catholic Missal, but typically change "through him, with him, and in him" to "through Christ, with Christ, and in Christ. . . ." One Eucharistic Prayer published by the Order of Saint Luke retained a version of the opening portion of the Roman Canon and, by interpolating six Christological images from the Fourth Gospel, offered a more communal expression of the doxology. The OSL prayer concludes,

> In, with and through Jesus Christ our Light, our Bread, our Wine, our Way, our Truth, and our Life in your blessed triune glory.[420]

One exception to this usage is found in The Great Thanksgiving of the "Service of Word and Table" (1989) of the United Methodist Church which restored the full ecclesial reference with the phrase, "in your holy church" within the Trinitarian doxology.[421] It would seem that the United Methodist Church and, subsequently, the Evangelical Lutheran Church in America, were intentional in recovering this fragment of early church Eucharistic praying. The two denominations voted to enter into full communion with each other in 2009 recognizing each other's beliefs and practices concerning baptism, Eucharist, and ministry.[422] On the other hand, there is some irony in the continued absence of any commemoration of the saints within the UM Great Thanksgivings except for the most fitting occasion of All Saints. This latter anaphora, then, represents a restoration of the Eucharistic intercessions and the ecclesial reference in the doxology for the first time in almost fifteen hundred years! (The significance of this is perhaps lost on most United Methodists or ecumenical colleagues.)

Amen and Amen

The early examples of Eucharistic praying prior to Nicaea all conclude the anaphora with the assembly's assent of "Amen." This very Jewish acclamation finds its way with ease from the berakah prayer form to the earliest Christian table blessing contained in the Didache. As Justin interprets the Christian mysteries (c. 150 C.E.) to the emperor, his son, and "to the sacred Senate and to the whole Roman people," he is careful to document the words and actions that conclude the Prayer of Thanksgiving:

> When he (the "president") has finished, all the people present acclaim it saying: "Amen." Amen is a Hebrew word which means: so be it.[423]

What Justin did not add to his interpretation of the "Amen" was the broader Jewish meanings of something being established, firm, and true.

This certainty of, or at least a longing for, the completion of God's truth is also connoted in the Septuagint; the Greek translation of "Amen" reads, "Would that it be so."[424] As Justin had not published this implication of Amen, he also refrained from adding that for his Christian assembly, the futurity implicit in the "Amen" is now confessed as being fulfilled in Jesus Christ. Therefore, the "Amen" is "a triumphant proclamation that Jesus, the Amen to the everlasting Yea of God, had himself passed into the Messianic Kingdom and the world to come."[425]

During the post-Nicene era, numerous theologians and bishops comment on the significance of the Great Amen. St. Jerome, for example, celebrates the Christians in Rome, adding that "nowhere else does the Amen resound so loudly, like spiritual thunder, and shake the temples of the idols."[426] Given the ubiquity of the Amen as the assembly's conclusion to Eucharistic praying in both East and West, its communal expression was lost in the Roman Canon by the early medieval period. The "Silent Canon" practice meant that no one in the congregation could hear the doxological cue for the Amen and "the bizarre custom"[427] emerged of the presiding cleric answering himself! For the Continental reformers, the Amen was excised from the consecratory prayer, with Martin Luther shaping a movement directly from the Institution Narrative to Communion and John Calvin ordering a sequence from his extended admonition and discourse on the Supper to Communion.

The situation was otherwise in England; Cranmer concluded his Prayer of Consecrations in both the 1549 and 1552 *Books of Common Prayer* with a doxology and Amen. In Methodist practice prior to the reforms of the Ritual in 1989, the Amen was retained, but the doxology was dropped from the consecratory prayer. Later revisions of both the Lutheran Service and various Reformed churches restored the doxology and the Amen to the Eucharistic Prayer.[428] In the reforms of the liturgy following the Second Vatican Council, the Great Amen was restored to its historic location and church musicians created settings for it, as well as for the Sanctus/Benedictus, and the Acclamation.[429]

Homiletical Implications

One approach when considering the Trinitarian doxology in Eucharistic praying would be to stake out rather sclerotic boundaries of orthodoxy within which preaching is to abide. Such a use of doxology, however, may have as its outcome a community hardened into fixed notions of God, devoid of all mystery, marked boundaries of right belief and right action, and settled definitions of appropriate piety and praise. On the other hand, such uses of doxology can also generate reactive communities of disbelief, ironically sharing the same absence of mystery, the same wooden boundaries of belief and praxis, and the same hardened convictions as to insider and outsider. No, this sad dialectic is not built upon a biblical notion of doxology; "doxology," notes Catherine LaCugna, "has a logic all its own, the logic of overflow, freedom, and generosity."[430] LaCugna continues,

> Praise generates more praise; glory adds to glory. Praise works by overflow and contagion; it invites others to join in. God is made *our* God when creation and humanity render praise to God . . . the giving of praise to God has the power to bring about our union with God, to put us back into a right relationship with God. It is a discipline, not slavish duty, by which we let God be *God for us*.[431]

The problem in our preaching bursts into view right at this point: we moralize, develop learned essays on all sorts of topics, exegete or deconstruct Scriptural texts, and enter the political fray on behalf of all sorts of causes. Yet, as Mike Graves asks in commenting on the first line of the Fosdick hymn (God of Grace and God of Glory), "why does so much of our preaching sound anything but gracious and glorious?"[432] One chronic symptom of this pathology is the paucity of resources many preachers have when the sermon turns to "naming grace."

One assignment in my Introduction to Preaching courses is that of developing a sermon sketch loosely grounded in the Prologue of the Gospel of John. The first move is "The world is a world of darkness" and the second move is "But Jesus Christ is the light of the world." The sermon sketch assignment asks for no introduction or conclusion, but does focus on shaping each move well and especially looks for the strategies of concretion—the illustration, example(s), and imagery by which each move gains particularity. Again and again, I will receive sermon sketches in which the "darkness" move is abundantly, even excessively imaged. Sometimes, the illustrations and examples stumble over each other; the congregation would be overwhelmed by the differing types of illustration and by their abundance. On the other hand, often when the student turns to the "light move," there is sincere and pious talk about grace and praise and gospel, but the imagery is almost completely absent. The listener to such a sermon sketch is left chiefly with bad news. However, when the context of proclamation is the full service of Word and sacrament, the doxology of the Great Thanksgiving not only signals the ending of the Prayer over the Gifts, it establishes the theological and rhetorical grounding for the sermon.

Theologically, preaching as doxology proclaims the eschatological finality of that time when, as N.T. Wright puts it, God will put the world to rights. Preaching, then, keeps its eye on that prize while pointing to the Paschal mystery in which God has begun this new creation. And preachers will gesture toward the ways in which the Spirit works "in the lives of men and women, bringing them to the faith by which alone we are identified as belonging to Jesus."[433] Preaching that anticipates the liturgical doxology at the anaphora's ending will be imprinted with this eschatological passion—the praise of God *per omnia saecula saeculorum*, "world without end." And preaching that anticipates the sacramental doxology will be guided by a Trinitarian point of view for interpreting the Scriptures and construing the life of God's people, gathered for praise and scattered for the mission of God in the world. Rhetorically, the sermon leaning towards the sacramental doxology will have about it a resonance with praise; like the folk preachers of the African American church, we will "never quit praise'n God."[434]

There is a counter point, however, of lament. At times biblical lament seems not only in opposition to doxological praise, but even comes as a darkness threatening to suffocate the light. The psalms sing of lament along with praise, trust, penitence, and thanksgiving. Lament is that distinct response of a biblical people who turn to the God of their faith and praise with anger and grieving. Preachers, then, cannot avoid this task of "naming grief" (by suppression of lament), and offering a chronic focus only on "celebration." (One "lead pastor" of a mega-church some time ago announced on Palm Sunday—when there were no palms—"Hey, we're going to try something new this year, a Good Friday "celebration!" Not only were there no psalms on Palm Sunday, there was no Psalm 22 at the Good Friday "celebration.") But an ideology of perpetual celebration is simply not compatible with the gospel and, ultimately, with human life this side of the Parousia.

Lament, we may be discerning with a recovering sacramental life, is not a foe of doxology, but is intimately intertwined with it, both in the Paschal mystery and in our Christian journey. "Naming grief", as well as "naming grace," is perennially in juxtaposition in faithful proclamation. Mary Catherine Hilkert expands on this paradox:

> Naming grief is an integral part of the process of preaching hope in the resurrection because the first step toward overcoming suffering is finding a language that leads one out of the prison of silence. Good news is to be found already in the language of lament and tears. Naming pain and claiming forgotten memories are parts of a larger journey toward healing, wholeness, and joy, although that future hope cannot be seen at every step on the journey.[435]

Note, however, that for Hilkert the grief being named homiletically is provisional, not proleptic; it is "for a time" and not "forever and ever."

Hence, naming grief is an essential aspect of Christian proclamation but is not our thoroughgoing message. The act of lament is incumbent within the liturgy and the sermon, especially within the Lenten season (and during other occasions of loss and tragedy). Once more, the context of the Eucharist signals the shape of the sermon: Doxology finds expression in two dominant forms, those of praise-giving and lament-making. Catherine LaCugna summarizes the juxtaposition of these two expressions of doxology as follows: "Lamentation is not the opposite of praise but a form of praise in which God is rightly held accountable to God's promises. . . ."[436] Within the psalms of lament—including the Psalm from the Cross (Ps. 22)—only Psalm 88 is absent an explicit turn back towards praise. All others make the turn to doxology, even though that movement is perplexing, even baffling to the person or community engaged in lament. However, given LaCugna's insight, even Psalm 88 is a form of praise; God's promises are held up by those who suffer before the holy, covenant God. The same dynamic obtains in our preaching. We may encourage resistance to the principalities and powers, confess the broken state of Christ's church, and weep with those who suffer. But all of these essential homiletical duties are located within the praise of the triune God, "In Christ, with Christ, and through Christ." The preacher, then, will give witness to God's people, that lament is only a "for the time being" activity; in the fullness of time, "the Lamb at the center of the throne will be their shepherd, and he will guide them to springs of the water of life, and God will wipe away every tear from their eyes" (Rev. 7:17).

The ecclesial interpolation ("in the church") within the doxology of both East and West seems to have flourished for a season in the pre-Nicene church and then faded from the scene in the West with the emergence of the Roman text. As has been noted, the Sixteenth Century reformers either carved off any liturgical material following the Institution Narrative (thereby rendering any retrieval of the ecclesial reference null and void) or, with Cranmer and the *Book of Common Prayer*, first simply translated the Roman Mass' doxology and secondly eliminated all post-Institution Narrative material. It has also been noted that, whether intentional or not, the United Methodist and Evangelical Lutheran Church in America reforms of Eucharistic praying retrieved this ecclesial reference, "in your holy church," from the dust bin of liturgical history. With regard to Trinitarian theology, the ecclesial interpolation nicely extends the mystery of the *oikonomi*a within the Godhead to that of the koinonia between the Holy Trinity and the holy church.

This cascade of koinonia is deeply rooted in the Fourth Gospel, for example, as seen in the "High Priestly Prayer" of John 17: "so that they may be one, as we are one" (John 17:11). Homiletical implications of this ecclesial interpolation come immediately to mind. They include:

1. *Priority of Community*—For Trinitarian faith, the interpretation of Scripture will heed its communal context and not succumb to the individualism of our spirit of the age. David Buttrick therefore argues that biblical texts address a communal consciousness, personal, yet not one of individualistic isolation. Thus,

    > Virtually everything in scripture is written to a faith-community, usually in the style of communal address. Therefore, biblical texts must be set within *communal* consciousness to be understood…texts *do not* address individuals in individual self-awareness.[437]

    If the texts of Scripture are written "in holy Israel" and "in the holy church," then any individualistic reading involves a grievous distortion. Just one example of such distortion, Buttrick notes, is to be found in the widespread practice of some kind of therapeutic preaching. The genre is saturated with an appeal to an individualistic self-consciousness. (The same may be said for most prosperity gospel preaching.)

2. *Within the Church*—With the communal identity of Scripture in mind, along with the "communal consciousness" appropriate to biblical interpretation, the sermon is spoken *within* the holy church.[438] Consequently, the one called to preach is set apart within a congregation or communion, but that preacher's identity remains "in the holy church." Paul Janowiak, a Jesuit priest, echoes the Reformation principle

that "the individual preacher acts in the name of the priesthood of all believers, and it is the Church that grounds the one who speaks in the name of Christ."[439] However, the Spirit's work in the church to call and equip persons to preach the gospel is not always synchronous with a particular ecclesial community's definitions as to who should be called and authorized to exercise this vocation on behalf of the baptized.

So, while a convention, denomination, or communion may set in place the processes and procedures for assessing and authorizing those who will assume the ministry of the Word, the Spirit moves as well outside such structures to call and equip others to the ministry of proclamation. The ordination of women to the ministry of Word and sacrament in the face of long-standing prohibitions of that calling, continues to pit the Spirit's movement against hardened church traditions. In some cases, the refusal of a church body to welcome Spirit-graced women to preach has led to the necessity of forming a separate, more welcoming institutional entity.

Another scenario that has been repeated on numerous occasions is that of the eventual accommodation of the institutional church body to the pressure of the Spirit's work of calling and equipping women and men to the ministry of Word and sacrament. The Lutheran Church recently celebrated the fortieth anniversary of the ordination of Elizabeth Platz, the first woman ordained within that tradition in the United States. United Methodists also recently celebrated fifty years of full ordination rights for women called to the ministry of Word and Table.[440]

A third version of this on-going tension between the Spirit's movement to raise up preachers, and the institutional church's formal and informal resistance, may be witnessed within Roman Catholic contexts. Here, most women called and graced to the ministry of the Word remain in communion with the church and yet seek homiletical training even if their preaching be termed a "reflection" rather than a "homily." In every instance, the Spirit calls men and women to preach "within the holy church." The priesthood of all believers grounds this Spirit-filled vocation even when a particular church does not yet acknowledge the call of the one who preaches in the name of Christ.

3. *To the World*—Given this inherent ecclesial context of the ministry of preaching, it is also the case that proclamation is not only a holy activity *within* the church, but *to* the world as well. Preachers call the assembly to its ministry in the world, and also are charged to build up the body of Christ (Eph. 4:11-12). With regard to the latter, this gift and call to the preacher to build up the body of Christ, a lively interplay and mutually edifying dynamic occurs between the sermon and the sacrament. The Eucharist is the great gift of the Triune God to the church, a gift that nourishes life in Christ and grounds its unity. The Eucharistic hymns of Charles and John Wesley rehearse this unitive gift of Christ in the sacrament repeatedly. For example,

> How happy are thy servants, Lord,
> Who thus remember Thee!
> What tongue can tell our sweet Accord,
> Our perfect Harmony!

> Who thy Mysterious Supper share,
> Here at thy Table fed,
> Many, and yet but One we are.
> One undivided Bread.[441]

Finally, it is important to stress what is often a less emphasized role of the sermon as pertains to the church's koinonia. It may be said, that "the homily is a unifying moment in the celebration of the liturgy, deepening and giving expression to the unity that is already present through the sacrament of baptism."[442] By extension, we may add that the homily should serve, as well, to deepen and give expression to the unity that is recalled, envisioned, and experienced anew in the Sacrament of Holy Communion.

Conclusion

The end of the Great Thanksgiving comes as the assembly, with the minister at the Table, joins as one voice to pronounce the final acclamation, "Amen." It may be spoken or sung, but since the reforms of the liturgy at the Second Vatican Council, it is voiced by the entire congregation. The sense of the ending of Eucharistic praying is simply that the faithful hear the doxological praise being proclaimed as a cue for them to take a deep breath, open their mouths, and together speak or sing out the Amen. Now the Great Thanksgiving is come to its "meet, right, and salutary" ending. Homiletical implications will be diverse when considering this sense of the ending, but this much should be clear: sermon conclusions "are designed to conclude."[443]

Despite this rather obvious conclusion about sermon concluding, most anyone who has joined with other members of the body of Christ on the Lord's Day, has experienced sermons that just do not seem to have the capacity to, well, end. Pious talk may keep circling around in a sort of holding pattern, seemingly never getting clearance to land; or, preachers feel that only by repetition are listeners convinced of overheated demands that the congregation get about being saved/inclusive/more financially open-fisted/missionally involved, etc.

Other sermon conclusions have a way of revisiting the introduction, thereby tying things neatly in a package. (Buttrick cautions that such overly neat summation "totally destroys motivation.")[444] Homiletician Eugene Lowry expands on this same insight:

> Preachers often doubt the quality and integrity of their work, and hence feel obligated to explain—to unpack—what might just have been released. Nervously, we may suggest this specific consequence, these four places for proper application, these two most important challenges to our faithfulness. The congregation feels the unneeded reiteration of duty and feels its integrity being questioned in the process. As an actor once told me—when the play is powerful, people do not want a tour of the building.[445]

In spite of the skein of sermon conclusions that either refuse to provide any sense of an ending on one hand or, on the other, the tightly packaged conclusions that in fact over-conclude by way of summary, the best conclusion of a homily embodies an intention which is latent in the movement of the sermon through its sequence of moves. That is, the conclusion deals with matters tersely stated by the question "So what?" The question, of course, assumes that built into the very shape of most any sermon on the Lord's Day is an energy tending toward some sort of performative ending, an arrival by preacher and congregation at that place where all discern what this Word has as its call, its invitation, its demand.

In African American preaching, the "Amen" of the sermon's ending—as distinguished from the "amens" of call and response—is often associated with the celebration. "Finally," James Earl Massey notes, "black preaching is intended to produce a climax of impression for the hearer."[446] Whether the celebration erupts at the sermon's conclusion (the majority practice), or at some other location within the homiletical plot (a minority approach), several characteristics will be shared between the celebration and the conclusion.

Of course, this assertion becomes a truism if the celebration and the conclusion are one and the same thing. However, when approaching the "Amen" that is the sermon's conclusion, these rhetorical qualities will gain prominence if: (1) The sermon will now be about evoking a congregational sense of climax that brings together images and themes from earlier contexts. The intent is not that of argumentative closure, but evocative open ended performance. Therefore, Gerald Davis argues that, "closure is rarely found at the end of the African American sermon. . . ."[447] Its energy, Davis adds, will extend beyond the time and place context of the particular sermonic event. (2) The language of the conclusion is concrete and immediate rather than discursive and dispassionate. The speech of celebration may turn more rhythmic and shift in tempo (by either moving toward a faster pace or a more deliberate beat). As a consequence, the conclusion's rhetoric will evoke emotion along with thoughtful reflection. (3) A conclusion is not, especially if it moves toward celebration, the occasion for additional, new material to be introduced to the listeners.

New conceptual material in either celebration or conclusion, Frank Thomas adds, will "shut down the emotional flow."[448] Thomas adds that "it is difficult to celebrate and digest new cognitive truth at the same time."[449] So at the end of Eucharistic praying, the assembly sings its "Amen." That word does not signal closure to a theological treatise on the sacrament, but a "So be it" that leads to the Holy Meal itself, a feast that gives bread for the journey. So, too, the "Amen" that is the conclusion of the sermon does not entail closure as much as evocation and assent. And the trajectory for the proclaimed Word is always beyond the scope of the liturgical homily; it opens up into God's world and into the promises of God's kingdom to come.

9

The Lord's Prayer

"Pater noster, qui es in caelis, sanctificetur nomen tuum."

Worship at a cathedral Mass is a commixture of the familiar and the foreign for visitors from other locales and other traditions. The architecture is not familiar, even if its style is recognizable. The Ordo remains, along with the propers of the Sunday or festival. But the presiding minister, the deacons, lectors, and acolytes are all unknown. Even the cathedral parish newsletter, distributed as the worshippers enter seems to visitors both somewhat familiar—there will be a parish dinner following Mass next Sunday—and yet filled with unknowns. But the musical setting of the Eucharistic Prayer is familiar (wonderfully, composed by a Lutheran musician!) and following the Great Amen, the assembly rises as they are able for the Lord's Prayer. The "regulars" know what to do, raising their arms and clasping the hands of their neighbor. Visitors and parishioners alike, become physically connected as the celebrant announces, "At our Savior's command and formed by divine teaching, we dare to say:"[450] Now with one voice and bound together as one Body, the assembly joins in prayer: "Our Father, who art in heaven, hallowed be thy name . . ."

Investigating the Rite

Given the attention devoted to the Lord's Prayer (Matt. 6:9-13) by Pre-Nicene commentators, it would be quite odd if the prayer did not find its way into the daily prayer, rites of initiation, and the Eucharist of the faithful. Tertullian, Cyprian, and Origen all engage in theological and formational reflections on what

Tertullian refers to as a "new form of prayer."[451] However, while scholars have speculated on possible uses of the Prayer in Pre-Nicene worship (Jungmann, for example, assumes such usage in house church worship prior to its appearing "in liturgical monuments as part of the liturgy"),[452] the core liturgical text of the early third century, Hippolytus' *The Apostolic Tradition*, demonstrates no evidence of the Lord's Prayer in either Eucharistic rite.[453] Instead, it is in the Eucharistic Prayer of Cyril of Jerusalem that the Lord's Prayer is first in evidence,[454] while both Ambrose of Milan and Augustine of Hippo note its use in the West prior to the beginning of the fifth century.[455] When the Prayer does begin to appear in Eucharistic liturgies, East and West, several issues confront the church with regard to its interpretation, location, and translation (in the Latin West).

Initially, a widespread consensus emerges as to the liturgical location of the Lord's Prayer. The Prayer will follow the Great Thanksgiving and serve as a primary Communion Prayer. What varies among the liturgical traditions is whether the Prayer should serve as the immediate precursor to Communion—this being the Eastern Church's solution—or the contiguous prayer following upon the Great Thanksgiving—inaugurated in the West beginning with Pope Gregory the Great (c. 540-604)). Prior to Gregory's initiative, it would seem that the Lord's Prayer was widely used in the West at the Eucharist, but in a position shared with the East. In a letter to one critic of this innovation (to John of Syracuse in 598), Gregory argues that the Prayer is of sacred origin, being delivered to the church by the Lord himself and it should therefore be closely bound to the Eucharistic Prayer. Moreover, "the Lord's Prayer is said by the priest alone, whereas, Gregory writes, 'among the Greeks [it] is said by all the people.'"[456] Thus Rome joins with other Western traditions in locating the Lord's Prayer immediately following the canon and prior to the fraction.

Perhaps one of the most significant factors in the Gregorian alignment of the Lord's Prayer with the canon was provided by Augustine in his catechetical homilies to the "competentes." As John Anthony McGuckin notes,

> In the early church (certainly by the third century) the Lord's Prayer was communicated to catechumens in the pre-baptismal Lenten instruction and was expected to be learned by heart (a catechetical practice that has marked the church ever since). . . . By the fourth century it was commonly recited at the Eucharist (Cyril of Jerusalem, Catechetical Lectures 23.11).[457]

In his own version of such catechetical lectures, Augustine interprets the "daily bread" petition as embodying three levels of meaning. First, there is the literal meaning—our Lord recognizes that daily bread is necessary; "without bread we cannot live."[458] However, remaining on the level of literal meaning, Augustine views the petition as more extensively referring to all human needs appropriate to sustain life. "The whole is understood in the part," the bishop teaches; "When we ask for bread, we thereby understand all things."[459] Beyond this more expansive literal meaning—as readers of his treatise on rhetoric, *De Doctrina Christiana* would expect—came a spiritual meaning, the daily bread for which the faithful petition is also the spiritual food which comes from God. The daily bread of the faithful relates to those liturgical practices by which they are also fed, including the singing of hymns and the hearing of sacred texts.

Rather than being added as a third level of meaning, Augustine extends the spiritual meaning of the daily bread to its fulfillment at the Eucharist. Therefore the petition is prayed "that we may live in such sort, as that be not separated from the Holy Altar."[460] Once more, the competentes hear further meaning broken from this "daily bread:" there is an eschatological teaching embedded in the petition as well, once the provisional character of the petition is fathomed. Coming in the fullness of time, our pilgrimage brings us into the presence of the Eternal Word, Jesus Christ. No longer will the faithful need to ask for daily bread, for they will dwell with the angels and heavenly hosts in the presence of the Word. Thus, this petition, Augustine adds, "is necessary for us in this life."[461]

In addition to questions of meaning and liturgical placement which are internal to the Lord's Prayer, two related questions needed to be addressed. On one hand, the churches were aware that the Greek text in the Gospel of Matthew concluded the Prayer without a doxology, ending ". . .*apo tou ponerou.*" Some Eastern churches in the fourth century (including the liturgy of St. Chrysostom) did conclude the Prayer with a doxology. But in both East and West, the question arose as to the seam between the Matthean text and the doxology. One solution, adopted by the churches in the West along with many in the East, was to locate an embolism between the end of the biblical text and the doxology. That embolism in the Roman rite took up the theme of the final petition by beginning, "Deliver us lord, . . ." (*"Liber nos, quaesumus Domine..."*) and ending with its own petition for peace. In the Latin missals, a series of intercessions petitioning several saints constituted the middle section of the embolism. However, in the missals of 1969 and 2011, the intercessions are removed and the embolism connects "Deliver us . . ." nicely with "graciously grant peace. . . ."[462]

The second issue related to the liturgical use of the Lord's Prayer at the Eucharist related to the variations extant in the Latin texts of Matthew 6:9-13). An important variance in translating "daily" had emerged by virtue of Jerome's translation of the Scriptures later termed the "Vulgate." In both the Matthean and Lukan versions of the Lord's Prayer, the word *epiousion* appears, a term widely held to be unique to the tradition held in common by these two gospels.[463] Based on prevailing Greek commentaries and the possible influence of Origen, Jerome deployed "*supersubstantialem*" (meaning "bread necessary to sustain our life [or substance]") rather than the more mundane "*quotidianum*," ("daily") the former being "an unattractive word, but an accurate rendition of Eastern interpretation."[464] Interestingly, though, when the first full Western text of the Lord's Prayer appears in the liturgy—in the Gregorian Sacramentary—the less distinctive term, "*quotidianum*," is used.

Clearly, the West was employing old Latin translations for liturgical use prior to Jerome. "The Lord's Prayer," Nicholas Ayo correctly concludes, "was translated into Latin for the liturgy before the Vulgate of Jerome."[465] Even Gregory the Great acknowledged the more venerable tradition in the translation of "*quotidianum*" in Roman Eucharistic practice rather than shift to Jerome's translation of the petition regarding our "daily bread." The Latin text for the Prayer remains unchanged in the Roman Missal through the centuries and councils of the church; it is the foundation of all vernacular translations of the Mass today.[466]

The first of the sixteenth century Reformers, Martin Luther increasingly devoted himself to the excision from the Mass of all of the corruptions he believed Rome had added, especially those connoting works righteousness and priestly notions of sacrifice. On the other hand, Luther personally was deeply devoted to the Lord's Prayer and its use in his theological and liturgical reforms. His sermons and meditations on the Prayer reflected the late medieval context of his setting, along with his role as reformer. Consequently, we note both aspects of continuity with Augustine and the medieval doctors regarding the thematics and number of the petitions (after all, Luther is an Augustinian!). On the other hand, Luther suppresses Augustine's spiritual meaning of the daily bread petition while expanding the scope of its literal meaning (to encompass all human needs). Thus,

> Luther's view of the Lord's Prayer has something patristic, something medieval, and something Reformation about it. It is patristic, in that the prayer has a narrative in which the believer (particularly in the latter part) is caught up; it is medieval, in that the believer is aware of inadequacy and sinfulness; and it is Reformation, in that God is seen to act regardless of human beings and institutions, and the believer is put passively in the position of receiving divine grace.[467]

In Luther's first major attempt to reform the Mass—his Formula Missae of 1523—he retained the Latin where used previously, and engaged in his alterations in a careful, conservative manner. The result, Luther Reed celebrates, "was Luther's greatest liturgical writing."[468] Within the canon, Luther moved the Verba to a location following the usual preface but preceding the Sanctus. Thus, in keeping with the medieval "moment of consecration," the blessing of the bread and wine has been accomplished before the Sanctus. He therefore conflates the elevation with the Benedictus after which the Lord's Prayer follows immediately, introduced with a different invitation, "Let us pray, taught by thy saving precepts. . . ."[469] The embolism is omitted as are any manual acts related to the consecrated bread and cup (the elevation having already occurred during the singing of the Benedictus).

Being confronted with a need to respond to such vernacular liturgies as the Strasbourg masses which, according to Reed, "seemed to be seeking novelty at the expense of stability,"[470] Martin Luther came out with his own German language service, the German Mass of 1526. The Lord's Prayer now tip-toes into the liturgy even earlier, preferably located following the sermon, and offered in a paraphrase rendition. Stevenson refers to this shift in liturgical positioning and from biblical text to paraphrase as a transformation of the Lord's Prayer "into a devotional paraphrase in preparation for communion."[471] Once more, the radical Luther acts in accord with the medieval Luther: devotional paraphrases in the Lord's Prayer were abundant and widely circulated to meet the needs of laity whose inactive stance in the Mass was in need of a supplementary diet. However, Luther now transfers such supplementary fare to the Eucharist itself.

Ulrich Zwingli, on the other hand, came to provide Martin Luther with as serious a theological, and liturgical opposition as did Rome. For Zwingli, the notion of sacrament was abolished entirely, and the notion of the real presence was retained only in a spiritual sense—a position with which Luther disagreed vigorously. "Representation" or "symbolic" interpretations of the presence of Christ in the sacrament were contrary to Christ's plain words: "This is my body." "The bread did not stand for 'my body,'—it *is* 'my body.'"[472]

It is to be expected, therefore, that Zwingli's liturgical reforms would embody his radical and anti-sacramental convictions; in this we are not disappointed. Zwingli's gold standard liturgy is his *"Action oder Bruch des Nachtmahls"* of 1525 (Use of the Lord's Supper). The liturgy as a whole is clearly not based upon the Sunday Eucharist's ordo, but upon the monastic office (to which the sermon has been appended). When the Zwinglian service is enhanced for the Lord's Supper—urged at the medieval frequency of communing four times a year—the liturgical material leading to communion takes the form of four prayers, "none including the formula of distribution."[473] After a further exhortation, the congregation is directed to kneel and pray the Lord's Prayer. The embolism, as one would also expect, has been omitted along with the doxology (which one might not expect). Then, following further exhortation and prayer, the Words of Institution are read and the elements served.

John Calvin also engaged in sharp disagreement with Martin Luther regarding sacramental theology in general, and the notion of "ubiquity" in particular (Calvin objecting to what he perceives is a logical contradiction in Luther's doctrine of the real presence.) Christ's body, for Calvin, cannot be "everywhere" in every Eucharistic celebration after the Ascension, but only resides gloriously in heaven. Therefore Calvin argues,

> Even though it seems unbelievable that Christ's flesh, separated from us by such great distance, penetrates to us, so that it becomes our food, let us remember how far the secret power of the Holy Spirit towers above all our senses, and how foolish it is to wish to measure his immeasureableness by our measure.[474]

The sacramental efficacy of the Eucharist resides in the power of the Spirit to elevate the faithful to where Christ dwells on high in a Holy Communion.

Given this Divine penetration of the worshippers, it is not surprising that Calvin would regard the Lord's Prayer as of sacred worth and liturgical importance. The Prayer is "a table" which contains "all that (Jesus) allows us to seek of him, all that is of benefit to us, all that we need to ask."[475] If we believed this conviction would seem likely to lead Calvin to privilege the Lord's Prayer in his services of the Lord's Supper, though, we would be disappointed. Recall first, that at Strassbourg and Geneva, the civil authorities limited the observance of the Holy Meal to a quarterly schedule; and second, that a catechesis on the Lord's Prayer follows the Creed in the former rite and does not appear at all in the latter. These liturgical realities create an "ambiguity" of Calvin's interpretation of the Lord's Prayer for public worship, because he seems to understand the Prayer as "a scriptural warrant about prayer, not a liturgical text." To this observation, Stevenson adds that "this was not the solution that was to stand the test of time."[476] Contrary to its presence in Western rite Eucharistic practice since Gregory the Great, the Lord's Prayer mostly was not present in John Calvin's Lord's Day services, both by his own determination, as well as that of the civil authorities.

Somewhat late to the occasion, the English Reformation had one additional factor to take into consideration as its liturgical directions were being forged. The challenge for Archbishop Cranmer as he set about those liturgical reforms culminating in the 1549 and 1552 Prayer Books was that several English Bible translations of the Lord's Prayer were already in circulation. Both the Tyndale (1534) and Coverdale (1536) translations shared much in common while differing in ways that remain in variance among English-speaking congregations. Tyndale gave the church "trespasses" while Coverdale preferred "debts." Also, Tyndale chose to go with later Greek texts and added the concluding doxology (as would the Geneva Bible of 1560, a translation strongly influential for the Scottish Church).[477]

The first Prayer Book, however, would provide the version that would remain normative for many English-speaking Christians:

> Our Father which art in heaven,
> Hallowed be thy name.
> Thy kingdom come,
> Thy will be done in earth,
> As it is in heaven.
> Give us this day our daily bread.
> And forgive us our trespasses,
> As we forgive them that trespass against us.
> And lead us not into temptation,
> But deliver us from evil. Amen.[478]

Given the relative stability of the Prayer Book text, the prayer's liturgical locations and rubrical directions changed with a dizzying regularity. In the first Prayer Book of 1549, the Lord's Prayer appears twice, first as the opening prayer of the entire liturgy and then, in its more traditional location, in train with the Prayer of Consecration. In both cases, the priest offered the prayer although upon the second use, the laity responded, "But deliver us from evil. Amen."[479] Following the Lord's Prayer in the 1549 BCP, Cranmer then located the penitential rite and Prayer of Humble Access, all preceding the Communion.

In the much more Protestant Prayer Book of 1552, however, the Prayer disappears from the opening rite of the service which now begins with the Collect for Purity of Heart. The Lord's Prayer also disappears from its usual location in the Western ordo following the canon with the Words of Institution leading directly to the Communion (not even with an "Amen" following the very abbreviated consecration). However, the Lord's Prayer was not entirely suppressed, but simply displaced from its traditional location. Now, following Communion, a rubric instructs: "Then shall the priest saye the Lordes prayer, the people repeating after him every peticion."[480]

No text of the Lord's Prayer is included at this point, so the question as to the inclusion of the doxology remains open. However, in the 1662 Prayer Book, as with the first Prayer Book, the entire liturgy begins with the Lord's Prayer being said by the priest prior to the Collect for Purity of Heart. That opening version ends with "But deliver us from evil," the people responding "Amen." But in keeping with the practice of the 1552 Prayer Book, the second use of the Lord's Prayer is located immediately following the Communion; the rubric indicates: "Then shall the priest say the Lord's Prayer, the people repeating after him every petition."[481] In this version of the Prayer Book the text of this after-Communion Lord's Prayer is provided and it does include the doxology. Again, the translation of the Prayer remains stable, though with the doxology now in place at least by 1662, while the locations and repetitions of the Prayer oscillate from version to version of the BCP.

When John Wesley commended his Eucharistic rite to the American Methodists, he had hoped that weekly Communion would continue to be normative for members of his movement in the newly born United States. Although he specified his Sunday Service of Word and sacrament for use "every Lord's day," his American followers did not follow "Father John" in the matter of frequency of Holy Communion (reverting to quarterly Communion for a number of reasons). The *Sunday Service* sent by Wesley was an abridgement of the Service of Holy Communion Book of Common Prayer. The Lord's Prayer was retained in both its locations, first in the opening rite of the Ante-Communion and then at the Lord's Supper following Communion. .[482]

Following Wesley's death in 1791, the 1792 Conference added a rubric to the Service of Holy Communion that would have far-reaching implications for American Methodist Worship, including the use and location of the Lord's Prayer. This rubric read: "If the Elder be straightened for time, he may omit any part of the service except for the prayer of Consecration."[483] What began to trend by the mid-nineteenth century was the practice of appending the "short form" of the Service of Holy Communion to the preaching service that is best described by James F. White as the camp-meeting come indoors.[484] In the preaching service—as opposed to the shape of the Sunday Service of Word and Sacrament or "Morning Prayer and Sermon" in Episcopalian usage—the revivalist purposes of worship organized the service into first a series of elements of a preparatory mode, then the climactic moment of the message, and, finally, the invitation.

Among those acts of worship that were gathered in no particular order in the preparatory part of the service, was the pastoral prayer which was typically followed by the congregation joining in the Lord's Prayer. Employing the discretion offered by the 1792 rubric, Methodist elders were given the option of utilizing the Service of Holy Communion found in the succession of Methodist hymnals or of appending the "short form" to the already normative preaching service. Since the Lord's Prayer had already been prayed following the pastoral prayer, it was usually deleted from the Communion rite (or, one can imagine, was again prayed twice, providing yet another twist on the dual-Pater Noster of a number of the Anglican rites).[485] However, throughout the succession of revisions to the Wesleyan-Anglican Service of Holy Communion, the location of the Lord's Prayer (with doxology) remained either in Wesley's location (following Communion) or, by the merger *Hymnal* of 1935/39, again as part of the opening rite following the Prayer of Humble Access.

After the publication of the 1964 *Book of Worship*, and given the abundant fruits of the liturgical movement and the reforms of the Second Vatican Council, Episcopal liturgical scholar Massey Shepherd wrote to a member of the Order of St. Luke in some dismay. Shepherd lamented the many "traditional and conventional" aspects of the Sunday Service of Holy Communion just approved by the 1964 General Conference. Among them he notes "the unhappy position of the Lord's Prayer"[486] (it unhappily remaining lodged in the opening rite following the Prayer of Humble Access). Of course, the cautious tweaking of the Prayer Book service by Methodists, in a marvelous and ironic juxtaposition, was rolling off the presses at the same time that the Roman Catholic Church was meeting in the Second Vatican Council and drafting and approving its first statement, "The Constitution on the Sacred Liturgy." The Methodists' mild and liberal revisions of the Sunday service were obsolete upon publication. The Holy Spirit has a way of outstripping our careful fine-tuning of comfortable locations and practices. But then, the people of God called Methodists should have learned that from their Bible and their liturgical Bible, the Eucharistic hymns of John and Charles Wesley.

Homiletical Implications

The possibilities for preaching provided in the Lord's Prayer are endless and expansive. Books and internet sermon series abound with the implicit or explicit title, "Preaching on the Lord's Prayer." Moreover, since the Lord's Prayer was one of the "instruments" delivered to the catechumens by the bishops during the Nicene and Post-Nicene eras, homilies on the Prayer of Jesus appear in multiple variants by such saintly catechists as Ambrose, Augustine, Cyril, and Chrysostom. For the purposes of this present exploration of the homiletical implications of the Eucharistic setting of the Lord's Prayer, it is crucial to recognize the chasm that has opened between the immovable centrality of the kingdom of God in the Prayer, and the American church's relative abandonment of that vision. As David Buttrick observed, "all of a sudden in the twentieth century, the kingdom of God seems to have vanished from our preaching." Buttrick continues: "Like Lewis Carroll's remarkable Cheshire cat, the kingdom had faded from sight, and not even a smile remains."[487]

A whole skein of reasons can be identified for this odd avoidance of proclaiming the kingdom of God in contemporary American preaching. (Indeed the development is somewhat ironic given that Jesus came to Galilee after the Baptist's arrest "proclaiming the good news of God, saying 'The time is fulfilled, and the kingdom of God has come near; repent and believe in the good news.'" [Mk 1:15]) Buttrick suggests that among the principal causes for the growing disinterest in the reign of God in churches is the turn toward a "past-tense biblical world"[488] by Protestant neo-orthodox theology which came to dominate the latter two-thirds of the twentieth century. Moreover, he adds, the venerable old individualism of American culture morphed into yet another form of pietism that centered on a personalistic "gospel" of self-fulfillment and therapeutic reinterpretations of the Good News.

One further factor is proposed which diminishes any serious attention to God's reign—a between-the-times place of fatigue and self-absorption that characterizes eras like our own. An age in which "[n]othing seems to work anymore, yet, [we are] afraid to lose what we have, America seems strangely frozen; we resist change."[489] In a post-9/11 America, however, these analyses all necessitate some revision or correction by addition.

The individualism and self-absorption of church and society have accelerated the chronic features of the prosperity gospel into hyper-drive. On the opposite side of the same coin, the culture's "strangely frozen" sense has only grown more frozen following 9/11, the Great Recession, and the decay of American exceptionalism. The Zombie population explosion in film and popular culture is one important expression of this "walking dead" frozen world. Other expressions in film and media include a plethora of dystopic films featuring an assessment of the earth as either environmentally doomed, technologically imperiled, or the place of consignment to those "left behind." These all serve as our culture's rejection of God's reign that will make all things right, including a new heaven *and* a new earth.[490]

Preachers who "make bold" to lead the assembly in the Lord's Prayer at the Holy Eucharist, will most certainly need to recover from this fearful place to which we may have retreated. This proclamation of God's reign also requires those of us called to preach to violate David's Buttrick's criticism; we must be about a hermeneutics of retrieval of other seasons in the tradition of the church as when Christians were a minority, scorned if not persecuted, and dismissed as irrelevant to the spirit of the age. Among other aspects of such retrieval, we need the saints back in our personal and communal praise and prayer (this said for those of us who inherited Protestant traditions in which the noble endeavor of reforming the place of the saints in worship and devotion resulted in a widespread rejection of the *communio sanctorum*). Thankfully, there are occurring significant signs of recovery of the presence of the saints in both liturgical resources and theological reflection among a number of these Protestant traditions.[491] A significant sign that Christ's faithful are catching on to the new context for the American church is the recovery of the adult catechumenate,[492] a journey for those seeking faith in

Christ and membership in the Body of Christ that includes both teaching on the Lord's Prayer and the discipline of praying it. Christians, as Tertullian famously observed, "are made, not born."[493] One of the ways we make Christians is by teaching seekers to pray, including forming them to join in the Lord's Prayer on the way to their baptism and continue in that praying all their days.

As regards those of us called to preach the gospel, we are, most of us, coming to grips with the demise of Christendom in Western culture and are thereby becoming aware that the kingdom of God is not some improved version of American values. We are coming to a place where God's disturbing and mysterious reign has again become a necessary context to faithful biblical preaching. In fact, it would not be surprising to find some statistics that demonstrate that we are not as fearful a college of preachers as David Buttrick proposed, but to be sure a number of us are certainly unskilled in this ancient-modern task. That is, preaching the reign of God places a burden on preachers to image the radically discontinuous nature of that Divine promise and intervention, to offer imagery that captures the cosmic scope of the reign of God (involving the creation as well as human history), and to provide images of the fullness of what God intends for the world when all things are made right. Put simply, rather than being mostly a fearful pulpit, the pulpit may well be more impoverished in its capacity to effectively be about "naming kingdom," analogous to its difficulty in "naming grace."[494] There may be considerable "talk about" God's reign, but what is imaged in many sermons has more to do with imaging "the kingdoms of this world." So, as a project in "naming kingdom," several aspects of this multivalent concept will be explored:

1. *The surprising mystery of this discontinuous kingdom*—As David Buttrick indicated in *Preaching the New and the Now*, the parables of Jesus—these "parables of the kingdom"—have a way about them that reverses conventional definitions of world, faith community, and even God. Buttrick's selection among the parables to provide an exemplar of this quality of unsettling reversal and mysterious Divine purpose is the parable of the mustard seed. (Mark 4:30-32) He notes, with Bernard Brandon Scott, Robert Funk, and others,[495] that the parable has as its essential setting the story of Israel's triumphalist vision of the glorious cedar tree of Ezekiel 17:22-24 and 31:1-9. "Although tiny and impoverished, Israel dreamed that, someday, she would be like a great cedar of Lebanon towering toward the sky." Buttrick continues, "And 'birds of the air,' the pagan nations, would have to flock to Israel in order to be redeemed."[496] But in his preaching, Jesus offers a powerful and disturbing counter-vision of God's reign. A mustard seed is planted (notice the resonance with the image of God planting a sprig upon the heights in Ezek. 17:22) and becomes "a plant as insubstantial as milkweed and as attractive as skunk cabbage while, at the same time, employing Ezekiel's familiar language."[497] The parable lends itself nicely to a four-move homiletical plot that embodies the reversal of expectations and mysterious ponderings as to this strange kingdom of God. The four moves shake out nicely:

Move 1. *Look up at Israel's image of power and glory—the mighty cedar of Lebanon. One day, God will plant us there on the mountain heights. And our oppressors? They will be like little birds who come to find shelter in our branches.*

> **Imagery:** Ezekiel provides the image here—the majestic cedar, and, equally important, the point of view. The trodden-down faithful will look up in hope to the mountains. One does not even find cedars in Israel, only up in Lebanon's mountains.[498] The savvy preacher will establish the upward-looking point of view as the image of the majestic cedar is established in the congregational

consciousness. This point of view provides much of the significance and affective tone for both the first and second moves.

Move 2. But, look. *Most all of us have our images of power and glory. We carry around visions that can promise a future with a freedom from fear, and want, and doubt.*

Imagery: (Note that this move is the second half of the move set with the tone and imagery of Move 1. In order for the image system here to resonate with that in the first move, it will not retain the same content, but share in a common point of view. So, on one hand, we will not depict another grand and majestic tree—or worse, have one ready to project on a screen at this point. But, rather ask, what are some images that function analogously to Israel's great tree and share a common point of view? An example system is deployed spanning national, cultural, and ecclesial images of power and glory. Such a move could read:

Just imagine you are along on a youth group trip to the nation's capitol. The bus ride takes most of the night, but in the morning, you're there, and the bus pulls to a stop at the bottom of a knoll. Everyone gets off and looks up. The Washington Monument stands proudly in the morning sunlight, white granite on green grass and blue sky, . . . and surrounded by fifty American flags already waving in the early breeze. An image of American power and glory.

We watch it being dedicated, the new World Trade Center building in New York City. The camera pans up from across the plaza—1776 feet it rises, to a height where, as the pamphlet says,"that crowning structure is never to be added to, never to be taken away."[499] *A soaring image of America recovering power and glory.*

In Nashville, Tennessee there's one street that should be named "Denomination Boulevard." You drive along and look up at each building—they seem to have been in a "steeple chase" to see who would be number one. But it is clear who the winner is. Oh, the congregation had to use four different styles of architecture to get to the height it needed, but they outdid everyone else along the block. Driving away, though, the proportions are all wrong. It looks like the steeple tower will lever the church building out of the ground and into the air. But still, weren't they all playing a game of churchly power and glory?

Move 3. *Then Jesus turns the tables on all of our dreams of glory and power. He turns to us and says, the kingdom of God is just like a mustard seed, . . . put it in the ground and it grows and it grows and it grow up to be a mustard shrub. And you look down at that shrub and a thought comes to mind. "God," you cry, "what happened to my great tree?"*

Imagery: After developing more fully the problem with controlling mustard plants—something like Palestinian kudzu—the point of view for regarding the mustard shrub-like reign of God is developed. We also will not forget to provide the congregation with at least one nesting bird.

On a pilgrimage to the Holy Land, imagine that we have stayed overnight at an agricultural kibbutz. Today, our host and guide is showing us all the wonderful fruits and vegetables grown there. You think, after seeing the rows of lemon trees weighed down with their fruit, and palm trees swaying up high, "Wow, all they need is some milk and honey here." Instead, the guide takes us over to a small section by itself. "And just for you," she announces, "we have a mustard plant." We look down at the shrub and walk around it. Then someone notices, "Look, over here. A bird is on her nest!" Mustard shrub, nesting bird, . . . and then someone reads from St. Mark: "With what

> *can we compare the kingdom of God, or what parable will we use for it? It is like a mustard seed. . . ."*(Mark 4:30-31a).

Move 4. *So maybe Jesus is telling us to look for the places where the kingdom is being born, we will need to look around us at mustard shrub level. Not upwards towards a power and glory church, but down where the miracles of God's reign are hid like a nesting bird.*

> **Imagery:** Since we deployed an example system—three towering images—in the second move, we will move to another means of providing an "eyewitness account" of this mustard shrub kingdom. A brief narrative from the early church will be used, retaining the point of view that gives feeling and conviction to this "grace move."

They have excavated the baptistery from the fourth century under the glorious "duomo," the cathedral in Milan, Italy. You buy a ticket and descend to a large room where Bishop Ambrose had the eight-sided baptismal pool built. You can see the ducts that were connected to the water system that kept the baptismal waters flowing, living. It was here, in 387 at the Easter Vigil that Bishop Ambrose baptized Augustine in the Triune Name. Ambrose had taught him the Lord's Prayer and delivered the Creed to him during the Forty Days. Now, Augustine was "planted" down in the waters and rose in Christ to be one of the Lord's saintly mustard shrubs.

2. *God's kingdom embraces all creation*—Anticipating the sequence of lections during Advent, Year B, the preacher may be drawn to Isaiah's vision of God's reign referred to as "the peaceable kingdom" (Isaiah 11:1-11). Here is given the prophetic word of a restoration of all creation that God will accomplish. The lection is placed here on the Second Sunday in Advent because it opens with the promise of a shoot coming

from the stump of Jesse, one upon whom "the spirit of the Lord shall rest" (Isa. 11:2). In the fullness of time, that coming of the little child will be of cosmic consequence; all creation will live in harmony upon God's holy mountain.

The issue for the preacher here is once again to "name kingdom." To be sure we will need to engage in "talk about" this vision of cosmic shalom, but once again Dr. Mitchell challenges us to provide an eyewitness account of the prophetic word.[500] The problem for congregation and preacher is that the same scenes of tranquil creation have been used and reused until they have become dormant speech. Sunsets, mountains, and lighthouses out on a craggy spit of land are the usual fare of such homilies. They are not heard.

So what is the imagery available to preachers that is grounded in Isaiah's vision and embraces the human family and all creation? On one hand, if the issue is simply the glory of God revealed in the creation, instead of those sunrises or sunsets, we could image the stunning computer-generated photos from the Hubble space telescope of the far reaches of the universe. The opportunity here is to depict the Hubble space telescope's photos of the "Pillars of Creation" *rising out of a nebulae that ejected these pillars, each several trillion miles long. Each one is a cloud of dust and other matter giving birth to stars all along its unimaginable span.* As stunning as this Hubble image is, it does not include all creatures great and small here upon our good earth, nor does it connote the redemption of humanity.

On the other hand, there is an image that does depict the Isaiah text, an image repeated with subtle variations almost one hundred times by colonial American painter, Edward Hicks. Here are the creatures of Isaiah's vision: bears and oxen, lions and sheep, and in their midst a child—in several of the renditions, the child pets the muzzle of a docile leopard sleeping beside him. Here are all earth's creatures at peace in God's new creation. But true to his Quaker virtues,

Hicks has another scene occurring in the background. William Penn and a group of Native Americans are making a treaty that will bring peace. Now the prophecy of Isaiah is captured in its completion. The church locates the lection in Advent and the context provides its own lens of interpretation. The little child will soon be born of Mary and "the earth will be full of the knowledge of the Lord as the waters cover the sea" (Isa. 11:9).

3   *The Feast of the Kingdom Come*—In no other aspect of the church's life is the Eucharist more crucial as a context and resource for proclamation than when announcing our eschatological hope. Put simply, it is during the service of Word and Table that we proclaim the Word within a liturgical celebration that embodies the sign of the fulfillment of God's reign. We join at Holy Communion and anticipate the heavenly banquet through our Eucharistic feast. But the scope of the fulfillment of God's reign is not limited only to those who gather at a local Holy Meal in a particular location. Rather, as mentioned above, the Eucharistic feast is a sign of what God intends for all creation.

The joint Roman Catholic-United Methodist statement on Eucharist and ecology, therefore, affirms, "The Eucharist gives us a foretaste of the redemption for which all of nature groans."[501] In the metaphor of kingdom-as-heavenly-banquet, the completion of God's purposes extends to the entire cosmos. However, the Eucharist texts bear testimony to the One whose heavenly banquet is promised and whose Presence graces the Holy Meal. For this reason the Preface for the Feast of Christ the King (the Reign of Christ), in the Roman Catholic Missal proclaims that by virtue of the sacrifice of Christ on the cross, there is secured,

> an eternal and universal kingdom,
> a kingdom of truth and life,
> a kingdom of holiness and grace,
> a kingdom of justice,

love and peace.[502]

Three levels of the heavenly banquet are implied or explicitly stated in the preface, all available to the preacher who proclaims the coming kingdom of God. First, the Eucharist is the unambiguous sign that the reign of God is a "kingdom of justice." The Eucharist is a justice sacrament, modeling the time when all are fed with daily bread along with the Bread of Life. Put simply, yet profoundly, "In the symbolism of the eschatological banquet, absolutely no one goes hungry!"[503] One resource for imaging this simple and profound meaning of the Eucharist is a hymn text from the Iona community, "Till all the jails are empty and all the bellies filled;"[504] The heavenly banquet will be that glorious feast when hunger is no more; the Eucharist is the sign and seal of that promise.

At another level of significance, the Eucharist as eschatological sign of the heavenly banquet proclaims the communal quality of God's kingdom in Christ. In that day, "people will come from the east and the west, from north and south, and will eat in the kingdom of God" (Luke 13:29); the sacrament of Holy Communion is never a private, solitary Meal. To the contrary, the Meal is always communal, even if communed of necessity alone; the saints are not far off. Here is provided another perspective on John Wesley's insistence that the Eucharist is a "converting ordinance." Rather than emphasizing the role of Holy Communion as an evangelistic tool for converting the non-believer, Wesley's intent was that the faithful move "from being baptized but with weak faith to being baptized and having a lively assurance of faith."[505] The Eucharist as sign of the heavenly banquet, then, "converts" the communicant from any individualism toward a deeper sharing in the Body of Christ and from a solely "here and now" interest in the benefits of the sacrament toward a vision of its fulfillment when many will be gathered to eat in the kingdom of God. A further conversion offered in the Eucharist is that from chronic solemnity and stone-faced piety to the joy of the Banquet with its glorious feast and risen Host. Here, a wise preacher may well image this significance of the Holy Meal when preaching on the "Parable of the Prodigal Son" (Luke 15:1132) during Year C of the Lectionary.

The dominant level of significance regarding the heavenly banquet and the Eucharist, relates to the Christological center of both the former—the banquet—and the latter—the Holy Meal—which is sign and seal of the promise of the culminating feast. That is, lacking its Christological center, sermonic pleas to help the poor and feed the hungry remain important humanitarian duties, but are ungrounded in the central strength of our faith. Similarly, sermons that speak out against the structures and institutions that dehumanize and exploit persons, but avoid grounding such resistance in the work of Jesus Christ can become chronic lamentation and blaming without any real sense of redemption. Only the life, death, resurrection, and ascension of Christ establishes the foundation for authentic hope; the Eucharist is the liturgical event whose sacramental trajectory leads the assembly to share in the victory of the Lord in the midst of this already, but not yet reality. "For one who understands sacramental reality, the eternal banquet is already under way."[506]

With regard to imaging the eschatological banquet, a number of Orthodox icons have been written that feature either Christ at the Eucharist or with the communion of saints. According to the particular slant of the move in the sermon, one or the other would serve well as the image. One caution, however, needs to be made of a more theological variety. In a search for images of the Last Supper, Salvador Dali's painting will typically appear on an internet search (or perhaps come to mind because it hangs in the pastor's office). In that painting, Jesus at the table hovers over the earth in a kind of diaphanous transparency—you can see right through him! The picture is remarkably docetic, taking Jesus out of our world for the Supper. This interpretation of the Lord, however, does not bring him closer to the heavenly banquet in the coming kingdom. Rather, it evokes a non-material, timeless Christ whose life is removed from ours. Ironically, the more the Eucharist is "grounded" in human life, the better it becomes at proclaiming that the eternal banquet is already under way.

10

AGNUS DEI/BREAKING OF THE BREAD

*"Lamb of God, you take away the sins of the world:
Have mercy on us."* [507]

The image of Jesus as Lamb of God continues to pulse through assemblies of the Christian faithful. The "Pie Jesu" of Andrew Lloyd Webber's Requiem[508] *(Requiem Mass) continues to minister to families and communities of faith in the time of loss; and in contemporary music, the image of Jesus as lamb of God is frequently encountered, mostly associated with the atonement.* [509] *It is through such cultural usages, even while the United Methodist Church has set this Eucharistic text aside, that the image and language of the Agnus Dei continues to abide in popular piety and remains pastorally and theologically important.*

Investigating the Rite

Following the rendition of the Prologue, the Fourth Evangelist reintroduces John the Baptist (already brought to the fore in John 1:6-7) and invites the Baptizer to elaborate on his identity—who he is and who he is not. The boundaries on his ministry and identity are in relation to "the one who is coming after me," as John explains to the Pharisees (1:27). Then, on "the next day" Jesus comes to where John is teaching and baptizing, and the Baptist proclaims, "Here is the Lamb of God who takes away the sin of the world!"(1:29) The Baptist's words eventually eased their way into the Service of Word and sacrament, continuing for generations of Christians their confession concerning Jesus. He is "the Lamb of God." The formula itself may well have been among the traditions received and reinterpreted by the Fourth Evangelist, with Luke (Acts 8:32), Paul (1 Cor. 5:7), and the author of the Petrine Epistles (1 Pet. 1:19) having identified Jesus as the Paschal lamb.[510]

The trajectory of this Christological image continues, of course, in the New Testament Book of Revelation. There Christ is the triumphant Lamb, the One fitting to open the scroll (Rev 5:5-7), the source of our salvation (Rev. 7:10), and the One to eternally reign over the New Jerusalem (Rev.22:3). When Jesus is first introduced by the Baptist as Lamb of God, the work related to that identity is taking away the sin of the world, a statement that would seem to support the doctrine of the substitutionary atonement. However, as numerous commentators have discerned, the Passover Lamb was not a sin offering in the Temple, but the symbol at the heart of the domestic feast recalling Israel's deliverance from bondage in Egypt.

Two terms aligned with "Lamb of God" must be explored within the context of the Johannine witness, "sin" (*hamartian*) and the action of "taking up" (*airō*) that sin. The former, the sin that is "taken up," has numerous meanings in Scripture, but the distinctive cluster of characteristics in the Gospel of John relates to the adamant failure to see the truth and to believe, to prefer the darkness, and to oppose those who bear witness to the light. The latter term, the action of being lifted up, is associated in other appearances with references to the Passion when Jesus will be lifted up on the cross and, ironically, in glory. Jo-Ann Brant expands on the implications of this Johannine skein of meanings related to two terms:

> The action of taking up suggests an understanding of sin more ontological than psychological. Jesus does not remove guilt. The sin of the world is failure, corruption, degradation; it is a dying, decaying thing. Jesus takes away death and brings life.[511]

This perspective on the Johannine witness concerning sin is nicely congruent with the Dominical action of "taking up," rather than simply the exculpatory activity of "taking away."

In the Fourth Gospel, there are repeated references to Jesus being "lifted up" at his hour, an hour that, at the first sign in Cana of Galilee, the Lord announces as having "not yet come" (2:4). When that hour does arrive, Jesus promises that he "will draw all people to myself" (12:32). Brant notes the ironic function played by *airo* ("lifted up") in this mystery: Christ is lifted up on a cross and in glory at once and in tandem. "In John, the act of lifting Jesus up onto the cross becomes an act of exaltation. . . . [H]is death signifies glorification and not humiliation."[512] The Orthodox icons of the crucifixion embody this mystery much more abundantly than do the Western depictions of the crucified Christ (the latter expressing a more Markan image of poured out forsakenness). The Icon of the Crucifixion in Orthodoxy presents Christ as being lifted up, both on the cross and yet already lifted up in glorification. It is this testimony of the icon that is proclaimed as well in the Gospel of John.

Given the locus of the Fourth Gospel with regard to the Christological image of "Lamb of God," it would be natural to expect that the first liturgical evidence for the employment of the text would be in the Eastern Church. That assumption, moreover, would be correct. In the liturgies and piety of the East, the term

"Lamb" was used "to designate both Christ and the consecrated bread of the eucharist."[513] An anaphora from West Syria, for example, contains the single text, "Lamb of God . . ." to be prayed during the breaking of the bread. Early versions of the Gallican rite—until replaced by the Roman Mass—contained references to Christ as the Lamb, drawing on the Isaiah 53 portrayal of the suffering servant. The first clear evidence of the use of the Agnus Dei in the West was during the papacy of Sergius I (687-701) where, consistent with Eastern practice, the chant was deployed to accompany the breaking of the bread.[514] The most ancient Western practice, then, was for the choir and assembly to chant the Agnus Dei during the fraction conducted by the bishop or priest.

During this initial stage of development, the "Lamb of God line would be chanted by the choir with the people responding, *miserere nobis*" (have mercy on us). This responsory chant would be repeated for as long as the presiding minister needed to complete the breaking of the bread. The sequence of liturgical acts following the Great Amen, therefore, proceeded from the Lord's Prayer to the Peace, and continued to the fraction/Agnus Dei before Communion. Again, given this location, the Agnus Dei served as the vehicle through which the congregation and choir entered into a solemn time of sung prayer to Christ, present on the altar as Lamb of God. However, the sequence suffered severe disruption as the fraction "was gradually abandoned after the ninth-tenth century."[515]

The meaning of the Agnus Dei also experienced a change as a result of this loss of the fraction. Now, the chant became a Communion song, soon to have as its companions other chants provided by the choir. One possible explanation for the loss of the fraction—now thankfully recovered in many Western

Eucharistic liturgies—is that as the use of leavened bread was suppressed in favor of unleavened wafers, the time needed for an extended singing of the Agnus Dei was drastically abbreviated. In its new location at Communion, there was no need for an extended responsory chanting of the text. Now, the triplet stanzas familiar in the West became the norm, with the last response becoming "*dona nobis pacem*" (grant us peace). [516] During the same era (the 11th-12th centuries) the Angus Dei was modestly edited when sung at a Requiem Mass. The first and second responses became "*dona eis requiem*" (grant them rest) while the last response sang "*dona eis requiem sempiternam*" (grant them rest eternal).

The familiar pattern of the liturgical reforms of Martin Luther, along with Archbishop Cranmer, repeats itself with regard to the Agnus Dei. In both the *Formulae Misse* and the 1549 *Book of Common Prayer,* the chant is retained and, in continuity with the medieval Mass, is located so as to provide a Communion song. For example, referring to the Eucharistic duties of the bishop, Luther instructs that following the Lord's Prayer and the peace, "let him communicate himself first, then the people; in the meanwhile, let the *Agnus Dei* be sung."[517] Similarly, the 1549 *Book of Common Prayer* instructs in a rubric: "*In the Communion tyme the Clarkes shall syng*," followed by "O Lambe of God. . . ."[518] Likewise, the more Protestant revisions of Luther's *Deutsche Messe* and the 1552 *Book of Common Prayer* simply delete the Agnus Dei entirely as, we have also come to expect, is the case in the liturgical revisions propounded by John Calvin at Strassburg and Geneva.

Later revisions of the Sunday service within various Lutheran synods restored the hymn text, most notably in *The Common Service of 1888*.[519] On the other hand, the Anglican churches resisted the recovery of the Agnus Dei through the succession of prayer books from 1552 to 1928. Luther Reed, therefore ponders that, "It is difficult to understand the strength of the opposition to the Agnus in the Anglican Communion."[520] The strength of that opposition was again manifest with the publication of the 1979 Episcopal *Book of Common Prayer*. Neither "Holy Eucharist I" or "II" contained any reference to the Agnus Dei whatsoever. On the other hand, *The Hymnal*, 1982 provides a number of "Fraction Anthem" settings, several of which are of the Agnus Dei.[521] Consequently, the rubric stating that "hymns, psalms, and anthems may be sung"[522] during Communion allows for the use of the text. *The Hymnal*, therefore, restores the place and purpose of the hymn at the Breaking of Bread when the Agnus Dei is chosen.[523] Finally, the Episcopal supplementary resource, *Enriching our Worship 1*, recovered the Agnus Dei as one of several texts designated as "Fraction Anthems."[524]

A corollary of this Anglican opposition to the hymn is a derivative Methodist disinterest in its recovery. Hence, the successive Rituals of the Methodist Church through the *Book of Worship* of 1939 include no hint of its existence. However, the Agnus Dei was finally recovered in the Eucharistic practice of the Methodist Church in the *Book of Worship* of 1965—the last prayer book of the Methodist Church to have its location within the Anglican, Cranmerian tradition. The various trial liturgies of the United Methodist Church related to the Sunday service, beginning with "The Sacrament of the Lord's Supper: An Alternative Text" in 1972, once again deleted the Agnus Dei from its historic location at or adjacent to the Fraction. Put simply, the hymn had a brief appearance in Methodist/United Methodist euchology from 1965 to 1988! One metrical hymn version of the Agnus Dei is provided in the U.M. Hymnal, 1989 and it is included in the U.M. Book of Worship, 1992 "A Service of Word and Table IV." The Order of Saint Luke, on the other hand, lists for optional use the Agnus Dei in its "A Lukan Liturgy of Word and Table."[525] The OSL publication also provides four musical settings for the text (19-22). The Roman Catholic Missal of 2011, along with its predecessor, continues to locate the Agnus Dei in its ancient location during the fraction. No longer a Communion hymn, since the restoration of the fraction following the Second Vatican Council, the text of the hymn is provided under the heading, "Fraction of the Bread."[526]

With the recovery of the Breaking of the Bread, the Agnus Dei's absence in churches of the Reformation should have been corrected as a companion reform. For those traditions which soldiered on with the suppression of the hymn or, in the case of the United Methodist Church, flirted briefly with the text before again sidelining it, the underlying reasons range from the doctrinal to simple institutional inertia. Regarding the former, the doctrinal issues, perhaps the core objection to the Agnus Dei was the suspicion that its use at this particular location in the liturgy "might foster erroneous notions concerning the adoration of the host."[527] A more modern liberal and feminist stance against the text relates to its assumed unreconstructed ideological commitments to atonement theology, particularly to the substitutionary theory of the atonement. Most famously, one theologian at the "Reimagining Conference" in 1993 told the group, "I don't think we need a theory of atonement at all. . . . I don't think we need folks hanging on crosses, and blood dripping, and weird stuff. . . ."[528] On the other hand, Mark Heim comments on the need for atonement theology within the core loci of Christian doctrine:

Belief that Christ's death has fundamentally changed the world seems so integral to the grammar of faith that its absence amounts to a debilitating speech defect. A church that falls silent about the cross has a hole where the gospel ought to be.[529]

Again it is important to return to the Johannine context for the Agnus Dei and its distinctive atonement perspective.

Several key images in the Fourth Gospel come together with the proclamation by the Baptist that Jesus is the Lamb of God. The first is the Lamb itself, the Paschal Lamb recalling Israel's deliverance from bondage at the Passover and the suffering servant lamb of the prophet Isaiah. Then, the Johannine images of "lifting up" and "taking up" come into juxtaposition with the Lamb of God image. The work of the Lamb in the crucifixion, then, focuses on his "exodus," from death to eternal life and the Lamb leads the way for the children of God to be healed from their sin, from oppression, and from death. And since our need for forgiveness and healing and eternal life is so profound, what the Lamb lifts up is the sin of the world. The term is singular, "sin," not "sins." "This Lamb will," Wes Howard Brook observes, "change the situation in which 'the world' finds itself."[530] By proclaiming that Jesus is the Lamb of God, the Baptist gives witness to this world-changing event. The Word has become flesh and lived among us. As the bread is broken, and before the assembly communes on the bread of life, it joins in song to the Lamb, asking mercy, peace, and eternal rest.

Homiletical Implications

For preachers blessed with Eucharistic liturgies in which the Agnus Dei has been restored at the Breaking of Bread, the song of the people to the Lamb may echo during the sermon as well as at the fraction. Obviously, the Agnus Dei brings a distinctively Johannine Christology and spirituality to the Sunday Service of Word and sacrament. The images of Jesus as the Lamb—suffering and triumphant—are carved into wooden altars and chiseled into cathedral granite. They are stitched into vestments, paraments, and flannel banners created in Vacation Bible School. The image of the Lamb of God is shaped from myriad shards of stained glass, forming huge and dazzling icons of light. How odd in some cases that churches and cathedrals graced with these images of the Lamb continue in the liturgy to suppress the Agnus Dei. Still, preachers in those traditions might gesture in their preaching towards the Lamb of God embodied in fabric and glass and stone, if not in song. With such "echoes of the Lamb" preachers are gently guided and formed in their vocation in certain distinctive directions. The homiletical implications of the Agnus Dei include at least the following:

1. *The binary Lamb*—Now, just before the assembly comes to the Table to feast on the bread of life and the cup of salvation, the lines of the Agnus Dei are echoed throughout the worship space: "Lamb of God, . . . Lamb of God, . . . Lamb of God. . . ." As noted above, the image of Jesus as Lamb is a binary composite in the New Testament. On one hand, the image draws deeply on the Isaian vision of the suffering servant, chosen and chrismed by God. Isaiah 42 speaks of his suffering: "He will not cry or lift up his voice. . . ."(Isa. 42:2). Then, in a later expansion of the role and identity of the servant, Isaiah gives these familiar words,

> He was oppressed and, and he was afflicted, yet he did not open his mouth; like a lamb that is led to the shearer, and like a sheep that before its shearers is silent, so he did not open his mouth. (Isa. 53:7)

Whether construed as an individual within the covenant, or as a faithful remnant, the work of the servant will be to suffer on behalf of the entire people and through that vicarious suffering, "make many righteous" (Isa. 53:11b). The vicarious nature of his suffering is clear; "the Lord has laid on him the iniquity of us all" (Isa. 53:6). But this affirmation raises the question for this fourth Servant Song as well as for the one the Fourth Gospel identifies as the Lamb of God. R. E. Clements asks, "In what sense can a human being remove the sins of a community?"[531] The answer, the author argues, is found in the Deuteronomic interpretation of the figure and role of Moses.

> [Deuteronomy] treats the death of Moses as an action which had become necessary because of Israel's sins in the wilderness, so that the Servant suffers both for, *and with*, the community he represents. [He] became a victim of the broken holiness which resulted.[532]

Jesus, the Lamb of God, is the fulfillment of this Mosaic office as priest and victim; this Lamb of God decisively and finally suffers for the community he represents. That community, within the Johannine witness, is both God's people Israel, and the world (*hō kosmos*).

On the other hand, in the Book of Revelation, the Seer envisions a new heaven and a new earth presided over by the Triumphant Lamb, the Lamb upon the throne (Rev. 22:3). Just as the Agnus Dei, as we shall see, plants in the Eucharist an essential tension between the already in Christ and the not yet, so this hymn holds in juxtaposition the suffering servant Christ, the Lamb nailed to the cross, with the glorious vision of the Lamb upon the throne. The tension between the Lamb's suffering and the Lamb's final victory cannot be relaxed until the end of the age.

So preachers whose words are perennially triumphalist and who encourage listeners to lives of individualistic prosperity have erred to the point of heresy. The Lamb also was oppressed and afflicted, but did not open his mouth. Then, too, those preachers who have become so immersed in the struggles against the principalities and powers, yet without the hope engendered by the resurrection of the Lord who is the Lamb that will reign, will also slip into angry reaction and possibly schism. Within these aberrant expressions of Christian preaching emerge ironic, polar construals of discipleship. On one hand, preachers invite the faithful to join with the Triumphant Lamb here in this life—a "best life now." They preach the certainty that right faith and belief will result in individual lives of happiness and prosperity. On the other hand, other preachers teach with equal certainty that sin is exhaustively social and only its elimination is an adequate goal of discipleship.

The ironies among these opposing models of interpretation are also binary; the systems share first, foundational assumptions that suffering is an extrinsic feature of theological anthropology. Put more simply, both depict suffering as an accessory to the human condition, to be put aside by right belief, therapeutic procedures, and celebration worship or by combating the principalities and powers until they are expunged from human institutions. In both cases, then, in the words of Luke Timothy Johnson, "suffering is excluded from discipleship."[533] Second, each approach, vastly distorting the virtue of humility, "is totally certain of being right."[534]

2. *The Care of Souls*—Two early medieval evolutions in the responsory phrase of the Agnus Dei enlarged the chant's pastoral and liturgical meaning beyond that of an adoration of

the Lamb of God as the Breaking of the Bread continued. First, as noted above,[535] once the Eucharistic bread shifted to that of the unleavened host, the chant no longer was needed to extend through the entirety of time needed for the Fraction. Now, instead of a chant of indefinite length—requiring the one repeated response, *"Miserere nobis"*—the Agnus Dei settled into the three-part text sung during the very brief Fraction of the unleavened host. A rhetorical change was therefore required to signal that the sequence concluded after the third trope; thus by the tenth and eleventh centuries, the last response became *"dona nobis pacem."*[536] Now, the concluding phrase of the song was a plea for peace, both in its inward and spiritual sense, as well as the social and public meaning of the term.

Soon, "the whole *Agnus Dei* was regarded as a prayer for peace. . . ."[537] During this same medieval era, as noted above, a further change was made to the text at the Requiem Mass. Now the tropes for the Mass at the Burial of the Dead tended to comingle with the more traditional responses petitioning the Lamb of God for mercy and forgiveness. The responsory texts shifted from "have mercy on us" and "grant us peace" to "grant them rest" and "grant them rest eternal." The plaintive quality of the prayer of the faithful and the compassionate grace of the Lamb abiding within the Requiem Agnus Dei infused the more penitential tonalities of the anthem proper of the Sunday Eucharist. This rich intermingling of compassion and grace with penitence and forgiveness are now the liturgical context for proclamation when the Agnus Dei is present in the liturgy. The pastoral weight of the hymn widened to embrace petitions for peace and eternal rest; the meaning of the Agnus Dei now included the Care of Souls.

A homiletical mystagogy will be alert to the need for discerning the fused meanings inherent within the Agnus Dei, especially in traditions (including at present the United Methodist) where the hymn has been mostly omitted from the Eucharist. Preachers will be sensitive to the ways in which the Agnus Dei in its Requiem version serves as a profound pastoral (sung) prayer, for example at the time of national crisis such as the multitude of memorial liturgies following 9/11. Preaching that anticipates the spirituality of the Agnus Dei, therefore, will, from time to time, address the homiletical domain best described as "care of the soul." This domain of preaching, teaches Cleophus LaRue in *The Heart of Black Preaching*, is "a sphere or realm that covers a broad but specified area of black experience and also provides a category for sermonic reflection, creation, and organization."[538] Such domains for LaRue include personal piety, care of the soul, social justice, corporate concerns, and maintenance of the institutional church.[539]

While elicited and expanded particularly for the African American church, the domains also have a ubiquity about them, reaching out to provide useful templates for the categorizing of most all North American preaching. Translation, however, is critical to this latter endeavor. For example, in some suburban majority churches, the maintenance of the institutional church may take on a sermonic recitation of the teachings of the church growth movement of the 1980s and '90s. Hispanic preaching in the domain of corporate concerns, on the other hand, may focus on the need for basic human welfare resources (food, medical care, education, etc.) as well as immigration policy reform for recent immigrants to this country. In any event, the five domains of preaching in the Black Church provide "a means of categorizing broad areas of black lived experience and . . . once identified and understood, they afford an endless resource of ideas for the content of the black sermon."[540] Moreover, by extension, once both understood and appropriately retranslated for other social and ecclesial contexts, they provide the same benefits to all preachers: a means of categorizing broad areas of experience and a rich resource for sermonic content.

The care of souls, then, is one of these core domains of preaching, both within the black church and, as carefully translated, other congregational and cultural contexts as well. The preacher fortunate enough to be called to the ministry of proclamation within church traditions that have retained or recovered the Agnus Dei (or preachers wise enough to initiate such a recovery in spite of the recent liturgical tradition) is reminded at each Eucharist of the domain of care of the soul. Within the Agnus Dei, moreover, that domain is woven into one tapestry, featuring the anamnesis of the sacrifice of Christ, the welcome of penitents to the Holy Meal, an abiding peace both with Christ and within the Body of Christ, and deep comfort for the mourner and those who grieve.

The care of souls, then, is embedded within this rich tapestry in such a way that it cannot be isolated, considered unilaterally, and debased into preaching that emphasizes only a therapeutic gospel. Preaching that anticipates the congregation's petitions for healing, solace, and forgiveness to the Lamb of God is authorized by the risen Lord who asks Simon Peter the question in triplicate: "Do you love me?"(John 21:16). After hearing the apostle stumble through his pained responses, the Lord answers, "Feed my lambs," "Tend my sheep," "Feed my sheep"(John 21:15-17). The assembly will now move to be fed at the Eucharistic Meal by the presence of the Lamb of God who is also our Good Shepherd.

Those of us called to preach are asked the same questions as Simon Peter and we, too, stammer out our ambivalent faith. And like Peter, we are called to feed and tend. Here is a most explicit interconnection between the ministry of the Word and that of the Table. At the Holy Meal, the Lord Jesus will feed the flock with his precious body and blood. But at the liturgical occasion of the homily, we are mandated to feed and tend the children of God through the proclaimed Word. One writer pondered this interconnection of Word and sacrament with regard to the preacher, and reflected that, "Tending the word is the purest form of tending to the people of his (or her) parish."[541] The Agnus Dei nurtures and makes explicit this feeding and tending that is to be provided both in proclamation and in Holy Communion. In both expressions of the Word, Christ feeds and tends his own.

3. *The eschatological Lamb and "the world"*—The precedents in the Hebrew Scriptures for the Baptist's announcement of Jesus as the Lamb of God already bring to that term several distinctive references to Israel's future hope. The central image of the Passover Lamb is a complete example of anamnesis, because it is a distinctive and lively sharing in that saving event by the contemporary covenant community. However, since the time of the Exile, the Passover came to have distinctive elements of futurity as well as remembrance. Gradually, the meal was celebrated with a place and cup for Elijah, precursor to the coming of the Messiah. Prayers for the restoration of God's people and for the peace of Jerusalem

become a feature of the Berakoth prayed after most every meal and were to be found in the Passover ritual itself.

While the servant lamb of Isaiah (Isa. 53:7-12) lacks specific messianic reference, it does, nevertheless, allude to a future in which the sufferings of the Lamb accomplish their work of vicariously healing the covenant people of their sins. While bearing the sin of many (53:12), the servant more than any, will also be vindicated by God. The servant lamb's days will be extended and "out of his anguish he shall see light" (53:11a). Once the vicarious work of suffering is accomplished, the future will be a season of blessing for all those whose sins have been borne by the Lord's servant. Moreover, the suffering servant will remain the vicarious lamb. Only now, it is the vindication of God that will raise up the servant lamb to have "a portion with the great" (53:12a).

In addition to the resonances of these meanings from the Old Testament, the Evangelist of the Fourth Gospel brings to the foreground some distinctive juxtapositions of the image of Jesus as Lamb of God and the Johannine construal of the future hope. The Lamb of God will be "lifted up" on the cross and in glory. "In John," notes Jo-Ann Brant, "the act of lifting Jesus up onto the cross becomes an act of exaltation. . . ."[542] Thus, the cryptic comment to the Mother of Jesus during the first sign at Cana regarding an "hour" that is not yet come, has been clarified in the Baptist's announcement just prior to that wedding. The hour is that time not yet ripened, when the Lamb will be lifted up on the cross and in glory.

However, in the act of identifying Jesus as the Lamb of God, the movement towards that hour is begun. Brant comments that "the Baptist's pronouncement marks Jesus for death, that Jesus is God's agent, and that his death signifies glorification and not humiliation."[543] Each of these thematics is in play as the Agnus Dei is prayed and as the assembly moves toward the Eucharistic feast. The Lamb is both victim and sacrifice, and the priest and the faithful are becoming children of God. They are graced to share sacramentally in this "hour" and to know eternal life begun here in the midst of the world and its darkness. Moreover, the Lamb of God is that fierce Lamb who will reign forever and ever.

The homiletical implications of this multivalent image of the Lamb of God are rich and diverse. Yet the preacher whose liturgical context is the Eucharist will discern the resources that the Agnus Dei offers to the children of God as they prepare to receive the bread of heaven. This discernment will begin with the examination of several core Johannine convictions with regard to our interest in the eschatological aspects of the Agnus that call for our attention as we preach. Central among them is the complex issue of "the world." By the time the Baptist announces Jesus as the Lamb of God, we have been well informed by the Evangelist in the Prologue as to the nature of "the world" (*hō kosmos*). On one hand, it was created through the Word, while on the other hand, it does not know him. The world is a place of darkness into which the light of the Incarnate Word has come. Simply put, "The light shines in the darkness and the darkness did not overcome it" (John 1:5). The world, then, remains simply ignorant of the light of the Word through which it was created. Moreover, the world's condition is not that of simply having need of further education about the light; it is a place that adamantly refuses the Word-made-flesh and revels in its darkness. The irony of the world's condition is not exhausted as we note that it loves the darkness and refuses the light by which it came into being; the fullness of irony here is that God loves the world and gives his only Son, "so that everyone who believes in him may not perish but have eternal life" (3:16).

What is signaled as the Baptist makes his Agnus Dei pronouncement is, that in Jesus, the Word has become flesh and dwells within the world. The truth and grace of the Father are now revealed in the Son, and the Lamb of God will gather children of the light from the world's darkness. The motif of the Lamb's "hour" is then developed as that time of fulfillment when the Lamb will be slain for the sin of the world, a death that the world will intend as humiliation (crucifixion being the most shameful form of death in the ancient Roman world), while to those who are becoming children of God, a death that is the Lamb's glorification. As the hour that had not yet come at the Wedding in Cana draws ever nearer, its significance is revealed in narratives such as the Raising of Lazarus (11:1-44) and its immediate consequences (11:45-57), Mary's Anointing of Jesus' Feet (12:1-8), the Triumphal Entry (12:12-19), and the Foot Washing account (13:1-30).

One often overlooked scene in the midst of these narrative indicators, however, points to a profound new linkage between the construal of "the world" and the purpose and scope of Jesus' "hour." At the conclusion of the Triumphal Entry, with its crowds celebrating the signs Jesus performed, the Pharisees turn to each other in fear and frustration and say: "You see, you can do nothing. Look, the world has gone after him" (12:19). The statement can be read as an anxious over-generalization evoked by the sights and sounds of the crowd with their palm branches and "Hosannas." But immediately following their comment, "the world" begins to lose its hold as the dominion of darkness. Some Greeks wish to see Jesus (12:20-27). Now the "hour" is at hand, for Jesus, for the children of God, and for the world. The reign of darkness is being overthrown and the world's dominion begins to suffer loss, all because Jesus' hour is now come. As the question of Jesus' hour is first raised, the Baptist points to him and announces, "Look, here is the Lamb of God" (1:36b). And in the midst of those huge narratives clustered about this Passover, the triumph of the light over the darkness is signaled in this modest yet decisive event. Some Greeks come to seek Jesus.

Now we may be able to propose several theses regarding "the world" while preaching at the Eucharist and anticipating the assembly's antiphon of the Agnus Dei as the faithful then come to join in the feast of the Lamb:

- Since the world, and all things, were made through the Word, and by virtue of the enduring love of God for the world, the preacher will not adequately proclaim that Word by way of a chronic, dyspeptic haranguing about its woes and evil deeds. God loves the world and has redeemed it in Jesus Christ. The household of believers is not built up in Christ through sermons that chronically deprecate God's world. A better model would acknowledge the darkness while extolling the light. The present creation is neither the all bad of evil, nor the all good that God first pronounced.
- The image of Jesus as the Lamb of God holds together the humility of the Suffering Servant with the glorification of the Lamb at his "hour" and at the end of the age. Thus, the servant model of the church is fully appropriate to teach and proclaim (see the Foot Washing pericope!). However, this model of the church will not suffice as the sole stance of the church in relationship to the world.[544] A most effective pairing for proclamation and mission is that

between the servant model of the church and the sacramental. It is oxymoronic, therefore, to encounter churches championing the servant model while simply ignoring the sacramental. (After all, Jesus did wash the disciples' feet at the Maundy Thursday Meal!) Likewise, the sacramental model of the church cannot stand alone, because the two images are not complete unless the assembly is blessed at the Heavenly Banquet, and washed, fed, taught, and sent into the world to be light.

- The world, however, remains set in its old ways time and again. It is the place of darkness, remaining adamantly opposed to the light. Moreover, the world would not have any knowledge of its darkness without the "contrast model"[545] of the church, a community that welcomes the truth and in Christ forsakes worldly power. For those of us called to preach, this juxtaposition between the community of the faithful and the world offers a practically inexhaustible resource. To amend by addition the quote from Eugene Lowry that a preacher needs "a thirst for chaos,"[546] she or he also needs a fervor for spotting oppositions.

It is crucial, though, to assess the resistance of the congregation to receiving the discrete components of the sermon—the "more" or "page" or "stage"—rather than simply backing off and regarding the sermon in its entirety for any resistance. My way of imaging this is by way of a homiletical version of the Ohm meter (one of my tools for the on-going restoration of an old British sports car). In the automotive version of this tester, if no resistance is to be had in a circuit, the needle points to zero. But with increasing resistance, the needle climbs up to measure the result. Those of us called to preach need a homiletical

Ohm meter by which we will test each component of our homily to assess the level of congregational resistance.

Rarely will there be no resistance by anyone in the assembly. In many cases, that resistance will be widely felt, but mild. In other cases it will be felt more emphatically, but by only one or two members of the parish. When our homiletical Ohm meter shows significant and widely held resistance, it is time to shape a means within that component part of the sermon to reduce the opposition to a level where the congregation will receive the conceptual material. So, if a component part of the sermon ("move," etc.) evokes some considerable resistance as it focuses on some attitude or action typical to the world, a counter-point expressing the gospel may be necessary.[547] (Notice that the congregation's resistance may stem largely from its over-identification with the world's "wisdom" and spirit of the age.)

- In our faithfulness as preachers of the gospel, therefore, we will resist calls for "relevance" and conformity to the latest wisdom of the world. So, as one preacher/blogger insists,

> I cringe when the preacher standing in the pulpit of the church talks about "the real world out there," as if what happens in the church is not the real world. It is the conviction of the New Testament that the real world is not "out there;" the real world is to be found in the church, the earthly embodiment of God's Kingdom. The world "out there" is not the real world God wanted in the first place. It is a world distorted because of sin. The church is to model for the world "out there" the reality of what God wants it to become.[548]

The contrary also holds. The world is most happy when the church seeks after relevance and, while doing so, gives away its proclamation of the "real world" of God in Christ.

Of course, a church that pursues such relevance will become a domesticated religious auxiliary to the principalities and powers of the world. So the alternatives would seem to be as follows: On one hand, the world is the "real" version, knows the real truth (or knows that no truth is ever reachable), and therefore if Christian faith is to be relevant, it must be so on the world's terms. On the other hand, the world's darkness blinds it to the "real" world of the gospel and the community of faith and, thusly, the church is best served by preachers standing against the world in condemnation, focused more intently on that "alternate reality" called the church.

There is another way to approach this quandary regarding the church and the world, a more nuanced and careful consideration of the relationship between the children of God and those living in the darkness. This third way is suggested by the mystery of the Incarnation embodied within the Agnus Dei which, in turn, is grounded in the witness of the Fourth Gospel. The explicit pronouncement of the liturgical text is that the world is one of sin—again, that more ontological quality of remaining apart from God and even opposed to God. However, the Lamb of God is affirmed to "take away" or "lift up" the sin of the world. So, the power of God working through the Incarnation has brought a new situation into being; the world is now in the process of being redeemed. The view that considers the church an alternate reality to the world also needs some reconsideration. At least this is certain: the children of God are called to be light in the darkness in order that those dwelling in darkness may be beckoned to live in the light, and therefore become children of God as well.

The less explicit dimension of the Agnus is the foremost Christological statement of the mystery of the Incarnation in the Gospel of John. Not only is the Lamb lifted up on a cross, but in the same mystery, the Lord is lifted up in glory. What the Lamb of God text in the Gospel, and in the Eucharistic liturgy, is declaring, is that both the Lord Jesus and the world are lifted up in the Paschal mystery; the Lord on the cross and in glory and the world lifted up as regards its sins and, in some amazing and hidden ways, lifted up towards its intended glory. The preacher, then, will be directed to preach toward the world, not only by way of counting its manifold examples of darkness, but by tracing along the paths of light-giving fissures that are the Spirit's intrusions into the ubiquity of the darkness and its hold on the human family and the creation.

Several writers have been drawn to a more auditory image; the world is susceptible to hearing the Word in arenas where an "echo of the voice" remains within the worldly ways of existence. N.T. Wright sees such echoes of the voice in the world's grappling with issues of justice, spirituality, relationship, and beauty.[549] Mary Catherine Hilkert speaks of the preacher's need to listen for "echoes of the gospel" which reverberate within the world, echoes that are pointers to human suffering and other depth experiences within human life.[550] Within each "echo" the world is being lifted up toward the truth of the Word— although left solely to its own resources, the outcome is frequently confused if not outright dangerous. (Witness the oscillation in contemporary culture between the values of security and privacy.)

From the perspective of homiletic method, then, the contrasting examples between the gospel and the world provide preachers with resources for opposition and contrapuntal imagery. But regarding issues and experiences in the world, where the fissures of light of God have already cracked through the darkness, the rhetorical strategy is much more one of analogy. In the latter context, the world yields "fragments of salvation," events and deep experiences where the preacher discerns the "surprise of the kingdom, the lavish extravagance of God, the reversal of roles and expectations that characterizes the gospel."[551] Liturgically, the household of faith should be on heightened alert for such gospel intrusions as it gathers around the Word and the Holy Meal. It is especially at such times that we may be graced to welcome some "Greeks" who wish to see Jesus.

Conclusion

Perhaps the chief liturgical innovation of Pope Sergius I was his introduction of the Lamb of God text into Western Eucharistic praying (Sergius also initiated a festive procession with candles at the Festival of the Presentation of the Lord in the Temple [February 2], becoming known then as "Candlemas"). The Agnus Dei has, as has been traced, a varied fortune in the churches of the West, becoming the triad of petitions to the Lamb of God with "have mercy on us" being the assembly's response to the first two lines and "grant us your peace" becoming the final reply. It was also the Fraction Anthem prior to Communion itself. The Agnus Dei, however, has also suffered loss in long seasons of the church's liturgical practice. So, later in the medieval period, the anthem was chanted only between priest and deacon and, again as noted, a number of Reformation churches simply set the prayer aside. Some have now recovered the Lamb of God as the Fraction Anthem while others, including United Methodists, remain mostly disinterested in this reform of the liturgy.

For those traditions and churches who have recovered the Agnus Dei as the Fraction Anthem in the Sunday Eucharist, a number of expressions of this image are available to the preacher and the congregation. These begin with our noting that when Sergius included the Agnus Dei in the Eucharistic liturgy, he brought us Western Christians (he was from Syria in the East) a liturgical prayer conveying a deeply Johannine imagery, doctrine, and spirituality. Later accretions emphasized the compassion of the Lamb of God, who brings peace. This means that preaching as pastoral care will remain one of the core domains of faithful proclamation.[552]

Nevertheless, at the heart of the anthem is the image of Jesus as Lamb of God, an ironic doublet in which the Lord is both the suffering Lamb of God, slain as the Fourth Gospel bears witness, on the Day of Preparation, and the triumphant Lamb, lifted up in glory and eternal reign. These two meanings signify that at various times and seasons preachers will gravitate toward the Suffering Servant Christology of the anthem. At other times and seasons, the image of the Lamb of God which also encompasses the One who is "lifted up" and glorified, the fierce, triumphant Lamb will inform the preacher's message; the Lamb of God will be "lifted up" in glory.

To homiletically dwell solely on one pole of the Agnus Dei ellipse will result in a shrunken gospel. The lectionary's shaping of the church year invites preachers to play about this ellipse of the Lamb exploring the mystery of the Lord who is lifted up both on a cross and in glory. At the Easter Vigil, though, both poles come together in one mystery. The Exsultet, the Easter Proclamation unique to the Great Vigil, proclaims the unitive mystery of the Lamb of God. One strophe of the Exsultet opens by proclaiming the suffering of the Lamb while concluding with the glorification of that same Lamb of God:

> This is our Passover feast,
>   when Christ, the true Lamb, is slain,
>   whose blood consecrates the homes of all believers...
> This is the night when Jesus Christ
>   broke the chains of death
>   and rose triumphant from the grave.[553]

We preach the compassionate Lamb of God who cares for the souls of the faithful. We preach the sacrificial Lamb of God, slain and risen. We preach the entirety of the Paschal Mystery.

11

THE COMMUNION

*"The Body of Christ given for you. **Amen.**"*
*"The Blood of Christ shed for you. **Amen.**"* [554]

A friend was appointed to a small parish in a poor section of Nashville, Tennessee. Anticipating her first "Communion Sunday," she baked a glorious loaf of bread at home and brought it to the Table. As she served the consecrated bread to the members of that little congregation, she noticed that the line of parishioners was not growing smaller. Instead, the hungry members were receiving the Bread of Life and returning to the line because their hunger for physical sustenance remained. The large loaf was entirely consumed as the people were fed.

Investigating the Rite

The culmination of Eucharistic praying in the action of the Communion is juxtaposed to the initiating acts at the Offertory. When the faithful are full participants in the offering of the Eucharistic Gifts, we consequently expect to find the early church's practice of the Communion of the clergy and the laity in both elements (bread and wine). Likewise, we note a correlation between this juxtaposition of lay participation in the Offertory and Communion and the recovery of the full Sunday service of Word and sacrament in traditions where frequent celebration of the Holy Meal had suffered longstanding erosion. It was not the case, as is widely known, in the liturgical practice of the early church. The solemn and joyful culmination of the Eucharistic feast—in the Meal itself—involved words and actions along with a developing sacramental grounding to the various orders of ministry. Moreover, the liturgical practices at Communion were revealing distinctive understandings of the identity and mission of the entire people of God.

With regard to the Communion itself, Gregory Dix states that it is "the climax and completion of the rite for all pre-Nicene writers."[555] Those same pre-Nicene writers also affirmed that in this culminating act of the Eucharist, the Communion was a solemn and joyous participation in the presence of Christ. One of those early writers, Justin Martyr, speaks for the orthodox position of the early church regarding the climactic event of the Eucharist:

> For we do not receive these things as common bread or common drink; but as Jesus Christ our Saviour being incarnate by God's word took flesh and blood for our salvation, so also we have been taught that the food consecrated by the word of prayer which comes from him, from which our flesh and blood are nourished by transformation, is the flesh and blood of that incarnate Jesus.[556]

The liturgical act of Communion is, itself, a complex of ritual words and actions, and, of course, the presence of the Eucharistic signs of bread and wine themselves. Each aspect of this complex of ritual is organically connected to the others, with the entirety holding in tension the Holy Mystery of which Justin speaks: the abiding signs of common bread and wine along with the real presence of the incarnate Jesus. Moreover, heeding the admonition of the Apostle Paul, this Communion is a koinonia among those graced as the body of Christ (1 Cor. 10:16-17).

Among the pre-Nicene writers, the first to provide successive generations with a liturgical text of the Eucharist (actually, two liturgies are provided) is that of the *Apostolic Tradition*. In the liturgies themselves, as well as its didactic commentaries, the *Apostolic Tradition* provides a "freeze frame" of liturgical practices in Rome in the early third century. Each component of the multivalent rite of Communion is in play as the *Apostolic Tradition* lays down its liturgies and interprets their context. The trajectory towards our present practices and theological reflections on the Communion will take as their point of reference the witness of the *Apostolic Tradition*. To reiterate, these components include ritual words and actions, as well as the Eucharistic signs themselves.

1. *The Eucharistic elements*—At the Easter Vigil, upon the completion of the rite of Holy Baptism, the *Apostolic Tradition* reports that the deacons present to the bishop the bread and wine for the Eucharist. This offertory, however, is distinctive from all other celebrations of the Holy Meal throughout the liturgical year. In addition to the bread and wine, other gifts are offered as well. Milk and honey are also offered and eucharized, signs of the fulfillment of the promises of God that a Promised Land would be provided for God's elect, the land "in which Christ gave his flesh."[557] Water is also presented to the bishop by the deacons as a sign of the washings and cleansing just accomplished by the Spirit as the catechumens descended into the font. All of the gifts are received by the bishop at the Offertory, and the presiding minister then proceeds with the Great Thanksgiving. At liturgical contexts other than the Easter Vigil, the Gifts of bread and wine are those offered, eucharized, and served to the assembly.

2. *The words of administration*—It may be surprising to contemporary members of the Body of Christ that Hippolytus reports that at the Paschal Vigil—which includes the Baptism of the catechumens—the bishop proclaims as the broken bread is given to the communicant, "The bread of heaven in Christ Jesus," to which the one receiving the morsel responds, "Amen."[558] The surprising note here is that this distinctly Johannine reference (see: John 6:25-51) appears in the liturgy of Hippolytus of Rome and not in sources identified with the Eastern Church. Whatever the reasons,[559] this imagery from the Bread of Life discourse in John 6 does not take root in either the West or the East. By one century later in both East and West the Pauline and Synoptic formula has displaced the imagery of the Fourth Gospel: "The Body of Christ," "the Blood of Christ." The response of the communicant is also ubiquitously one word, "Amen."

Modest elaborations to the Words of Administration were seen in the classic liturgical traditions such as with the Apostolic Constitutions where the second administering word was extended to say "The blood of Christ, the cup of life."[560] During the medieval era, a general practice at the Words of Administration was the following: "The body (blood) of our Lord Jesus Christ keep you in eternal life."[561] However, a later medieval distinction emerged with regard to the two Eucharistic elements. The bread was administered with a petition that the body of Christ preserve the communicant's body to eternal life while the wine was served—when served—with a prayer that the communicant's soul be preserved to eternal life.[562] The Tridentine Mass of the Latin Rite, however, conflates both petitions into the administrating word over the bread: "The body of our Lord Jesus Christ preserve your soul for everlasting life."[563]

The sixteenth century Reformers reworked the Words of Administration from widely different perspectives. Martin Luther, in his *Deutsche Messe*, does not mention the Words at Communion since the Prayer of Consecration ends with the Institution Narrative and proceeds directly to Communion. Hence, the Words of Institution serve as the Words of Administration. On the other hand, John Calvin expanded the Words of Administration from those in the Mass. In his Strassburg liturgy, they are to be said as follows:

> Take, eat, the body of Jesus which has been delivered unto death for you.
> This is the cup of the new testament in the blood of Jesus which has been shed for you.[564]

In the first Prayer Book of 1549, Archbishop Cranmer conflated the previous administration formula with both statements, "the body of our Lord Jesus Christ" and "the blood of our Lord Jesus Christ" both concluding "preserve thy body and soul unto everlasting life."[565] The 1552 Words of Administration adopt a much more Zwinglian note:

> Take and eat this in remembrance that Christ died for thee, and feed on him in thy heart by faith with thanksgiving.
> Drink this in remembrance that Christ's blood was shed for thee, and be thankful.[566]

The two versions of the Words of Administration—1549 and 1552—were joined together in the 1559 *Book of Common Prayer* and remained conjoined in the Episcopal Church until the 1928 Book. The Methodist Church adopted the more Zwinglian Administration Words in a succession of hymnals and worship books. So, in the 1935-1939 *Hymnal*, the sentences are as follows:

> Jesus said, "This is My body which is given for you." Take and eat this in remembrance that Christ died for you, and feed on him in your heart by faith with thanksgiving .
> Jesus said, "This cup is the new covenant in My blood, which is shed for you." Drink this in remembrance that Christ died for you, and be thankful.[567]

Providing both the more Catholic and more Zwinglian versions of the Words of Administration, a rubric in *The Book of Worship* of 1965 allows that "one or both of the sentences shall be said."[568] Whether in the practice of Episcopalians or Methodists prior to the reforms following the Second Vatican Council, the speaking of the "both-and" sentences during Communion will need to involve the serving of more than one communicant at a time. In the *Companion to the Book of Worship*, Joseph D. Quillian, Jr. notes that "The words of distribution often are said in the process of serving four or five people, the server saying words slowly as he moves along."[569] It may be assumed that a similar approach was employed in many Episcopal parishes.

In the Episcopal *Book of Common Prayer*, 1979, the traditional language in "Rite One" continues the joint statements of the 1549 and 1552 Prayer Books. However, in "Rite Two," the more contemporary language version of the Holy Eucharist, the bread and cup are given to the communicants with these words:

> The Body (Blood) of our Lord Jesus Christ keep you in everlasting life. [*Amen.*]
>
> *or*
>
> The Body of Christ, the bread of heaven. [*Amen.*]
> The Blood of Christ, the cup of salvation. [*Amen.*][570]

The most recent hymnal of the Presbyterian Church (U.S.A.), *Glory to God*,[571] provides for alternative statements related to the administration of the bread and cup:

> The bread of heaven. [*Amen*]
> The cup of salvation. [*Amen*]
>
> *or*
>
> The body of Christ given for you. [*Amen*]
> The blood of Christ, given for you. [*Amen*][572]

Likewise, *Evangelical Lutheran Worship*,[573] the latest hymnal of the Evangelical Lutheran Church in America, provides for the most succinct and to the point Words of Administration:

> The body of Christ, given for you.
> The blood of Christ, shed for you.
> (A rubric adds that "*each person may respond* Amen.")
> [574]

Following the reforms of the Council's "Constitution on the Sacred Liturgy," the Words of Administration at the Mass and within a wide span of the more liturgical Protestant churches were both simplified and spoken directly to each communicant.[575] So, in the Missal of 2011, the Words of Administration were as follows:

> *Communion Minister*: The body of Christ.
> **Communicant: Amen.**
> *Communion Minister*: The blood of Christ.
> **Communicant: Amen.**[576]

What is evident in all of these recent examples of Eucharistic praying, with the exception of "Rite One" of the Episcopal

Book of Common Prayer, 1979, is that the terse and direct Administration sentences are meant to be spoken to each communicant as she or he receives Communion.

3. *The liturgical actions*—Unless prohibited from Communion by present occupation in a long list of questionable activities and offices,[577] which the *Apostolic Tradition* notes, the assembly is communed at the Paschal Vigil in accord to the functions of the various orders of ministry. The bishop—as chief pastor, overseer, and sacramental priest—both completes the Fraction and distributes the fragments of bread to the assembly. Hippolytus interestingly ascribes first priority to the presbyters in administering the cup, although, "if there are not enough presbyters, the deacons also shall hold the cups, and stand by in good order and reverence. . . ."[578]

Each communicant drinks three times of the cup, each in the name of the respective Person of the Holy Trinity. Other presbyters and/or deacons there, also present themselves in good order and demeanor, and serve the distinctive additional gifts of milk and honey, this being the Great Vigil. Gregory Dix comments on further liturgical practice at these rites:

> We know from other evidence that communion was received standing, and that the clergy received before the laity. It seems that the ministers stood before the altar and that the communicants moved from one to another of them, instead of the ministers passing along a row of communicants as with us.[579]

Throughout the fourth and fifth centuries the liturgical actions of both East and West generally follow the practices mentioned in the *Apostolic Tradition*. The presence of milk and honey disappears during the immediate post-Nicene era and the serving of the cup for this reason is mostly assigned to the deacons (a practice that will diminish along with the more general "atrophy"[580] of the order in the West).

What is surprising, however, is how early in the church's Eucharistic tradition this full participation of the laity at both the Offertory and at Communion began to suffer loss. Following the high point of sacramental practice in the fourth and fifth centuries, Jungmann notes, "with unexpected rapidity, the frequency of reception, at least in some countries, took a sharp drop."[581] Several factors appear to have conspired together to assist in this slide toward infrequent communion by the laity. The overemphasis on the divinity of Christ along with a heightened emphasis on the sacrificial character of the Mass were major factors, along with the increasingly penitential rites and general ethos attending to Communion. A consequent elevation of the status of the priest as the sole communicant and thereby as the representative of the people in the act of communing gained popularity in many regions in the West by the early medieval period.[582]

As a correlate to this rationalization of the infrequency of lay communion, myriad private devotional acts arose, as well as the spiritualizing of Communion by the act of gazing upon the consecrated Host and contemplating the sacrifice of Christ. The individual worshipper "became a mere spectator and listener, without a 'liturgy' in the primitive sense at all."[583] The shift in the West from leavened bread to the unleavened Communion wafer—mostly accomplished by the eleventh century—then led to the communing of the laity directly on the tongue rather than in the hands. Linked to this significant shift from a loaf of bread to the unleavened host were further diminishments in the sacramental signs and actions that conveyed the Eucharist as a resurrection meal with Christ.

So, as Jungmann notes, "all of a sudden, the paten loses its function."[584] The last vestiges of Western medieval use of the paten were restricted to its holding the larger host that the priest would break at the fraction. "Its use no longer extends beyond the altar."[585] The withholding of the Chalice lagged behind these developments with regard to the consecrated bread, but by the twelfth century, the laity no longer communed in both kinds in most of the Western church. But the situation was even more dire regarding the frequency of communion of the people of God; the laity communed at Easter and, perhaps a few further times during the liturgical year.

In addition, the devolving of Communion to reception primarily by the celebrant was accompanied by dramatic increases in ceremonial action along with theological justifications of both the ceremony and the shrunken participation. For example, the reservation of the Blessed Sacrament was related to two pastoral contexts in the late classical period. On one hand, the faithful received enough consecrated bread to take home and commune during the week. On the other hand, there was a need to set aside some portion of the consecrated elements to take to the sick and the dying. Initially, this latter pastoral necessity was met by the priest simply placing some of the remaining elements on the altar to be used as needed throughout the week. Neither practice, however, could be maintained given the shifts in Eucharistic piety and theological interpretation. By the ninth century, the tradition of keeping the Blessed Sacrament in the homes of the faithful had come to an end. But while that aspect of "extending the table"[586] was trending toward total eclipse, the dynamics related to the reservation of the Eucharist were waxing throughout the medieval period.

From the simple and functional practice of setting aside some of the consecrated species in a small container to be left on the altar, the place of reservation moved to a sacristy or other small room. However, with the increasing emphasis on the adoration of the Blessed Sacrament (rather than the assembly's communing of it), the West trended toward wall tabernacles on the Gospel side of the Table and, most grandly, to the building of sacramental towers where the host could be seen and reverenced by the faithful. Such "towers," comments Cassian Folsom, "were actually a kind of monstrance, with a kind of permanent exposition of the Blessed Sacrament."[587] In place of the early church's Communion by celebrant and people, in the medieval Mass, in most cases, the priest communed and the people beheld the Host.

The sixteenth century reformers all strove to correct the distortions of the sacrament, seeking a return to the clear teaching and practice of Christ and the teachings of the New Testament. All three major centers of reform—the Lutheran, the Calvinist, and the Anglican—concurred with Martin Luther that "according to the institution of Christ, let both forms be both sought and ministered."[588] Early Lutheran practice retained the medieval administration of the bread directly into the mouth of the communicant, although a gradual movement toward receiving the wafer in the hand later prevailed. Moreover, the Lutheran Eucharistic tradition held either standing or kneeling as appropriate for communicants. "Luther," Reed adds, "approved kneeling, though he refers to standing."[589]

The Reformed churches, however, chose to sit at table or at their pews, with some exceptions. In the French Reformed congregations, for example, women and men, divided by gender, moved to the table in pairs and received the bread and wine standing. "The bread and wine," Lee Palmer Randel notes, "were both common to quotidian tables."[590] In Scotland, the Eucharistic practice involved the use of multiple tables with communion served to the congregants seated. According to Randel, the ritual meaning of seated communion was "the radical application of the principle of scriptural authority: if this is what Christ and his apostles did, then in obedience to God's Word—and in conscious rejection of human invention—so, too, the faithful were to gather seated."[591]

Such "human invention" was perceived as residing in the Roman Catholic practice of receiving the Eucharistic food kneeling, although more immediately, the "inventors" were the Anglicans. Polemics regarding the kneeling-standing controversy, however, worked both ways. Reed notes that in the second Prayer Book of the Church of England, a rubric was added that specified kneeling, "probably to meet the agitation for sitting which came from Scotland."[592]

After the initial momentum of the Eucharistic zeal of the early reformers wore down, the medieval issue of infrequent communion by the people reasserted itself even as that infrequent communion was served in both kinds in the hand. Whether kneeling, sitting, or standing, the descendants of the sixteenth century Reformers reverted back to old habits of communing between one and four times a year. The Scottish faithful, for example, typically communed only at Easter. Meanwhile, to the south, the minimum frequency of communion according to the *Book of Common Prayer*, 1552, was set at four celebrations—"at the three great festivals and around Michaelmas."[593]

Regional differences did exist within the English Church, with Wales, for example, manifesting a vigorous practice of monthly liturgies of Holy Communion on average. Still, the frequency of the services of Holy Communion did not automatically translate into occasions of parishioners communing together. Many worshippers would remain in the service through the sermon and subsequent Litany and then take their leave. One remarkable and bright exception, however, was the Eucharistic reforms of John and Charles Wesley in England during the eighteenth century. Both ordained priests of the Church of England, John noted that he communed regularly, about every four or five days, while Charles' diary shows him communing at least twice every month.[594]

In a sermon titled "The Duty of Constant Communion," John indicates that his homiletical purpose is to show "that it is the duty of every Christian to receive the Lord's Supper as often as he can."[595] Even the slightly more relaxed notion of "frequent communion" is regarded by Wesley as a frivolous compromise with the clear command of Christ. Moreover, the objection that one is unworthy is likewise swept aside:

> You say, "I am unworthy to receive it." And what then? You are unworthy to receive any mercy from God. But is that a reason for refusing all mercy? God offers you a pardon for all your sins. You are unworthy of it, it is sure, and he knows it, but since he is pleased to offer it nevertheless, will not you accept of it? . . . What can God himself do for us farther, if we refuse his mercy because we are unworthy of it?[596]

Further advocates of Eucharistic reform in England included the Tractarian movement[597] of Pusey, Newman, and others (the ninety tracts spanning from 1833 to 1841) as well as a proto-ecumenical group known as the "Catholic Apostolics."[598]

The former, more controversial and influential movement, advocated for the celebration of the sacrament on each Lord's Day and major festival of the liturgical year. The latter community, beginning in 1835, practiced weekly Eucharist. About the same time, but in a quite different context, Alexander Campbell and other leaders in the "Restorationist Movement," were advocating a recovery of what they determined to be the New Testament practice for worship on the Lord's Day. "All Christians are members of the house or family of God," Campbell proclaimed, "and called and constituted a royal priesthood, and may, therefore bless God for the Lord's table, its loaf and cup—approach it without fear, and partake of it with joy as often as they please, in remembrance of the death of their Lord and Saviour. . . ."[599] The descendent churches of the Stone-Campbell renewal movement celebrate the Lord's Supper each Lord's Day.

Lamentably, the children of John Wesley in the new United States soon suffered a "decline of Eucharistic observance and fervor."[600] However, this decline involved more than only the people called Methodists, and involved more than one single factor. Deterioration in the signs and actions at the Communion, though, were integral threads in the skein of issues at the heart of this loss of Eucharistic piety and practice within Methodism, and other Protestant denominations. The "one loaf" of which St. Paul wrote to the Corinthians had already become ambiguous as the churches in the West moved to individual wafers about a millennium beforehand. But now, the varieties of "Communion bread" included small cubes of sliced bread, little Communion "Chicklets" (hard tiny bits of bread), and pieces of saltine crackers.[601] In every instance, the Eucharistic sign of the one bread is compromised, and a pious individualism encouraged.

In a number of Protestant traditions, an analogous dynamic obtained with reference to the sacramental sign of the one cup. The mid-nineteenth century confluence of the temperance movement, the medical discovery of germs, along with the application of Pasteur's discovery to "the unfermented juice of the grape," all resulted in the individual communion glasses becoming the norm. Here, too, the fractured sign encouraged individualistic piety at the expense of a Holy Communion among the faithful. (Perhaps the nadir of these trends was reached when church supply houses began offering "Individual Pre-Filled Communion Cups," comprised of a small plastic cup containing the grape juice with a dime-sized wafer hermetically sealed in the lid!) Significant ecumenical reforms of the Eucharist in the West would, for the most part, await the fruits of the liturgical movement.[602] With the work of the Constitution on the Sacred Liturgy, and the companion reforms of various Protestant denominations in the post-Conciliar environment, participation in the Eucharist would once again be expanded toward its earliest roots. These reforms would address every aspect of Eucharistic theology and practice, including the Communion itself.

Homiletical Implications

The liturgical text at Communion is simple and direct: "The body of Christ: given for you," "The blood of Christ: the cup of salvation." With minor variations, these words convey the depth of sacramental faith that at this Holy Mystery we commune with the presence of Christ. As a counterpoint, the power and meaning of these words can be obscured if, on one hand, the Eucharistic minister uses the occasion to squeeze the open hands of the communicant in a gesture of warm-feeling fondness or on the other hand, the direct clarity of the liturgical words and actions can be buried by a server's overlay of pious verbal white noise. Lamentably, in all too many congregations, a communicant is liable at times to hear the minister spreading a coating of pious words over the actions of the rite, apparently not trusting the signs and acts to speak for themselves.

Faced with the need to speak in the sermon, and at the same time let the sign-acts of the communion speak for themselves, we must address the need for the economy of scale in an effective sermon. The question of the need for a generally terse shape to the sermon has been addressed as the Preface and its propers were explored, but there is room yet to discuss some of the particulars of the introduction, the illustrations, and the conclusion.

The introduction is first, not only in the sermon, but also in its importance regarding the need for a trim, focused deployment. Sermons that open with a series of rambling comments about yesterday's football game, the preacher's growing up years related to the present time of year, the latest attempt at humor from the pulpit, or even an extended discourse on the Sunday's location within the liturgical year, create distractions that impede the assembly's ability to attend to the first conceptual element following the introduction. Moreover, epic-sized stories do not serve well as introductory material to the body of the sermon; they tend to become the new "text" for the message that follows.

Similarly, within the body of the sermon the illustrative material, whether a story-illustration, an example, or a vivid image is especially crucial. Once again, those large and overdone stories, often downloaded from some internet source, will gain a life of their own and cease to function effectively within the homiletical plot. Taking into account the need to assess the communicant's experience at Communion, the wise preacher will attempt, in most instances, to shape examples and images from the point of view of the listeners.

Finally, a sermonic conclusion may be heard now and then which really does not succinctly conclude anything that has been said. Rather, a series of recaps may be attempted or simply a lengthy revisit of a type-scene ending (e.g., sharing the story of the preacher's conversion yet again) that has little or nothing to do with the content of the sermon. Conclusions to the homily will both embody the intention of the Scriptural text and conclude with a fitting style of speech and economy of scale. Exemplary of these virtues of a fitting and terse shaping of language is the following conclusion to a sermon on Isaiah 9:2-7:

> So rejoice, said Isaiah, without a shadow of irony. You who stumble in the dark, upon *you* has the light shined. All the light we cannot see. Until . . . until it is reflected. By the mirror of your life. And then *others* who walk in darkness will see a great light. Your mirror will give *them* cause to rejoice. "The zeal of the Lord of hosts will do this." Amen.[603]

In addition to the necessity for succinct communication in the sermon, is the need to avoid formulaic phrases which are intended to communicate with brevity and clarity, but actually muddy the waters of understanding by their repetitive or simplistic content. Just as some communicants hear brief snippets of extended, formulaic Administration Words, repetitive yet fragmentary, so, too, the congregation will become dulled to formulaic phrases from the pulpit, heard again and again. Whether heard seated at the sermon or kneeling at the Communion rail, these fragmentary phrases soon become devoid of immediate consequence; they entirely lose their ability to convey bright meaning.

So, if the preacher overly trades in such phrases as "saving the least, the last, and the lost" or "striving for peace and justice," the important meanings behind the formulae will grow increasingly more distant and vague. The same dynamic occurs if the often-repeated pulpit phrases are cyphers of denominational marketing slogans. (Some United Methodist congregations were pummeled by injunctions toward "radical hospitality" without that idea ever being imaged concretely in the least. The same outcome resulted; the phrase eventually became devoid of meaning and consequence.)

Within the Communion itself, the "tape loop" of lengthy, formulaic Administration Words fails because it is neither directed to one member of the faithful in particular nor to the distinctive community of the baptized who come for the sacrament. The homiletical analogue is the sermon that appears addressed to a generic congregation of persons about matters of what William Willimon labels the "general human condition."[604] Willimon adds,

> How many of our sermons speak as if no one in particular has gathered here, as if we are an audience of disinterested listeners, as if nothing like life or death were at stake in our speech? Such speaking is an affront to the dignity of the baptized.[605]

The analogy to the dynamics of the reformed Communion rites is striking, both as regards the assembly and the presiding minister. In the former, the faithful and their priest receive the Word become flesh through the power of the Holy Spirit in the particular time and place of the Eucharist. In the latter, the priest of the church is called to preside in the words and actions of the Holy Meal within a particular community of the faithful in a certain time and place (hence the importance of the propers). The homiletical aspect of the analogy also involves both congregation and preacher. For the assembly, their context shapes the wise preacher's sermon, taking into account the congregation's own story, their joys and hopes as well as their sorrows and losses. One of the core errors in preaching, notes Lenora Tubbs Tisdale, is that preachers "prepare sermons for generic humanity that never truly become enfleshed in the real-life situations of particular congregations."[606] For the preacher, the on-going task is that of "exegeting the congregation" in all its contextual distinctiveness "so that the preacher as 'priest' can best represent it in the homiletical process."[607]

Because it is a service of Word and Table, these notes about brevity, clarity, and contextuality in the homily are apt, but the Communion itself is centrally signs and actions. The problem for some preachers, perhaps, lies in a skepticism that the sacramental signs can speak for themselves without all our chatting at the rite. Another possible interpretation of such practices, is that the minister does not trust the efficacy of the sacrament of the Table. So, some "value-added" homily must accompany the serving of the bread and cup in order for the parishioners to take something relevant away from the service. We come, stand, and extend our hands to receive the Sacrament, or perhaps we sit or kneel and wait to be served. The rite of Communion has its ritual words, but the Mystery of Christ's presence is also conveyed through the Eucharistic signs and the actions of the ministers and the assembly at Communion. These signs and actions, then, are available to the preacher as a powerful means to name grace in the sermon. Their meanings are richly abundant and tensive; they express the entirety of the Paschal Mystery, a vigorous doctrine of creation, an assurance of spiritual feeding, the motive and means of the church's care for the poor and hungry, a strengthening for Christ's mission in the world, and an assurance of salvation and eternal life.[608]

Some specific ways in which the signs and actions at Communion may be deployed in the homily in order to address these thematics within various kinds of sermonic moves may be explored as follows. In every instance, the move's conceptual content and imagery are drawn from the Communion rite; each move, thereby, would find its location within a larger sermon plot.

- *So here's Saint Paul's math at work: "One loaf equals one body." Because there is one loaf, we, many as we are, are one body in Jesus Christ. "We all partake of the one bread," the apostle announces. That makes us all one in the Lord.* (Move within a homily on 1 Cor. 12:12-31a, Third Sunday after the Epiphany, Year C)

Image: We just can't get away from the image, can we? We enter the sanctuary, and there on a table in the back is the basket with the one loaf, ready to be offered along with the wine and our tithes and other gifts. Then we see the one loaf presented at the Altar/Table and we give thanks and ask the Spirit to come down. The one loaf, once blessed, is lifted for all to see after we sing "Amen," and pray the prayer our Lord taught us. We look and listen for the words—"Because there is one loaf, we, who are many, are one body, for we all partake of the one loaf."[609] That one loaf will be broken so that we might all be fed, and all might share in the body of Christ. But it is *"one* bread, *one* body,"[610] as the hymn puts it. We are all *one*.

○ *Here is the sign of our God's promise—that the Lord will give what is good. The land has yielded its increase, the good soil and the rain have nurtured the seed now grown into the finest wheat. Here is the fulfillment promised by our faithful God. The promises are fulfilled as we receive the abundance of creation, bread broken for us and wine poured out in love.* (Move within a homily on Psalm 85, Second Sunday of Advent, Year B)

Image: We offer the fruits of creation, the bread and the wine. They are blessed by the Spirit and broken for all of us to be fed. We open our hands and receive the bread of life, the Body of Christ. As we commune, the words of the song surround us: "You satisfy the hungry heart with gifts of finest wheat." [611] "Amen," we respond, in gratitude and in deep joy. (Psalm 85, Second Sunday of Advent, Year B)

○ *The Lord Jesus never gives up asking the church this question, "Where are we to buy bread for these people to eat?" Our Savior's care for the hungry and the poor never weakens, never is set aside. And the church sees the need and gives Phillip's response to the Lord: "Look, Jesus, we know of your care and concern, we have no way to help. Phillip's question is our own—look at us, never enough resources, members, money, even our faith is weak. And look at the need right in our own community let alone the world. With Phillip, we shake our heads in real regret. "No, Lord, we do not know where to buy enough bread for the world's hunger. In fact, we struggle to provide enough bread for ourselves.* (Move within homily on John 6:1-21, Ninth Sunday after Pentecost, Year B)

Image: So what would Communion look like at the "Church of St. Philip the Skeptical?" No doubt, the congregation would come forward looking solemn and sad. The choir would sing that familiar Communion song, "There's no bread to break together on our knees." The servers at St. Philip the Skeptical would hand out little pieces of paper to each of us as we come forward. The message would read, "No bread today. No Bread come down from heaven."

This image is a counterpoint to the reality of the gospel, exploring the consequences of Philip's despairing response to Jesus' question. A next move, however, would focus on the meager gifts of the poor boy who shares his five barley loaves and two little fish with the Lord. Then, a grace-filled move would celebrate the feast of abundance that Jesus provides for us and intends for all God's children.

o *So the earth has trembled and the tomb is flung open. Those on guard to prevent the exodus of our Lord Jesus from death to resurrection life also lie quaking on the ground. The bright Morning Star who came back from the dead sheds his peaceful light upon all creation. The pillar of fire glows in the midst of this night and heaven is wedded to earth. This is the night when Jesus Christ broke the chains of death and rose triumphant from the grave!*[612] (Move within a homily on Matthew 28:1:10, The Easter Vigil, Year A)

Image: Once again the "alleluias" will sound forth and the proclamation will be heard, "Christ our Passover is sacrificed for us." Joyfully, we see the one loaf broken for all. "Therefore let us keep the feast," we respond. "Alleluia!"[613] This move would be the final in a sermon at the Easter Vigil.

Conclusion

The words and actions at the Communion offer the preacher perhaps the richest and most abundant ways in which to "name grace."[614] Conversely, as seen in the contrapuntal example related to the Miraculous Feeding in John 6:1-15, the sermonic oppositions to the images of grace at the Communion range from skepticism as to Divine providence, all the way to a dogged resistance to the command of Christ to "do this." When we faithfully "do this," and celebrate the Holy Meal, every Lord's Day along with the great festivals of the church year offer a skein of grace-filled images for the preacher in prodigal abundance. It is at this Communion that the newly baptized now join with the assembly in their first Communion, still wet with the waters of their saving and foreheads glistening with the oil of their anointing. It is at this Communion that those newly covenanted in marriage engage in their first sacrament together. It is at this Communion that the grieving come close to their risen Lord and share in the feast with all the saints. It is at this Communion, week in and week out that the faithful are fed with the Bread of Heaven and the Cup of Salvation. These images and actions, traditions and promises are all offered to the preacher in every occasion when the community breaks bread together.

Here is the rich center for the proclamation of the gospel. God's people in Christ are fed at the "double feast," "the two tables of the Word (the proclamation of the Scriptures and the preaching) and of the Eucharist (Holy Communion)."[615] The challenge for the preacher is not "what to preach about," but to discern which particular promises out of this double feast will find their way into any particular proclamation. The preacher's proclamation at the Great Vigil is grounded in this gospel anthem:

> This is the feast of vict'ry for our God,
> for the Lamb who was slain
> has begun his reign. Alleluia.[616]

ENDNOTES

Introduction, [1]-18

[1] See: Edward Foley, *Preaching Basics: A Model and a Method* (Chicago: Liturgy Training Publications, 1998).
[2] Ibid., 13.
[3] Patricia Wilson-Kastner, "Preaching as Liturgical Prayer and Sacramental Act," *Doxology* 8 (1991): 16.
[4] Ibid. Daniel Benedict, Abbot of the Order of Saint Luke, adds, "Isn't it amazing that the sermon that purports to offer Christ, so often neglects to imagine the meal as the opportunity to meet him." Daniel Benedict, email message to the author, (January 18, 2014).
[5] See: Michael Monshau, ed., *Preaching at the Double Feast: Homiletics for Eucharistic Worship* (Collegeville, MN: The Liturgical Press, 2006).
[6] Augustine of Hippo, *Tractate 80 (John 15:1-3)*, 3, accessed March 4, 2013, http://www.newadvent.org/fathers/1701080.htm. "Take away the word, and the water is neither more nor less than water. The word is added to the element, and there results the Sacrament, as if itself also a kind of visible word."
[7] James A. Wallace, "Liturgical Ministry of Preaching," *The New Dictionary of Sacramental Worship*, ed. Peter E. Fink (Collegeville, MN: The Liturgical Press, 1990), 996.
[8] Ibid.
[9] Eugene Fairweather, "The Theological Basis of Celebration," *Celebrating the Word*, ed. James Schmeiser (Toronto, Ontario: The Anglican Book Centre, 1977), 53.
[10] R. H. Fuller, "Sermon," *The New Westminster Dictionary of Liturgy and Worship*, ed. J. D. Davies (Philadelphia: The Westminster Press, 1986), 485.
[11] James F. White, *A Brief History of Christian Worship* (Nashville, TN: Abingdon Press, 1993), 99.
[12] For the full text of the essay, see: Guilbert of Nocent, "A Book about the way a Sermon Ought to be Given," in O. C. Edwards, *A History of Preaching*, vol. 2 (Nashville, TN: Abingdon Press, 2004), 152-63.
[13] Ibid., vol. 1, 175.
[14] See: Alan of Lille, *The Art of Preaching*, trans., Gillian R. Evans (Kalamazoo, MI: Cistercian Publications, 1981).
[15] Ibid., 15-16.

[16] See, for example, Bernard's famous sermons in praise of the Virgin, "On the 'Missus Est'" in *Sermons of St. Bernard on Advent and Christmas* (London, UK: R. & T. Washbourne, 1909), 23-72. The sermons are also available online: accessed December 8, 2013, https://archive.org/stream/sermonsofstberna00bernuoft#page/22/mode/2up.

[17] See: Edwards, *A History of Preaching*, vol. 1, 14-17, for an analysis of the commonalities and distinctions between the two orders.

[18] James J. Murphy, *Rhetoric in the Middle Ages: A History of Rhetoric from Saint Augustine to the Renaissance* (Berkeley, CA: The University of California Press, 1974), 311-344, quoted in Edwards, vol. 1, 218.

[19] This is not to parody the need for studied biblical preaching on the sacraments from time to time. See: Craig A. Satterlee and Lester Ruth, *Creative Preaching on the Sacraments* (Nashville, TN: Discipleship Resources, 2001).

[20] See: Edward Farley, "Praxis and Piety: Hermeneutics Beyond the New Dualism," in *Justice and the Holy: Essays in Honor of Walter Harrelson*, eds. Douglas A. Knight and Peter J. Paris (Atlanta, GA: Scholars Press, 1989), 241-55, for an excellent analysis of individualism and "social-ism" in American religion.

[21] Regarding the 1965 Methodist *Book of Worship*, James F. White observed that, "Penitential piety was back in fashion; Methodists had discovered sin again after fleeing from generations of hellfire preaching." *Protestant Worship: Traditions in Transition* (Louisville, KY: Westminster John Knox, 1989), 167.

[22] One blogger provided a Communion meditation which focused on the grace toward defeated Germany in the Marshall Plan. The blogger then continued, "This is the same way with our Lord." See: accessed December 17, 2013, http://www.becomingcloser.org/supper/the_war_is_not_over.html

[23] "Let All Mortal Flesh Keep Silence," Presbyterian Church (U.S.A.), *Glory to God* (Louisville, KY: Westminster John Knox Press, 2013), 347.

[24] James A. Wallace, *Preaching to the Hungers of the Heart* (Collegeville, MN: The Liturgical Press, 2002), 89.

[25] Kathy Black cautions against the use of such words as "hearers" or listeners" when describing the members of the congregation attending to the sermon. The reference, she states, excludes non-hearing members of the assembly. Moreover, Black adds that "hearing is not necessary for faith" (this in opposition to Fred Craddock and David Buttrick, both of whom ground their

homiletics in the event of hearing the Word). In this exploration of preaching and its Eucharistic context, the terms "hearing" and listening" will be retained now and then, but with Kathy Black's caution in mind that not all worshippers may literally "hear" the homily. See: Kathy Black, *A Healing Homiletic: Preaching and Disability* (Nashville, TN: Abingdon Press, 1996), 100.

[26] Roman Catholic Church, National Conference of Catholic Bishops, *Fulfilled in Your Hearing: The Homily in the Sunday Assembly* (Washington, D. C.: USCC, 1982), 18.

[27] United Methodist Church, *This Holy Mystery: A United Methodist Understanding of Holy Communion*, 2004, 18, accessed December 8, 2013, http://www.umc.org/site/apps/nlnet/content2.aspx?c=lwL4KnN1L tH&b=4951419&ct=11623561. (Hereafter, *THM*.)

[28] The United Methodist statement on the Eucharist affirms that sacraments are "sign-acts, which include words, actions, and physical elements." *THM*, 8. Unfortunately, the document defines the role of preaching with regard to the sacrament largely in a didactic role. [Pastors should] "utilize proclamation, ritual, gestures, postures, and material signs in order to convey their full meaning." *THM*, 13.

[29] See, for example: William Harmless, "Mystagogy: Baking Bread, Fermenting Wine," *Augustine and the Catechumenate* (Collegeville, MN: The Liturgical Press, 1995), 300-345, and Craig Alan Satterlee, *Ambrose of Milan's Method of Mystagogical Preaching* (Collegeville, MN: The Liturgical Press, 2002).

[30] The Memorialist position, as opposed to the sacramental, is best articulated by the reformer Ulrich Zwingli (1484-1531). Zwingli "had little concern for the physical elements," but viewed the Supper as the occasion in which Christ transforms the congregation "by uniting it in a recollection of Christ." Thus, the elements are construed as symbols provided by Christ in order that the congregation may enter into this spiritual and communal remembrance. White, *A Brief History*, 124.

[31] Michael Joncas has quite a similar "homiletical mystagogy," which I first learned of from an address he presented at, "We Preach Christ Crucified: A Conference on Catholic Preaching," which was given at The University of Notre Dame in June, 2012. This conference happened only after the Introduction for this book was written. Joncas' lecture was later printed in a collection edited by Michael Connors. In his method, which could be considered a companion to my own, Joncas advocates a three step approach:
   1. Determine from official church teaching the intended function of a particular presidential text.

2. Study the structure and content of the liturgical text, exploring its original formulation and history of transmission if necessary.
3. Decide how the knowledge gleaned from this study will be communicated as catechetical (i.e., aimed at catechumens/elect) or mystagogical (i.e., the baptized) preaching, or both, in the context of a particular liturgy.

Jan Michael Joncas, "Preaching from and for the Liturgy," *We Preach Christ Crucified*, ed. Michael Connors (Collegeville, MN: The Liturgical Press, 2014), 47.

1 The Offertory, 19-34

[32] International Commission on English in the Liturgy (ICEL), "Liturgy of the Eucharist," *Basic Texts for the Roman Catholic Eucharist: The Order of the Mass*, compiled by Felix Just, new English translation of the *Roman Missal*, 3rd ed., 2010, accessed June 21, 2012, http://catholic-resources.org/ChurchDocs/Mass-RM3.htm.

[33] N.T. Wright, *After You Believe: Why Christian Character Matters* (New York: HarperCollins Publishers, 2010), 34. Wright adds that, "The 'cardinals' in the Roman Catholic Church are the 'hinge men,' the ones on whose ministry the rest 'hinges.'"

[34] Gregory Dix, *The Shape of the Liturgy*, new ed. (New York: Bloomsbury Academic, 2005). This magisterial work was first published in London in 1945.

Paul Bradshaw and Max Johnson speak for recent New Testament and early church scholarship when they argue that "it simply is not the case that all early Eucharistic meals followed either a sevenfold or a fourfold shape. . . ." The present use of the Dix four-fold shape of the liturgy derives from its seminal influence on the drafters of the anaphoras of so many communions following the Second Vatican Council. Paul F. Bradshaw and Maxwell E. Johnson, *The Eucharistic Liturgies: Their Evolution and Interpretation* (Collegeville, MN: The Liturgical Press, 2012), 20.

[35] Hippolytus, "The Apostolic Tradition of Hippolytus of Rome," in *Early Sources of the Liturgy*, ed. Lucien Deiss (Collegeville, MN: The Liturgical Press, 1975), 57.

Traditionally considered, among liturgical scholars, as a third-century Western document, Paul Bradshaw and Maxwell Johnson reflect a more recent consensus that, while the Apostolic Tradition "did not attain this form until the fourth century, it is also recognized that some of the language is more consistent with a second-century date and that therefore its core is probably much earlier than its final redaction." Bradshaw and Johnson, *The Eucharistic* Liturgies, 40. This emerging consensus also views the origin of this liturgical core to be in the West Syria area rather than Rome.

[36] Hippolytus, "The Apostolic Tradition," n. 1, 57.

[37] Michael McGuckian, *The Holy Sacrifice of the Mass: A Search for an Acceptable Notion of Sacrifice* (Chicago: Liturgy Training Publications, 2005), 67.

[38] Ibid.

[39] Bard Thompson, ed., *Liturgies of the Western Church* (Cleveland, OH: The World Publishing Company, 1961), 64-68. See: Joseph A. Jungmann, "The Offertory," in *The Mass of the Roman Rite: Its Origin and Development,* vol. 2 (Westminster, MD: Christian Classics, 1986), 1-100.

[40] Adolf Adam, *Eucharistic Celebration: The Source and Summit of Faith* (Collegeville, MN: The Liturgical Press, 1994), 52.

[41] Ibid.

[42] Louis Bouyer, *Eucharist: Theology and Spirituality of the Eucharistic Prayer*, trans., Charles Underhill Quinn (Notre Dame, IN: University of Notre Dame Press, 1968), 116.

[43] Adam, *Eucharistic Celebration,* 58.

[44] Martin Luther, *Martin Luther's Basic Theological Writings,* 2nd ed., ed. William R. Russell (Minneapolis, MN: Fortress Press, 2005), 307.

[45] Adam refers to this text as one "subject to a similar misinterpretation," 53. The revision of this text in the new third version of the Missal may also be subject to a misinterpretation. It provides a modest, stylistic revision of the prayer. See: ICEL (note 32 above).

[46] Episcopal Church, "Holy Eucharist II," *The Book of Common Prayer* (New York: The Church Hymnal Corporation, 1979), 361.

[47] United Methodist Church, "A Service of Word and Table I," *The United Methodist Book of Worship* (Nashville, TN: The United Methodist Publishing House, 1989), 36.

[48] Inter-Lutheran Commission on Worship, *Lutheran Book of Worship* (Minneapolis: Augsburg Publishing House, 1978), 66.

[49] Evangelical Lutheran Church in America, *Evangelical Lutheran Worship* (Minncapolis, MN: Augsburg Fortress, 2006), 128.

[50] William S. Skylstad and Timothy Whitaker, co-chairs, "Heaven and Earth are Full of Your Glory: A United Methodist and Roman Catholic Statement on the Eucharist and Ecology," April 20,

2012, para. 8, accessed April 28, 2013, http://www.usccb.org/beliefs-and-teachings/ecumenical-and-interreligious/ecumenical/methodist/upload/Heaven-and-Earth-are-Full-of-Your-Glory-Methodist-Catholic-Dialogue-Agreed-Statement-Round-Seven.pdf.

[51] Ruth Duck, "Give Thanks to the Source," *The Upper Room Worshipbook*, ed. Elise Eslinger (Nashville, TN: Upper Room Books, 2006), 126.

[52] Skylstad and Whitaker, para. 25.

[53] Ibid.

[54] Ibid., para 26.

[55] See: Omer Westerdorf, "You Satisfy the Hungry Heart," *The United Methodist Hymnal* (Nashville, TN: The United Methodist Publishing House, 1989), 629.

[56] See: Stephen Hawking and Larry Mlodinow, *The Grand Design* (New York: Bantam Books, 2010).

[57] See: Leigh Eric Schmidt, "Conservation, Ecology, and Worship in American Protestantism: From Arbor Day to the Environmental Sabbath," *Doxology* 9 (1992): 35-55.

[58] Guerric DeBona, *Fulfilled in Our Hearing: History and Method of Christian Preaching* (New York: Paulist Press, 2005), 42. Also: see my *A New Hearing: Living Options in Homiletic Method* (Nashville, TN: Abingdon Press, 1987), 95-132. The seminal statement of Fred Craddock's inductive method remains *As One Without Authority* (Nashville, TN: Abingdon Press, 1979). The book was originally published in 1971.

[59] See: David Buttrick, *Homiletic: Moves and Structures* (Philadelphia: Fortress Press, 1987).

[60] See: Lucy Lind Hogan and Robert Reid, *Connecting with the Congregation: Rhetoric and the Art of Preaching* (Nashville, TN: Abingdon Press, 1999).

[61] See: Lucy Atkinson Rose, *Sharing the Word: Preaching in the Roundtable Church* (Louisville, KY: Westminster John Knox Press, 1997).

[62] McGuckian, *The Holy Sacrifice of the Mass*, 64.

[63] Wes Howard Brook, *Becoming Children of God: John's Gospel and Radical Discipleship* (Maryknoll, NY: Orbis Books, 1994), 144.

[64] Ibid.

[65] One contemporary song expressing this reversal is from the Hispanic church: "*Cuando El Pobre*" ("When the Poor Ones") United Methodist Church, *The United Methodist Hymnal* (Nashville, TN: United Methodist Publishing House, 1989), 434.

2 The Sursum Corda, 35-44

[66] English Language Liturgical Consultation, *Praying Together* (Washington, D.C.: English Language Liturgical Consultation, 1988), 25. Electronic edition available at: accessed June 23, 2013, http://www.englishtexts.org/praying.pdf.

[67] The Methodist Church, *The Methodist Hymnal* (Nashville, TN: The Methodist Publishing House, 1939), 530.

[68] See: Thompson, *Liturgies,* 13-24.

[69] Hippolytus, *Hippolytus: A Text for Students*, trans. Geoffrey J. Cuming (Bramcote, UK: Grove Books, 1976), 10, quoted in James F. White, *Documents of Christian Worship: Descriptive and Interpretive Sources* (Louisville, KY: Westminster John Knox Press, 1992), 186.

[70] Ibid., 57.

[71] World Council of Churches, *Baptism, Eucharist and Ministry,* Faith and Order Paper 111, 19, accessed May 8, 2012, file:///C:/Users/RS%20Files/Documents/Baptism,%20Eucharist,%20and%20Ministry-WCC/BEM-text%20(1).pdf.

[72] At a United Methodist annual conference the bishop approached the Table to offer the Eucharistic Prayer, commenting that in order to save time, "we will skip over the people's parts." In so doing, this leader of the flock oddly deleted the community's authorization for him to exercise Eucharistic presidency. He was "on his own." More ironically, the service was the "Memorial Service of Holy Communion for the Honored Dead." By deleting the Sanctus, this bishop also attempted to shut out their eternal song as well!

[73] Melva Wilson Costen, *African American Christian Worship,* updated ed. (Nashville, TN: Abingdon Press, 2007), 92.

[74] Evans E. Crawford, *The Hum: Call and Response in African American Preaching* (Nashville, TN: Abingdon Press, 1995), 21.

[75] Ibid., 20.

[76] Ibid., 56.

[77] Craddock, *As One without Authority,* 54.

[78] Ibid., 56.

[79] David S. Cunningham, *These Three are One: The Practice of Trinitarian Theology* (Oxford, UK: Blackwell, 1998), 101, quoted in Mike Graves, ed., "God of Grace and Glory," *What's the Matter with Preaching Today?* (Louisville, KY: Westminster John Knox Press, 2004), 113.

[80] Some time ago, I visited a local expression of one rapidly growing mega-church/mini-denomination. After an opening and extensive session of being entertained by a high-quality band and praise team, the preacher then lectured the listeners for forty-five minutes on an extensive series of thematic points held dear by this movement and their leader. These were projected as bullet points on the screen and we were expected to copy them down in a space made available (and even numbered) in our handouts. We had been entertained as an audience and now transformed into javelin catchers!

[81] DeBona, *Fulfilled in Our Hearing*, 88.

3 The Preface, 43-74

[82] The Methodist Church Commission on Worship, *The Book of Worship for Church and Home: With Orders of Worship, Services for the Administration of the Sacraments and Other Aids to Worship According to the Usage of the Methodist Church* (Nashville, TN: The Methodist Publishing House, 1965), 19.

[83] See: Robert W. Hovda, *Strong, Loving, and Wise: Presiding in Liturgy* (Collegeville, MN: The Liturgical Press, 1976).

[84] See: Bouyer, *Eucharist,* 78-90.

[85] W. Jardine Grisbrooke, "Preface," *A Dictionary of Liturgy and Worship*, ed. J. G. Davies (New York: The Macmillan Company, 1972), 322.

[86] The Methodist Church Commission on Worship, *The Book of Worship*, 19. This last in the series of Communion Ritual services in the tradition of the Anglican Book of Common Prayer for American Methodists did contain four "Proper Prefaces for Certain Days" (Ibid., 23). In my own experience in both rural and urban Methodist churches prior to the reforms of the liturgy, these Proper Prefaces were rarely employed in place of the two-sentence Preface in the text of the Ritual.

[87] Thompson, *Liturgies*, 48.

[88] Catholic Doors Ministry, "Preface IV of Lent," accessed July 22, 2012, http://www.catholicdoors.com/prayers/english5/p03393.htm.

[89] Church of England, Archbishop's Council, "Preface for Trinity Sunday 1," *Common Worship: Services and Prayers for the Church of England* (London, UK: Church House Publishing, 2000), 509.

[90] "The United Methodist statement on Holy Communion witnesses to the 'in concert' roles of presiding minister and congregation by affirming that 'an elder or authorized pastor leads the congregation in praying the Great Thanksgiving, in which the whole assembly takes an active role.'" United Methodist Church, *THM*, 26.

[91] Stephen Reynolds, compiler, "The Birth of Saint John the Baptist," *For All the Saints: Prayers and Readings for Saints Days,* rev. ed. (Toronto, Ontario: ABC Publishing, 2007), 205.

[92] United Methodist Church, "The Great Thanksgiving for All Saints and Memorial Occasions," *Book of Worship*, 74-75.

[93] Episcopal Church, Standing Liturgical Commission, *Enriching our Worship 1: Supplemental Liturgical Materials* (New York: The Church Pension Fund, 1998), 50-71.

[94] Inter-Lutheran Commission on Worship, *Lutheran Book of Worship*, 68 and 88.

[95] Evangelical Lutheran Church in America, *Evangelical Lutheran Worship*, 132-33.

[96] United Methodist Church, "Service of Word and Table I," *Book of Worship,* 36.

[97] Ibid.

[98] A United Methodist "sacramentary," *At the Lord's Table*, was published during the trial use season for these "Supplemental Worship Resources." [Section on Worship of the Board of Discipleship of the United Methodist Church], *At the Lord's Table: A Communion Service Book for Use by the Minister*, vol. 9, Supplemental Worship Resources (Nashville: Abingdon, 1981). This "sacramentary" was republished in 1987 as: Hoyt L. Hickman, *Holy Communion, Supplemental Worship Resource 16* (Nashville, TN: Abingdon Press, 1987).Also see: Timothy Crouch and the Order of Saint Luke, *Offices and Services (Proposed): After the Usage of the Order of Saint Luke* (Hackettstown, NJ: Order of Saint Luke, 1984), 12-24.

[99] "The Great Thanksgiving IV," a Catholic Australian liturgical center notes, "is the most ecumenical of our eucharistic prayers in the sense that it has strong echoes of Eastern (especially Greek) forms." Liturgy Brisbane, "Eucharistic Prayers II, III and IV," *Liturgy Lines*, accessed February 7, 2013, http://liturgybrisbane.net.au/liturgylines/eucharistic-prayers-ii-iii-and-iv/.

[100] A. Fortescue, "Preface," *The Roman Catholic Encyclopedia* (New York: Robert Appleton Company, 1911), accessed June 14, 2012, http://www.newadvent.org/cathen/12384a.htm.

[101] Roman Catholic Church, National Conference of Catholic Bishops, Bishop's Committee on Priestly Life and Ministry, *Fulfilled in Your Hearing* (Washington, D.C.: Office of Pub. Services, United States Catholic Conference, [1982]), 18.

[102] Ibid., 17.

[103] William H. Willimon, *Peculiar Speech: Preaching to the Baptized* (Grand Rapids, MI: Wm. B. Eerdmans Publishing Company, 1992), 5.

[104] James A. Wallace, *Preaching to the Hungers of the Heart: The Homily on the Feasts and Within the Rites* (Collegeville, MN: The Liturgical Press, 2002), 92.

[105] See: Buttrick, *Homiletic,* 187-221.

[106] Ibid., 212.

[107] Ibid., 217.

[108] Cleophus J. LaRue, *The Heart of Black Preaching* (Louisville, KY: Westminster John Knox Press, 2000), 71.

[109] Ibid., 110.

[110] Charles L. Rice, *The Embodied Word: Preaching as Art and Liturgy* (Minneapolis, MN: Fortress Press, 1991), 31.

[111] See my: "'Fwd., Fwd., Fwd.': Mega-Story in the Untaught Homiletic," *Journal of Theology* (Summer 2002), 3-22.

[112] See: Buttrick, *Homiletic,* 137-170. Also see my: *The Web of Preaching: New Options in Homiletical Method* (Nashville, TN: Abingdon Press, 2002), 246-85.

[113] Only the lace-collecting preacher is an invention in my experience. For myself, I have a deep passion for aviation and am a Certified Flight Instructor in gliders. Since the realm of soaring obviously has applications within every sermon I am shaping, I will not mention gliders or flying in any of them!

[114] Several commentators have recently noted that post-millennial generational cohorts tend to depict themselves in mostly non-narrative ways. Thomas Long analyzes the claims of Galen Strawson that two quite distinct ways to be human are now evident: those persons who are "Diachronic," finding a narrative experience of life as both normal and normative and the "Episodic" ones for whom no narrative self-interpretation is needed or even possible. "As an Episodic," Long reflects, "Strawson lives in a series of present tense moments. . . . (He) has no narrative, wants no narrative, and needs no narrative." Thomas G. Long, *Preaching from Memory to Hope* (Louisville, KY: Westminster John Knox Press, 2009), 12. See: Galen Strawson, "Against Narrativity," *Ratio* (new series) 18, no. 4 (December 2004): 428-52.

[115] Church of England, *The Liturgies of 1549 and 1662*, ed. Orby Shipley (London, UK: Joseph Masters, 1866), 39.

[116] Eugene L. Lowry, *Doing Time in the Pulpit: The Relationship between Narrative and Preaching* (Nashville, TN: Abingdon Press, 1985), 23.

[117] Ibid.

[118] Buttrick, Homiletic, 291.

[119] The mode of immediacy, Buttrick insists, evokes a field of meaning in the congregations' hearing that involves a new understanding shaping to some particular faith consciousness. Among the vast suite of biblical genres, narratives and especially the parables lend themselves to being preached in the mode of immediacy. The goal is not to set the story at some distance and talk about it (emphatically not to draw moral truths from it), but to invite the congregation to hear the story and to form "immediate analogies of experience by which we understand and respond to the story as it moves along." Buttrick, *Homiletic*, 365.

[120] Ibid., 297.

[121] See: Higher Praise, "The Parables of Jesus: The Good Samaritan (Lk 10:25-37)," Higher Praise.com, accessed September 3, 2012, http://www.higherpraise.com/outlines/pa/pa_20.htm.

[122] See: Bernard Brandon Scott, *Hear Then the Parable: A Commentary on the Parables of Jesus* (Minneapolis, MN: Augsburg Fortress, 1989).

[123] In the Latin Mass prior to the Second Vatican Council, a rubric directs: "The priest now makes the sign of the cross, and, standing at the Epistle Corner, begins the Introit, which will be found in the Mass proper to the day." Thompson, *Liturgies,* 59.

[124] Roman Catholic Church, *Fulfilled in Your Hearing*, emphasizes that "The homily is not so much *on* the Scriptures as *from* and *through* them," 20.

[125] Marion Hatchett, *Sanctifying Life, Time, and Space: An Introduction to Liturgical Theology* (New York: The Seabury Press, 1976), 22.

[126] Ibid., 45.

[127] See: Andrew McGowan, *Augustine's Lectionary*, accessed November 23, 2015, https://augustine.villanova.edu/devotion-and-dissent/topics/books-and-reading/augustines-lectionary-revisited/.

[128] Peter G. Cobb, "The Liturgy of the Word in the Early Church," in *The Study of Liturgy*, eds. Cheslyn Jones, Geoffrey Wainwright, Edward Yarnold (Oxford, UK: Oxford University Press, 1979), 185.

[129] D.M. Hope, "Liturgical Books," in *The Study of Liturgy*, 66.

[130] Hatchett, *Sanctifying Life, Time, and Space*, 72-73.

[131] See: Luther D. Reed, *The Lutheran Liturgy* (Philadelphia: Muhlenberg Press, 1947), 450-575.

[132] Roman Catholic Church, "Constitution on the Sacred Liturgy," *The Documents of Vatican II*, ed. Walter M. Abbott (New York: The American Press, 1966), 155.

[133] A detailed history of the development of the reforms in calendar and lectionary within the North American churches is available in Hoyt L. Hickman, Don E. Saliers, Laurence Hull Stuckey, and James F. White, *The New Handbook of the Christian Year* (Nashville, TN: Abingdon Press, 1992), 28-33. Also see: The Consultation on Common Texts, "The Revised Common Lectionary," accessed August 4, 2014, http://commontexts.org/rcl/index.html.

[134] Roman Catholic Church, *Fulfilled in Your Hearing*, 20.

[135] Stanley Hauerwas, *Sanctify Them in the Truth: Holiness Exemplified* (Nashville: Abingdon Press, 1998), 237.

4 The Sanctus, 75-115

[136] English Language Liturgical Consultation, *Praying Together*, 27.

[137] Elise Eslinger. For the resulting musical setting see: United Methodist Church, "Musical Setting A," *The United Methodist Hymnal*, 17-18.

[138] Bryan D. Spinks, *The Sanctus in the Eucharistic Prayer* (Cambridge, UK: Cambridge University Press, 1991), 1.

[139] Bouyer, *Eucharist*, 120.

[140] Ibid., 127-28. Bouyer also argues for an early origin of the East Syrian tradition of Addai and Mari in which the Sanctus may also be found. (See: Ibid., 146-158.)

[141] Thompson, *Liturgies*, 17. Thompson reflects a pre-conciliar assumption when he equates the post-Sanctus with the Eucharistic Prayer.

[142] Dix, *The Shape of the Liturgy*, 219.

[143] Maxwell E. Johnson, "Recent Research on the Anaphoral Sanctus: An Update and Hypothesis," *Issues in Eucharistic Praying in East and West*, ed. Maxwell E. Johnson (Collegeville, MN: The Liturgical Press, 2010), 161.

[144] For example, see: Bouyer, *Eucharist*, 115-119 for the analysis of these connections between the berakah and early Christian anaphoras. Gregory Dix also devotes particular attention to the dynamics of the Last Supper and possible relationships to the berakah in *The Shape of the Liturgy*, 52ff. Bryan D. Spinks

provides an extensive summary and assessment of the alternative theories regarding a possible evolution of the Jewish berakah into the early Christian anaphora. See his: *The Sanctus in the Eucharistic Prayer*, 104-121.

[145] Willy Rordorf, ed., *The Eucharist of the Early Christians*, trans. Matthew J. O'Connell (New York: Pueblo Publishing Company, 1978), 7.
Historians of the liturgy have long argued whether the Didache represents the protocols related to a late first-century Jewish-Christian meal or a distinctive early Christian Eucharist. More recently, other scholars have argued that such a bifurcation between meal and Eucharist is premature within the context of the Didache. Thus, Paul Bradshaw and Maxwell Johnson state: "There are no grounds for distinguishing a sacramental Eucharist from other sorts of Christian meals in the earliest period: *agape* and Eucharist are synonyms at this time, and it was only much later that meal and Eucharist became separated from one another." Bradshaw and Johnson, *The Eucharistic Liturgies*, 24.

[146] Bouyer, *Eucharist*, 126.

[147] Bryan D. Spinks notes that each of these writers is employing the Sanctus by way of commenting on issues quite other than Christian liturgy in general or the Eucharist in particular. So, the author of *The Passion of Perpetual and Felicity* envisions the Hymn being sung as Christian martyrs ascend into heaven. Tertullian, in *On the Prayer*, employs the Hymn by way of meditating on the mystery of the God revealed in the Lord's Prayer. See: Bryan D. Spinks, *The Sanctus in the Eucharistic Prayer* (Cambridge, UK: Cambridge University Press, 1991), 51-52.

[148] Origen, First Principles, 4:3.14 , *Origen on First Principles*, ed. G. W. Butterworth (Gloucester, MA: Peter Smith, 1973), 311.

[149] The recent consensus regarding these third century writers' references to the Hymn of Isaiah 6 is that no anaphoral context is either stated or implied. See: Spinks, *The Sanctus in the Eucharistic Prayer*, 104-14.

[150] Clement of Rome, "The First Epistle to the Corinthians," Chap. 34, *The Early Christian Writings*, ed. and trans. Henry Bettenson (London, UK: Oxford University Press, 1956), 47.

[151] Ibid.

[152] W. C. Van Unnik, "1 Clement 34 and the Sanctus," *Vigiliae Christianae* 5 (1951), 245, quoted in Spinks, *The Sanctus*, 49.

[153] Dix, *The Shape of the Liturgy*, 165.

[154] The "climax theory" is so named because of E.C. Ratcliff's important paper in 1950 which argues that, in the earliest post-

New Testament Eucharistic prayers the expressions of thanksgiving for creation and redemption concluded with thanksgiving for the privilege of earthly worshipers to join with the heavenly host in the Sanctus. Thus the anaphoral Sanctus "climaxed" these early Eucharistic prayers. See: Johnson, "Recent Research," *Issues in Eucharistic Praying*, 162.

[155] Ibid.

[156] Ibid., 187.

[157] Ibid., 188. The desperate state of the Christian churches in Iraq and elsewhere in the Middle East resulting from intensified persecution led in 2001 to an amazing action by the Roman Catholic Church. The validity of the Assyrian form of the Eucharist of Addai and Mari was affirmed, establishing open communion between Chaldean Catholics and the Assyrian Church of the East. See: Nicholas V. Russo, "The Validity of the Anaphora of Addai and Mari: Critique of the Critiques," *Issues in Eucharistic Praying*, 21-62.

[158] Spinks, *The Sanctus in the Eucharistic Prayer*, 59.

[159] William Harmless, *Augustine and the Catechumenate* (Collegeville, MN: The Liturgical Press, 1995), 322.

[160] Ibid., 323.

[161] The quality of the mentoring Ambrose provided Augustine was far from the norm. On those well-known occasions when Augustine would approach the bishop for counsel, the sight of Ambrose reading while "his voice and tongue were silent" led him to quietly turn and move away. In the *Confessions* (6.3), Augustine notes—perhaps with frustration—that Ambrose entertained only questions that allowed responses marked by brevity. Most of the mentoring Augustine received was from afar, as part of the crowd who attended to the bishop's preaching. See: Augustine, *Confessions*, 6.3, trans. John K. Ryan, *The Confessions of St. Augustine* (New York: Doubleday, 1960), 136. Also see: Carl G. Vaught, *The Journey toward God in Augustine's Confessions: Books I-VI, Books 1-6* (Albany, NY: State University of New York Press, 2003), 140-46.

[162] Craig Alan Satterlee, *Ambrose of Milan's Method of Mystagogical Preaching* (Collegeville, MN: The Liturgical Press, 2002), 181.

[163] Cyril of Jerusalem, "Mystagogical Catechesis, 5:5," *Cyril of Jersualem*, ed. Edward Yarnold (London, UK: Routledge, 2000), 183.

[164] Ibid., "Mystagogical Catechesis," 5:7.

[165] Reed, *The Lutheran Liturgy*, 331.

[166] Spinks, *The Sanctus in the Eucharistic Prayer*, 120.

[167] Egeria, *Egeria's Travels to the Holy Land*, trans. John Wilkinson (Jerusalem: Ariel Publishing House, 1981), 133.

[168] This theory is propounded primarily by Gabriele Winkler in her *Das Sanctus: Über den Ursprung und die Anfänge des Sanctus und sien Fortwirken* (Rome: Orientalia Christiana Analecta, 2002), as translated in part, and interpreted in Johnson, "Recent Research," *Issues in Eucharistic Praying*, 169-181.

[169] Thompson, *Liturgies*, 70. For an analysis of the variations between the Vulgate Bible's texts of the hymns and the liturgical texts of the Latin Mass, see: Joseph A. Jungmann, *The Mass of the Roman Rite: Its Origins and Development*, vol. 2, (1951; repr., Westminster, MD: Christian Classics, Inc., 1986), 134-138.

[170] Thompson, *Liturgies*, 100.

[171] Ibid., 119.

[172] Thompson, *Liturgies*, 134. Luther D. Reed comments that this vernacular expression of the Sanctus "was the least happy of Luther's liturgical and hymnological endeavors. . . . [I]t gives only the story of Isaiah 6:1 and does not include the praise of the congregation." Reed, *The Lutheran Liturgy*, 332. Begging to differ, Bryan Spinks argues that "there seems to have been a clear logic behind Luther's suggestions." *The Sanctus in the Eucharistic Prayer*, 150. (See: 150-151 for Spinks' full argument.)

[173] Thompson, *Liturgies*, 185.

[174] Donald K. Kim, ed., *Calvin's Institutes*, abridged ed. (Louisville, KY: Westminster John Knox Press, 2001), 160.

[175] See: Martin Bucer, "Censura," in E.C. Whitaker, trans. and ed., *Martin Bucer and the Book of Common Prayer*, Alcuin Club Collections, no. 55 (Essex, UK: The Alcuin Club, 1974), 10-173.

[176] One of the factors in retaining the stand-alone Sanctus within Methodist and United Methodist churches until the adoption of a new Ritual in 1988 was its Merebecke musical setting. The sung Sanctus in numerous Methodist churches ended with a concluding "Amen." See: John Merebecke, "Holy, Holy, Holy," The Methodist Church, *The Methodist Hymnal* (Nashville, TN: The Methodist Publishing House, 1964), "The Ritual," 14-15.

[177] The various Protestant traditions engaged in the reforms of the Sunday service along with the Episcopal and Roman Catholic churches all drew on a common text of the Sanctus/Benedictus provided jointly by the Consultation on Common Texts (CCT) and the International Commission on English in the Liturgy (ICEL). This achievement provided North American Christians sharing the texts with a remarkably ecumenical foundation for their Eucharistic practice. Moreover, the texts in common offered

pastoral musicians the opportunity to write settings that could be shared across these traditions. Only with the promulgation of the Missal of 2011 did the Roman Catholic Church diverge from this ecumenical consensus.

[178] Johnson, "Recent Research," *Issues in Eucharistic Praying*, 183..

[179] United Methodist Church, *THM*, 20.

[180] The United Methodist statement on Holy Communion strongly cautions that "(b)oth 'self-service' Communion, where people help themselves, and 'drop-in' Communion, where the elements are available over a period of time, are contrary to the communal nature of the sacrament, which is the celebration of the gathered community of faith." United Methodist Church, THM, 23.

[181] Reed, *The Lutheran Liturgy*, 331.

[182] Pius Parsch, *The Liturgy of the Mass*, trans. H. E. Winstone, 3rd ed. (St. Louis, MO: Herder, 1957), 212. A more intriguing insight emerges when the Gloria in Excelsis is aligned with the Benedictus. In Luke's Gospel, the two hymns serve as bookends to the narrative. In the earlier (2:14) the angelic hosts sing peace to earth while in the latter, the Triumphal Entry in Luke, the disciples and women followers of Jesus antiphonally complete their Benedictus by adding "Peace in heaven, and glory in the highest heaven" (19:38b).

[183] Reed, *The Lutheran Liturgy*, 330.

[184] See: Karl Barth, *The Epistle to the Romans*, trans. Edwyn C. Hoskyns (Oxford, UK: Oxford University Press, 1968).

[185] See: John Dominic Crossan, *Jesus: A Revolutionary Biography* (New York: HarperCollins Publishers, 1994).

[186] "Exultet," *The New Handbook of the Christian Year*, 195.

[187] "Let All Mortal Flesh Keep Silent," *United Methodist Hymnal* (Nashville: United Methodist Publishing House, 1989), 626.

[188] Leonora Tubbs Tisdale, *Preaching as Local Theology and Folk Art* (Minneapolis, MN: Fortress Press, 1997), 18.

[189] See: "All Saints Icon | The Great Cloud of Witnesses," *A Reader's Guide to Orthodox Icons*, accessed March 23, 2014, http://iconreader.wordpress.com/2013/07/01/all-saints-icon-the-great-cloud-of-witnesses. The great cloud of witnesses, as the *Reader's Guide* commentary explains, includes the biblical saints from both Testaments, more recent saints and martyrs, angels and archangels, along with Adam and Eve, lying prostrate toward the lower side of the icon. At the center of the circle of saints is Christ, seated in glory. Even the non-canonized pious and holy ones are part of this cloud of witnesses.

[190] See: Brad R. Braxton, *Preaching Paul* (Nashville, TN: Abingdon Press, 2004).
[191] See: Ross Gregory Douthat, *Bad Religion: How We Became a Nation of Heretics* (New York: Free Press, 2012).
[192] *Ibid.,* 191.
[193] Thomas G. Long, *Preaching from Memory to Hope*, 120.
[194] Excerpted from the "Te Deum Laudemus," Episcopal Church, *The Book of Common Prayer*, 1979), 95.
[195] Douthat, *Bad Religion*, 219.
[196] Ibid., 221. Alyce McKenzie summarizes this New Age "virtue for living" as a "confidence that God's will is indistinguishable from our own good intentions." See: Alyce M. McKenzie, *Preaching Biblical Wisdom in a Self-Help Society* (Nashville, TN: Abingdon Press, 2002), 88.
[197] Thus, for example, Eckhart Tolle insists that "spiritual masters of all traditions have pointed to the Now as the key to the spiritual dimension." Tolle adds that "The end is an idea, a point in the mind-projected future. . . . Eckhart Tolle, *The Power of Now: A Guide to Spiritual Enlightenment* (Novato, CA: New World Library, 1999), 59. By denying that Day when God will make all things right, not only is eschatology rendered void, but the persistence of evil in the "Now" will be viewed as presenting occasions for acceptance and surrender, leading to "an inner peace and serenity. . . ." Ibid., 220.
[198] Douthat, *Bad Religion*, 216.
[199] Tolle, *The Power of Now*, 9.
[200] Douthat, *Bad Religion*, 216.
[201] Deepak Chopra, *The Ultimate Happiness Prescription: 7 Keys to Joy and Enlightenment* (New York: Harmony Books, 2009), 119.
[202] Douthat, *Bad Religion*, 216.
[203] Chopra concludes at this point that "righteousness never solved anything. It just fuels more anger; it provokes deeper antagonism." Chopra. *The Ultimate Happiness*, 79.
[204] Douthat, *Bad Religion*, 216.
[205] Chopra, *The Ultimate Happiness*, 89.
[206] Ibid, 122-123.
[207] McKenzie, *Preaching Biblical Wisdom,* 86.
[208] See: Christine Smith, *Preaching as Weeping, Confession, and Resistance: Radical Responses to Radical Evil* (Louisville, KY: Westminster John Knox Press, 1992).
[209] Tolle, *The Power of Now*, 18.
[210] Ibid.

[211] M. Basil Pennington, *Centering Prayer: Renewing an Ancient Christian Prayer Form* (Garden City, NY: Doubleday & Company, Inc., 1980), 14.
[212] Ibid.
[213] Richard Rohr and Andreas Ebert, *Discovering the Enneangram*, trans., Peter Heinegg (New York: Crossroad Publishing Company, 1990), xiv.
[214] Thomas E. Clarke, "Finding Grace at the Center," *Finding Grace at the Center*, eds. Thomas Keating, M. Basil Pennington, and Thomas E. Clarke (Still River, MA: St. Bede Publications, 1998), 57.
[215] Thomas Keating, *The Mystery of Christ: The Liturgy as Spiritual Experience* (New York: Continuum Publishing Company, 1996), 1.
[216] Pennington, *Centering Prayer*, 96-97.
[217] Douthat notes that it is "startling how little moral exhortation there is within the pages of the God Within literature." *Bad Religion*, 224.
[218] Thomas G. Long, *Preaching from Memory to Hope*, 72.
[219] Tolle, *The Power of Now*, 15.
[220] Long, *Preaching from Memory to Hope*, 73.
[221] Ibid., 76.
[222] Tolle, *The Power of Now*, 62.
[223] Don E. Saliers, "Then Sings My Soul . . . In the Word and at the Table," *Doxology* 6 (1989): 14-15.

5 The Post-Sanctus Narrative, 116-140

[224] Presbyterian Church (U.S.A.), *Book of Common Worship* (Louisville, KY: Westminster/John Knox Press, 1993), 127.
[225] Dennis C. Smolarski, *Eucharistia: A Study of the Eucharistic Prayer* (New York: Paulist Press, 1982), 28.
[226] Ibid., 16.
[227] Walter D. Ray, "Rome and Alexandria: Two Cities, One Anaphoral Tradition," *Issues in Eucharistic Praying in East and West,* ed. Maxwell E. Johnson (Collegeville, MN: The Liturgical Press, 2010), 104.
[228] See: "The Liturgy of St. Basil," Bouyer, *Eucharist*, 292-96.

[229] United Methodist Church, "A Service of Word and Table," *The United Methodist Hymnal* (Nashville, TN: United Methodist Publishing House, 1989), 10.

[230] Episcopal Church, "Holy Eucharist II," *The Book of Common Prayer*, 1979, 362.

[231] The new Presbyterian hymnal, *Glory to God* was published in September of 2013. See: Presbyterian Church (U.S.A.), *Glory to God* (Louisville, KY: Westminster John Knox Press, 2013). Electronic edition available at: accessed May 5, 2014, http://www.amazon.com/Glory-God-The-Presbyterian-Hymnal-ebook/dp/B00GLSJYF2.

[232] Presbyterian Church (U.S.A), "The Service for the Lord's Day," *Glory to God*, 10.

[233] ICEL, "Eucharistic Prayer IV," *Liturgy of the Eucharist*, 2011.

[234] "Constitution on the Sacred Liturgy," *Documents of Vatican II*, 148.

[235] See: Avery Dulles, "The Church: Community of Disciples," *Models of the Church*, expanded ed. (New York: Doubleday, 2002), 195-217.

[236] See: Buttrick, *Homiletic*.

[237] Adolf Jülicher, *Die Gleichnisreden Jesu* (Freiburg: J. C. B. Mohr, 1899).

[238] See my: *The Web of Preaching*, 77-79. Bernard Brandon Scott adds that "A methodology that seizes on the one point of likeness as a parable's meaning destroys the parable." *Hear Then the Parable*, 45.

[239] The Second Sunday in Lent in the Roman Catholic Lectionary and the Last Sunday after the Epiphany in the Revised Common Lectionary. See my: "Transfiguration: A Multiple Feast," *New Proclamation Year A, 2007-2008 Advent through Holy Week* (Minneapolis, MN: Fortress Press, 2007), 154-156.

[240] Warren H. Stewart, *Interpreting God's Word in Black Preaching* (Valley Forge, PA: Judson Press, 1984), 52.

[241] See: Marjorie J. Thompson, *Soul Feast: An Invitation to the Christian Spiritual Life* (Louisville, KY: Westminster John Knox Press, 2005).

[242] Fred B. Craddock, "Introduction," Eugene Lowry, *The Homiletical Plot: The Sermon as Narrative Art Form,* expanded ed. (Louisville, KY: Westminster John Knox Press, 2001), xi-xii.

[243] Long, *Preaching From Memory to Hope*, 20.

[244] Robert Reid and Lucy Hogan bring a nifty comic commentary to bear on such overdrawn pulpit self-reference: "A cartoon in *Leadership Journal* once depicted a congregation cheerfully providing a pastor their gift of a massive multivolume series of

books recounting the stories he told about himself, his wife, and his children." Robert Stephen Reid and Lucy Lind Hogan, *The Seven Deadly Sins of Preaching* (Nashville, TN: Abingdon Press, 2012), 34.

[245] Buttrick, *Homiletic*, 142.
[246] ICEL, "Eucharistic Prayer IV," *Liturgy of the Eucharist*, 2011.
[247] See my: *The Web of Preaching*, 83-90, for an interpretation of this narrative sermon method.
[248] See: David Schnasa Jacobsen and Robert Allen Kelly, *Kairos Preaching: Speaking the Gospel to the Situation* (Minneapolis, MN: Fortress Press, 2009).
[249] See: Eugene L. Lowry, *The Sermon: Dancing the Edge of Mystery* (Nashville, TN: Abingdon Press, 1997) and *The Homiletical Plot*.
[250] Lowry, *The Sermon*, 24.
[251] Ibid., 66.
[252] Ibid., 72.
[253] Ibid., 87.
[254] See: Buttrick, *Homiletic*, 23-79.
[255] Ibid., 127-70.
[256] See my: *Narrative and Imagination: Preaching the Worlds that Shape Us* (Minneapolis, MN: Fortress Press, 1995), 88-109.
[257] Buttrick, Homiletics, 57.
[258] Ibid., 57.

6 The Institution Narrative, 141-165

[259] Episcopal Church, *Book of Common Prayer*, 1979, 362.
[260] As noted by Owen F. Cummings, attempts to fix "the precise moment of consecration in respect of the Eucharistic words of Jesus was a phenomenon rather late in the development of Christian tradition. Historically there was no attempt to define a moment of consecration before the Middle Ages, and the rise of Scholasticism…" *Eucharist and Ecumenism: The Eucharist Across the Ages and Traditions* (Eugene, OR: Wipf and Stock Publishers, 2013), 44.
[261] See: Bouyer, *Eucharist,* 146-51.
[262] Paul F. Bradshaw, "The Barcelona Papyrus and the Development of Early Eucharistic Prayers," *Issues in Eucharistic Praying*, 132-133.
[263] Paul F. Bradshaw, "Did Jesus Institute the Eucharist at the Last Supper?" *Issues in Eucharistic Praying*, 9. Bradshaw is careful to add to this comment an important proviso: "Yet even after that,

liturgical formulae did not always conform their wording of the narrative of the Last Supper precisely to what was recorded in those venerable documents, but variants continued to flourish." Ibid.

[264] Dix, *The Shape of the Liturgy*, 275.

[265] See: Bouyer, *Eucharist,* 366-79.

[266] See: John H. McKenna, "The Emergence of the Moment of Consecration Question," *The Eucharistic Epiclesis: A Detailed History from the Patristic to the Modern Era*, 2nd ed. (Chicago: Hillenbrand Books, 2009), 70-92. McKenna concludes his survey of medieval developments by adding that, "The 'moment of consecration' was not an issue for the early Christian writers." Ibid., 92.

[267] Martin Luther, "The Babylonian Captivity of the Church," *Three Treatises: Martin Luther, 1520*, trans. A. T. W. Steinhäuser (Philadelphia: Muhlenberg Press, 1960), 152.

[268] Ibid., 158.

[269] Reed, *The Lutheran Liturgy*, 349.

[270] Ibid., 355.

[271] Frank C. Senn, *"*Martin Luther's Revisions of the Eucharistic Canon in the Formula Missae of 1523," *Concordia Theological Journal* 44 (1973): 118.

[272] Ibid.

[273] Robin A. Leaver, *Luther's Liturgical Music: Principles and Implications* (Grand Rapids, MI: Wm. B. Eerdmans Publishing Co., 2007), 179.

[274] See: Thompson, *Liturgies*, 123-37.

[275] Leaver, *Luther's Liturgical Music,* 180.

[276] John Calvin, "The Form of Church Prayers," Thompson, ed., *Liturgies*, 207.

[277] Church of England, "The Book of Common Prayer," 1549, Thompson, *Liturgies*, 257. Cranmer was careful to delete any implication of saintly intercession although retaining prayers for the faithful departed.

[278] Thompson, *Liturgies,* 235.

[279] See: Bucer, "Censura." Also see: D. F. Wright, ed., *Martin Bucer: Reforming Church and Community* (Cambridge, UK: Cambridge University Press, 1994).

[280] Ulrich Zwingli, "Action or Use of the Lord's Supper," Thompson, *Liturgies,* 149.

[281] Ibid., 143.

[282] Southern Baptist Convention, "Baptist Faith and Message," accessed December 22, 2012, www.sbc.net/bfm/bfm2000.asp.

[283] William S. Kervin, "Beyond the Last Supper," *Touchstone* 27, no. 2 (May 2009): 25-26.

[284] Lucien Deiss, *Springtime of the Liturgy: Liturgical Texts of the First Four Centuries* (Collegeville, MN: The Liturgical Press, 1979).

[285] See: United Methodist Church, "A Service of Word and Table I," *The United Methodist Book of Worship*, 1992, 37. Also see: the Eucharistic Prayers for various occasions, 54-79. The Great Thanksgivings for "Christian Marriage I" and "The Service of Death and Resurrection" are on pages 124-26 and 152-54 respectively.

[286] Episcopal Church, "Eucharistic Prayer A-D," *The Book of Common Prayer,* 1979, 361-376.

[287] Inter-Lutheran Commission on Worship "Holy Communion, Setting One," *Lutheran Book of Worship* (Minneapolis: Augsburg Publishing House, 1978), 69.

[288] Evangelical Lutheran Church in America, "Holy Communion, Setting One," *Evangelical Lutheran Worship*, 130. (In both the *LBW*, 1978 and *ELW*, 2006, the right hand column offers a Post-Sanctus option that moves directly from the Sanctus to the Institution Narrative.)

[289] See: ICEL, "Eucharistic Prayers I-IV," *Basic Texts for the Roman Catholic Eucharist.* Only Canon I employs the word "precious" in the Institution Narrative. Canons II-IV simply state, "he took the chalice. . . ."

[290] See: Gail Ramshaw, "Yesterday's Language," *The Christian Century*, September 6, 2011. Accessed October 3, 2014, https://www.christiancentury.org/archives/issues/2011.

[291] Dwight W. Vogel, ed./compiler, *The Book of Offices and Services of the Order of Saint Luke,* 20.

[292] An even more appalling example of this dissonance is watching the presiding minister attempt to offer the Eucharistic Prayer while stationed at the pulpit!

[293] See: Buttrick, *Homiletic*, 127-170.

[294] Ibid., 116.

[295] The mural, "The Freeing of the Slaves," was painted by John Steuart Curry.

[296] *Babette's Feast,* directed by Gabriel Axel (1987), DVD (MGM Pictures, 2001).

[297] Priscilla Parkhurst Ferguson, *Accounting for Taste: The Triumph of French Cuisine* (Chicago: University of Chicago Press, 2004), 194.

[298] Buttrick, *Homiletic,* 119.

[299] Ibid.

[300] See: Mary Catherine Hilkert, *Naming Grace: Preaching and the Sacramental Imagination* (New York: Continuum, 1999).
[301] Ibid.
[302] Ibid., 53.
[303] See: Samuel D. Proctor, *The Certain Sound of the Trumpet: Crafting a Sermon of Authority* (Valley Forge, PA: Judson Press, 1994).
[304] Buttrick, *Homiletic*, 119.
[305] Ibid., 120.
[306] See the refrain of a setting of Psalm 23 by Fr. Tobias Colgan: "O Jesus, Gentle Shepherd and Living Bread: Feed us, Guide us to the Land of Everlasting Life," Elise Eslinger, ed., *The Upper Room Worshipbook*, (Nashville, TN: Upper Room Books, 2005), 246.
[307] Buttrick, *Homiletic*, 120.
[308] Martin Luther's dialectical naming of the human condition: "Righteous and simultaneously a sinner."
[309] United Methodist Church, *THM*, 14.
[310] See, for example, The Methodist Church, "The Lord's Supper or Holy Communion," *The Methodist Hymnal*, 1964, 534.
[311] ICEL, "The Order of Mass, 2011," *Basic Texts for the Roman Catholic Eucharist*.
[312] Roman Catholic Church, United States Conference of Catholic Bishops, "Liturgy of the Eucharist: Eucharistic Prayer," accessed May 12, 2014, http://www.usccb.org/prayer-and-worship/the-mass/order-of-mass/liturgy-of-the-eucharist/index.cfm.
[313] Taking their cue from Eastern Church theology—which has never moved to a Moment of Consecration position in Eucharistic praying—the practice within several Protestant communions is to elevate the Gifts as the Verba are spoken, but to wait to reverence the consecrated bread and wine until the Eucharistic Prayer culminates with the Great Amen.

7 Anamnesis/Oblation/Epiclesis, 166-209

[314] United Methodist Church, *The United Methodist Hymnal*, 1989, 10.
[315] Bouyer, *Eucharist*, 104.
[316] Ray Carlton Jones, "The Lord's Supper and The Concept of Anamnesis," *Word & World,* Luther Seminary, 6/4, (1986), 438.
[317] See: Deiss, ed. "Didache 9-10," *Springtime of the Liturgy*, 74, n. 3.

[318] Willy Rordorf, "The Didache," *The Eucharist of Early Christians*, 4.
[319] Hippolytus, "The Apostolic Tradition of Hippolytus," Thompson, *Liturgies*, 21.
[320] Sarapion of Thmuis, "The Euchology of Serapion of Thmuis," in *Early Sources of the Liturgy*, 116.
[321] See: Marcel Metzger, "The Didascalia and the Constitutiones Apostolorum," *The Eucharist of the Early Christians*, 194-214. Also see: Bouyer, *Eucharist*, 250-68.
[322] The name is pseudonymous as the compiler presents the Apostolic Constitutions as being written by the much earlier Pope Clement of Rome.
[323] Metzger, "Didascalia and Constituiones," 207. John H. McKenna comments that because of its extraordinary length, "it has raised doubts that this part, at least, was ever intended for use in the liturgy." McKenna, *The Eucharistic Epiclesis*, 12.
[324] Bouyer, *Eucharist*, 239.
[325] Reed, *The Lutheran Liturgy,* 354.
[326] Thompson, *Liturgies,* 258.
[327] Episcopal Church, *Book of Common Prayer*, 1928, 80.
[328] The Methodist Church, *The Methodist Hymnal*, 1939, 530.
[329] The Methodist Church, *The Book of Worship*, 1964/65, 20.
[330] See: Enrico Mazza, *The Eucharistic Prayers of the Roman Rite*, trans., Matthew J. O'Connell (Collegeville, MN: The Liturgical Press, 2004), 164-68.
[331] "Liturgy of the Eucharist: Eucharistic Prayer," accessed June 3, 2014, http://www.usccb.org/prayer-and-worship/the-mass/order-of-mass/liturgy-of-the-eucharist/index.cfm.
[332] Episcopal Church, *Book of Common Prayer*, 1979, "Holy Eucharist II," 363.
[333] Evangelical Lutheran Church in America, *Evangelical Lutheran Worship*, 2006, "Setting One," 109.
[334] The Order of St. Luke, *The Book of Offices and Services*, Fourth ed., "Great Thanksgiving Three," 20.
[335] United Methodist Church, *The United Methodist Hymnal*, 1989, "A Service of Word and Table I, 10.
[336] Deiss, *Springtime of the Liturgy*, 131.
[337] Metzger, "Didascalia and Constitutiones, 210-11.
[338] Bouyer, *Eucharist*, 237.
[339] Thompson, *Liturgies,* 73, 75.
[340] Ibid., 258.
[341] See: McGuckian, "The Meal Theory of Sacrifice," *The Holy Sacrifice of the Mass,* 78-89 and 107-110. The author concludes

that the Eucharist is a sacramental sacrifice juxtaposing the meal sacrifice with the one Sacrifice of Christ.

[342] United Methodist Church, *THM,* 8.

[343] Episcopal Church, "The Collect for Purity of Heart," *Book of Common Prayer*, 1979, 355.

[344] Deiss, *Springtime of the Liturgy*, 131.

[345] Paul Bradshaw, "The Barcelona Papyrus," *Issues in Eucharistic Praying,* 131. Also see: John H. McKenna, "The Epiclesis in the Early Anaphoras," *The Eucharistic Epiclesis*, 7-39.

[346] Hippolytus, "The Apostolic Tradition," 4.12. Quoted in McKenna, *The Eucharistic Epiclesis*, 8. McKenna notes, however, that the authenticity of the Hippolytus epiclesis has been questioned by a number of historians of the liturgy. See: Ibid., 9, n. 25.

[347] Bouyer, *Eucharist*, 204.

[348] Bradshaw, "The Barcelona Papyrus," 131.

[349] Bouyer, *Eucharist*, 296.

[350] Michael Zheltov, "The Moment of Consecration in Byzantine Thought," *Issues in Eucharistic Praying,* 270.

[351] John McKenna presents an extensive and thorough analysis of the developments of the epiclesis in early Christian Eucharistic praying. See: McKenna, *The Eucharistic Epiclesis*, 7-70.

[352] Adolf Adam notes that in the first of the two epiclesis prayers, "the Holy Spirit is not explicitly named." *The Eucharistic Celebration: The Source and Summit of Faith* (Collegeville, MN: The Liturgical Press, 1994), 77.

[353] The *te igitur* text ("To you, therefore") follows the Sanctus and Benedictus Qui Venit and has long been identified as the beginning of the Roman Canon. The English translation in the Missal of 2011 now reflects the Latin text more closely:
To you, therefore, most merciful Father, we make humble prayer and petition through Jesus Christ, your Son, our Lord: that you accept and bless + these gifts, these offerings, these holy and unblemished sacrifices, which we offer you firstly for your holy catholic Church.
See: *Basic Texts for the Roman Catholic Eucharist: Eucharistic Prayers I-IV*, 2011, (from the 3rd Edition of the *Roman Missal*, English Translation, 2011), accessed June 12, 2014, http://catholic-resources.org/ChurchDocs/RM3-EP1-4.htm.

[354] Bucer, "Censura," 54.

[355] Ibid.

[356] Ibid., 62.

[357] See: ICEL, "Liturgy of the Eucharist," 2011. Some minor variation may be discerned among the four epiclesis prayers, however, they all function to invoke the Spirit's sanctifying work, making the bread and cup the Body and Blood of Christ.

[358] Ibid.

[359] Evangelical Lutheran Church in America, *Evangelical Lutheran Worship*, 2006, "Rite One," 109.

[360] United Methodist Church, *United Methodist Book of Worship*, 1992, 38.

[361] Presbyterian Church (U.S.A.), "The Service for the Lord's Day," *Glory to God*, 11.

[362] Episcopal Church, *Book of Common Prayer*, 1979, 375.

[363] *Didache*, 9.4, Dix, *The Shape of the Liturgy*, 90. For a more extensive discussion of the unitive aspects of the epiclesis, see: McKenna, "Epiclesis: An Appeal for Unity," *The Eucharistic Epiclesis*, 140-44.

[364] See: Peter K. Stevenson and Stephen I. Wright, *Preaching the Atonement* (Louisville, KY: Westminster John Knox Press, 2009) and *Preaching the Incarnation* (Louisville, KY: Westminster John Knox Press, 2010).

[365] The next revision of the Methodist Ritual, *The Book of Hymns* of 1966 does have one significant elaboration of this anamnesis. Now, the sacrament is "in remembrance of his passion, death, and resurrection," (The Methodist Church, *The Book of Hymns*, 1966), 15.

[366] Stevenson and Wright, "Introduction," *Preaching the Atonement*, xi.

[367] Ibid., 1-53.

[368] Ibid., 7.

[369] "Charles Wesley, "O the Depth of Love Divine," *The United Methodist Hymnal, 1989*, 627.

[370] See: Gail Ramshaw, *Richer Fare for the Christian People: Reflections on the Sunday Readings of Cycles A, B, C* (New York: Pueblo Publishing Company, 1990).

[371] The number and selection of the lessons of the Easter Vigil vary from tradition to tradition and, in some cases, the worship leaders are encouraged to select among the longer listing of options. For example, Hickman et al., *The New Handbook for the Christian Year* offers that while the number of readings may vary, "there should always be at least three from the Old Testament, including Exodus 14" (196). The Episcopal Church, using the Revised Common Lectionary, lists nine lessons while indicating that "[a]t least two of the following Lessons are read, of which one is always the Lesson from Exodus." Episcopal Church, "The

Lessons Appointed for Use on The Great Vigil of Easter," *Revised Common Lectionary*, accessed June 14, 2014, http://www.lectionarypage.net/YearB_RCL/Easter/BEasVigil_RCL.html.

[372] Stevenson and Wright, *Preaching the Incarnation*, xiii-xiv.

[373] Bouyer, *Eucharist*, 251.

[374] Ibid., 263.

[375] Stevenson and Wright, "Introduction," *Preaching the Atonement*, xi.

[376] See my: *The Web of Preaching*, 188-189.

[377] See: Alyce McKenzie, *Preaching Biblical Wisdom*, 115-17.

[378] Church of England, "The Book of Common Prayer, 1549," Thompson, ed., *Liturgies,* 258. (In the Second Prayer Book of 1552, after Bucer's *Censura*, Cranmer shifted this oblationary statement to the Prayer after Communion.)

[379] It is clear that pulpit or ambo is not the only places for proclamation within the Sunday liturgy. Mobility certainly has a place as long as the preacher is not "wandering around the worship space like Odysseus." Long, *From Memory to Hope*, xiv.

[380] See: Kathy Black, *A Healing Homiletic: Preaching and Disability* (Nashville, TN: Abingdon Press, 1996).

[381] J. Sergius Halvorsen, "The Context of the Liturgy," in *Preaching at the Double Feast: Homiletics for Eucharistic Worship*, ed. Michael Monshau, (Collegeville, MN: The Liturgical Press, 2006), 125.

[382] See: Jungmann, *The Mass of the Roman Rite*, 2: 86-103.

[383] Michael Monshau, ed., "Introduction," *Preaching at the Double Feast*, vii.

[384] Regarding the significance of the preacher and presider's need to be fed on behalf of the ministry to which they are called, it is interesting to note the popular practice in some churches and seminaries for the ministers at the Table to serve themselves last. Certainly this is a practice born of a certain anti-hierarchical sentiment along with egalitarian feelings. However, the "after supper" feeding of the Eucharistic ministers actually calls more attention to themselves than had they supped first. It also conveys a contrary message to that at the heart of Meal oblation. We are first fed by the Lord of his Body and Blood so that we may be strengthened to feed the flock. Ironically, the "after supper" Communion of the Eucharistic ministers conveys exactly an erroneous message—that we can serve Christ without first being served. In the "Communion breakfast" on the beach (John 21:1-19), the Beloved Disciples along with the others are first served by the Lord before they are instructed to feed his sheep.

[385] Hebrews 8: 1 (NRSV)
[386] "Accept, O Holy Father. . . ." The *Suscipe* is the prayer of the priest at the Offertory in which the presider acknowledges his unworthiness and of the need for the atonement for sins. See: "Mass of the Faithful," *Tridentine Mass - Side by Side in Latin and English*, accessed June 14, 2014, http://www.liturgies.net/Liturgies/Catholic/TridentineLatinEnglish.htm.
[387] Thomas B. Dozeman, *Holiness and Ministry: A Biblical Theology of Ordination* (Oxford, UK: Oxford University Press, 2008), 38.
[388] Ibid., 133.
[389] Paul Janowiak, *The Holy Preaching: The Sacramentality of the Word in the Liturgical Assembly* (Collegeville, MN: The Liturgical Press, 2000), 183.
[390] Long, *Preaching from Memory to Hope*, 35.
[391] Ibid.
[392] Mariano Margrassi, *Praying the Bible: An Introduction to Lectio Divina* (Collegeville, MN: The Liturgical Press, 1998), 3.
[393] John Calvin, *The Institutes of the Christian Religion*, 4.14.10, trans. Ford Lewis Battles (Grand Rapids, MI: Wm. B. Eerdmans Publishing Company, 1989), 89. Quoted in Janowiak, *The Holy Preaching*, 180.
[394] James A. Forbes, *The Holy Spirit and Preaching* (Nashville: Abingdon Press, 1989), 19.
[395] Ibid.
[396] Ibid., 82.
[397] Peter C. Bower, ed., *The Companion to the Book of Common Worship* (Louisville, KY: Geneva Press, 2003), 25
[398] Presbyterian Church (U.S.A.), "The Service for the Lord's Day," *Glory to God*, 5. Further resources are provided in *Glory to God* for Prayers for Illumination as well (90-91). Also see: United Methodist Church, "A Service of Word and Table I," *United Methodist Hymnal*, 6.
[399] Luke A. Powery, *Spirit Speech: Lament and Celebration in Preaching* (Nashville, TN: Abingdon Press, 2009), 49.
[400] Ibid.
[401] "Prayers for Beginning and Ending Sermons," *Ship of Fools*, accessed August 9, 2016, http://forum.ship-of-fools.com/cgi-bin/ultimatebb.cgi?ubb=get_topic;f=70;t=025852.
[402] Powery, *Spirit Speech*, 49.
[403] United Methodist Church, *Services for the Ordering of Ministry in The United Methodist Church, 2013-2016 as Approved by and Further Revised in Accordance with Actions of the 2012 General*

Conference (Nashville, TN: United Methodist Publishing House, 2012), 47.

[404] Ibid., 50.

[405] Ibid., 51.

[406] Ibid., 21.

[407] Recalling that two core criteria for the use of end-of-sermon set pieces in African American preaching include a judgment as to performance and a consideration of that epic's fit within a specific sermon. So, with celebration epics available that will take the congregation either to the Cross or to the Empty Tomb, when preaching on "The Rich Man and Lazarus" (Luke 16:19-31), the more righteous celebration will be a Resurrection Day joyous, even ecstatic encounter with the risen Christ.

[408] It is striking when shifting from a church whose Lord's Day worship embraces the full Ordo of Word and Sacrament to one featuring praise and worship "celebrations" how much variety and richness is lost with regard to the liturgical leadership of the laity. In the latter, the chief "on-stage" opportunities for lay leadership relate to instrumental and vocal music while "off-stage" technical leadership involves sound board operators and camera and lighting specialists. The former—a church whose worship is shaped by the Ordo of Word and sacrament—invites manifold lay ministries and, just as critically, tends to rotate those ministries across a broader spectrum of the congregation. Not just musical and technical "specialists" are set apart.

[409] Examples of such limited circumstances include the prior announcement of the use of someone's sermon other than the preacher by way of such mitigating circumstances as illness and other disruptive events, a last-minute fill-in for the scheduled preacher by another homilist, and, as noted above, the proclamation of St. Chrysostom's Paschal Homily during one of the liturgies of Easter Eve and Day.

8 Doxology and Amen, 210-228

[410] United Methodist Church, *United Methodist Book of Worship*, 1992, 38.

[411] Lucien Deiss, *Visions of Liturgy and Music for a New Century* (Collegeville, MN: The Liturgical Press, 1996), 72.

[412] Bouyer, *Eucharist,* 117.

[413] Ibid., 149.

[414] Deiss, ed., *Early Sources of the Liturgy*, 176.

[415] Thompson, *Liturgies,* 111.
[416] *Ibid.,* 206.
[417] Bouyer, *Eucharist,* 169.
[418] Ibid., 205. ("The Euchologium of Serapion.")
[419] The ecclesial reference, "in your holy church, in the Doxology was added in "Holy Communion, Setting One" and "Setting Two" in Evangelical Lutheran Church in American, *Evangelical Lutheran Worship,* 109, 131.
[420] Order of Saint Luke, *The Book of Offices and Services,* 21.
[421] United Methodist Church, *The United Methodist Hymnal,* 10. This usage is followed in all seasonal and occasional Great Thanksgivings in *The United Methodist Book of Worship,* with the exception of "Service of Word and Table IV" and two alternative uses on pages 79-80.
[422] See: United Methodist Church, The Council of Bishops, Office of Christian Unity and Interreligious Relationships, "ELCA-UMC Full Communion Frequently Asked Questions," accessed April 8, 2014, http://www.gccuic-umc.org/index.php?option=com_content&task=view&id=364&Itemid=295.
[423] Justin Martyr, "Apology I, 65," in *Early Sources of the Liturgy,* 24.
[424] Dix, *The Shape of the Liturgy,* 129.
[425] *Ibid.,* 130.
[426] Jerome, *Preface to Galatians, Book 2* (C.E. 387), 19.
[427] Bouyer, *Eucharist,* 242.
[428] See, for example: Reed, *The Lutheran Liturgy,* 725.
[429] See: the musical settings of the Eucharist in the *United Methodist Hymnal,* 1989, 17-25.
[430] Catherine Mowry LaCugna, *God for Us: The Trinity and Christian Life* (New York: HarperCollins Publishers, 1991), 338.
[431] Ibid.
[432] Mike Graves, "God of Grace and Glory: The Focus of our Preaching," *What's the Matter with Preaching Today?,* 112. To this issue, Thomas Long relates the comment of one of his students that "the sermons she heard were often 'like listening to something on National Public Radio: well researched, very well written prose, clever and witty in places, well voiced, but oral religious essays, nevertheless.'" *Preaching from Memory to Hope,* 34.
[433] N. T. Wright, *Simply Christian: Why Christianity Makes Sense* (New York: Harper-Collins Publishers, 2006), 209.

[434] Frank A. Thomas, *They Like to Never Quit Praisin' God: The Role of Celebration in Preaching*, 2nd ed. (Cleveland, OH: The Pilgrim Press, 2013).

[435] Mary Catherine Hilkert: *Naming Grace: Preaching and the Sacramental Imagination* (New York: Continuum, 1997), 119

[436] LaCugna, *God for Us*, 341.

[437] Buttrick, *Homiletic*, 276-77.

[438] The context here is the Sunday service of Word and sacrament. Somewhat different dynamics obtain when preaching in an evangelistic setting. See: William H. Willimon, *The Intrusive Word: Preaching to the Unbaptized* (Grand Rapids, MI: Wm. B. Eerdmans Publishing, 1994).

[439] Janowiak, *The Holy Preaching*, 55.

[440] The United Methodist Church's celebration focused on the history of the former Methodist Church since the Evangelical United Brethren (EUB) denomination has ordained women with full clergy rights since 1889.

[441] "How happy are thy servants, Lord," ed. J. Ernest Rattenbury, *The Eucharistic Hymns of John and Charles Wesley* (1948; repr., Akron, OH: OSL Publications, 2006), 202.

[442] *Fulfilled in Your Hearing*, 7-8.

[443] Buttrick, *Homiletic*, 97.

[444] Ibid., 105.

[445] Lowry, *The Sermon*, 87.

[446] James Earl Massey, *The Responsible Pulpit* (Anderson, IN: Warner Press, 1974), 108.

[447] Gerald L. Davis, *I Got the Word in Me and I Can Sing It, You Know: A Study of the Performed African American Sermon* (Philadelphia: University of Pennsylvania Press, 1985), 80.

[448] Frank A. Thomas, *They Like to Never Quit Praisin' God*, 90.

[449] Ibid.

9 The Lord's Prayer, 229-255

[450] Roman Catholic Church, "Communion Rite," The Order of Mass, 2011.

[451] Tertullian, "On Prayer, 1," accessed April 4, 2014, http://www.newadvent.org/fathers/0322.htm.

[452] Jungmann, *The Mass of the Roman Rite*, 464.

[453] Jungmann assumes such usage in house church worship prior to its appearing "in liturgical monuments as part of the liturgy," Jungmann, *The Mass of the Roman Rite*, 464.

[454] Cyril of Jerusalem, *Catechetical Lectures* 23.11.
[455] See: Dix, *The Shape of the Liturgy*, 130-31.
[456] Kenneth W. Stevenson, The *Lord's Prayer: A Text in Tradition* (Minneapolis, MN: Fortress Press, 2004), 100. Later, the Latin practice will be slightly amended and the last line of the Prayer will be offered by the people as a sort of responsory.
[457] John Anthony McGuckin, *The Westminster Handbook to Patristic Theology* (Louisville, KY: Westminster John Knox Press, 2004), 209.
[458] Augustine of Hippo, "On the Lord's Prayer in St. Matthew's Gospel, Sermon VI. 10.
[459] Ibid., Sermon VI.7.
[460] Ibid., Sermon VI.10.
[461] Ibid., Sermon VI.7.
[462] ICEL, *The Order of Mass*, "Communion Rite." For further analysis of the embolism in the Latin Mass, see: Jungmann, *The Mass of the Roman Rite*, 466-70.
[463] W.D. Davies and D. C Allison, Jr. speak for this majority view: "The word has not, despite assertions to the contrary, been found outside the gospels, save in literature influenced by them. . . ." See: *A Critical and Exegetical Commentary on the Gospel According to Saint Matthew*, vol. 1 (London, UK: T. & T. Clark, 1988), 607.
[464] Stevenson, *The Lord's Prayer*, 75. The term, *supersubstantialem*, immediately gained meanings related to the Eucharist as well. For a more extensive survey of the problem, see: Brian Pitre, *Jesus and the Last Supper* (Grand Rapids, MI: William B. Eerdmans Publishing Company, 2015), 172-175.
[465] Nicholas Ayo, *The Lord's Prayer: A Survey Theological and Literary (*Lanham, MD: Rowman & Littlefield Publishers, Inc., 1992) 216.
[466] While the Latin text of the Lord's Prayer remained unchanged through the medieval era, extra-liturgical reflections abounded in popular piety and theological writing. See: Stevenson, *The Lord's Prayer*, 117-50.
[467] Stevenson, *The Lord's Prayer*, 160-61.
[468] Reed, *The Lutheran Liturgy*, 72.
[469] Martin Luther, "*Formula Missae et Communionis* for the Church at Wittenberg," *Sacraments and Worship: The Sources of Christian Theology*, ed. Maxwell E. Johnson (Louisville, KY: Westminster John Knox, 2012), 232.
[470] Reed, *The Lutheran Liturgy*, 76. See: Frank Senn, "Martin Luther's Revision of the Eucharistic Canon in the Formula Missae of 1523," *Concordia Theological Monthly* 44 (1973): 101-118.

[471] Stevenson, *The Lord's Prayer*, 162.
[472] Lee Palmer Randel, *The Eucharist in the Reformation: Incarnation and Liturgy* (Cambridge, UK: Cambridge University Press, 2006), 103.
[473] Bradshaw and Maxwell, *The Eucharistic Liturgies*, 262.
[474] John Calvin, *Institutes of the Christian Religion*, vol. 2, ed. John T. McNeill, trans. Ford Lewis Battles (Philadelphia: The Westminster Press, 1960), 1370.
[475] Stevenson, *The Lord's Prayer*, 164.
[476] Ibid., 166.
[477] Ibid., 174.
[478] Ibid., 175.
[479] Church of England, "The Supper of the Lorde, and the Holy Communion, commonly called the Masse," *Book of Common Prayer,* 1549, accessed July 3, 2013, http://justus.anglican.org/resources/bcp/1549/BCP1549.pdf.
[480] Church of England, "The Order for the Administracion of the Lord's Supper, or Holye Communion, *Book of Common Prayer*, 1552, accessed July 3, 2013, http://justus.anglican.org/resources/bcp/1552/Communion_1552.htm.
[481] Church of England, "The Order for the Administration of the Lord's Supper, or Holy Communion," *Book of Common Prayer*, 1662, accessed, July 3, 2013, http://www.eskimo.com/~lhowell/bcp1662/communion/index.html.
[482] John Wesley, *The Sunday Service of the Methodists in North America: With Other Occasional Services,* London, 1784, accessed June18, 2015, https://ia801702.us.archive.org/33/items/amernorfm00wesl/amernorfm00wesl.pdf. See: Karen B. Westerfield Tucker, *American Methodist Worship* (Oxford, UK: Oxford University Press, 2001), 119-126 for an interpretation of Wesley's ordo for the American Methodists and the consequent revisions of that by the American Methodists.
[483] Ibid., 126.
[484] See: James F. White, *A History of Christian Worship*, 3rd ed. (Nashville, TN: Abingdon Press, 2001), 164.
[485] It remains common in United Methodist congregations, that when the full Service of Word and Table is celebrated, the Lord's Prayer remains attached to the pastoral prayer and is omitted from the Communion rite.
[486] Westerfield Tucker, *American Methodist Worship*, 137.

[487] David Buttrick, *Preaching the New and the Now* (Louisville, KY: Westminster John Knox Press, 1998), 7.
[488] Ibid, 16. Buttrick adds that lacking a robust future expectation, the sense of God's presence "attaches to the past and our religion becomes a wake." Ibid., 23.
[489] Ibid., 17.
[490] See: N. T. Wright, *Simply Christian*, 217-37.
[491] See: Lutheran-Roman Catholic International Commission, *Communio Sanctorum: The Church as the Communion of Saints*, trans. Mark W. Jeske, Michael Root, and Daniel R. Smith (Collegeville, MN: Liturgical Press, 2004).
[492] This movement was led by the Roman Catholic Church's "RCIA," the Rite of Initiation of Adults. See: Roman Catholic Church, International Commission on English in the Liturgy, *Rite of Christian Initiation of Adults*, study ed. (Collegeville, MN: The Liturgical Press, 1988). Also see: Dennis Bushkofsky, Suzanne Burke, Richard Rouse, eds., *Go Make Disciples: An Invitation to Baptismal Living: A Handbook to the Catechumenate* (Minneapolis, MN: Fortress Press, 2012). For an ecumenical annotated bibliography on the catechumenate, see: NAAC: North American Association for the Catechumenate, "History and Theology," (accessed July 7, 2014), http://catechumenate.org/index.php?page=history-and-theology.
[493] Tertullian, *Apology*, 18, *Early Christian Writings*, trans., S. Thelwall, accessed July 9, 2014, http://www.earlychristianwritings.com/text/tertullian01.html.
[494] See: Mary Catherine Hilkert, *Naming Grace, Preaching and the Sacramental Imagination* (New York: Continuum, 1997).
[495] See: Scott, *Hear Then the Parable*; and Robert W. Funk, *Parables and Presence* (Philadelphia: Fortress Press, 1982). Also see: Mike Graves, "Except in Parable: Preaching the Riddles of Jesus," eds. Mike Graves and David J. Schlafer, *What's the Shape of Narrative Preaching? Essays in Honor of Eugene L. Lowry* (St. Louis, MO: Chalice Press, 2008), 175-92; and Eugene L. Lowry, *How to Preach a Parable: Designs for Narrative Sermons* (Nashville, TN: Abingdon Press, 1989).
[496] Buttrick, *Preaching the New and the Now*, 52.
[497] Ibid.
[498] Scott, *Hear Then the Parable*, 373-87.
[499] Antony Wood, Executive Director, Council on Tall Buildings and Urban Habitat, News Conference, November 12, 2013, Illinois Institute of Technology, Bronzeville, IL.
[500] Henry Mitchell, *The Recovery of Preaching* (New York: Harper & Row, 1970), 34.

[501] "Heaven and Earth are Full of Your Glory," C, 28.
[502] Roman Catholic Church, *Missal of 2011*, "Preface of our Lord Jesus Christ, King of the Universe," accessed October 12, 2015, http://www.catholicdoors.com/prayers/english5/p03491.htm.
[503] John A. Coleman, "How the Eucharist Proclaims Social Justice," *The Eucharist: At the Center of Catholic Life, C 21 Resources,* Boston College (Fall 2011): 21.
[504] Carl P. Daw, "Till All the Jails are Empty," *Upper Room Worshipbook*, 2005, 177.
[505] Dawn Chesser, "World Communion Sunday 2013 and Communion as a Converting Ordinance," *United Methodist Worship*, accessed July 8, 2014, http://umcworship.blogspot.com/2013/09/world-communion-sunday-2013-and.html.
[506] Brian Daley, "The Drug of Immortality: Eucharistic Liturgy and Eschatology (Part VIII)," *Liturgy and Life,* Notre Dame Center for Liturgy, Institute for Church Life (August 2011), accessed July 7, 2014, http://blogs.nd.edu/oblation/2011/08/18/the-drug-of-immortality-eucharistic-liturgy-and-eschatology-part-viii/.

10   Agnus Dei, 256-283

[507] ICEL, "Liturgy of the Eucharist," 2011.
[508] Andrew Lloyd Webber, *Requiem*, 1985.
[509] See, for example: Andy Makken, Darlene Zschech, Michael W. Smith, "I Am Yours" (2013) and Mary Elizabeth Miller and Thomas Miller, "O, The Blood" (2010).
[510] See: R. Alan Culpepper, *The Gospel and Letters of John* (Nashville, TN: Abingdon Press, 1998), 90.
[511] Jo-Ann A. Brant, *John* (Grand Rapids, MI: Baler Academic, 2011), 48.
[512] Ibid., 63.
[513] *A Dictionary of Liturgy and Worship*, ed. J. G. Davies (New York: The Macmillan Company, 1972), 2.
[514] Joseph Jungmann notes the clear evidence related to Pope Sergius' initiative regarding this liturgical interpolation, but he adds that there is further evidence that the introduction of the Agnus Dei in the Roman rite could have begun earlier in the sixth century. See: Joseph A. Jungmann, *The Mass of the Roman Rite: Its Origins and Development,* vol. 2, trans. Francis A. Brunner (Westminster, MD: Christian Classics, Inc., 1986), 333.
[515] Ibid., 337.

[516] Marion J. Hatchett comments that the concluding petition, "grant us your peace," was inserted "when the anthem became part of the exchange of the peace. . . ." However, the Peace was subsequently dropped in the medieval West and the anthem was lost to the laity as a communal sung prayer. See: Marion J. Hatchett, *Commentary on the American Prayer Book* (New York: Seabury Press, 1981), 381.

[517] Martin Luther, "Formula of Mass and Communion for the Church at Wittenburg, 1523," Thompson, *Liturgies*, 113.

[518] Church of England, "*Book of Common Prayer*, 1549," 261.

[519] See: Reed, *The Lutheran Liturgy*, 182-204.

[520] Ibid., 370.

[521] See: Episcopal Church, *The Hymnal*, 1982, S 157-S 166. The alternate "Fraction Anthem" is "Christ our Passover" which concludes most settings with the Alleluia; thus this anthem is suppressed during Lent. See: S 150-S 155.

[522] Episcopal Church, *Book of Common Prayer*, 1979, 365. *The Hymnal,* 1982, however, provides multiple settings of the Agnus Dei, the text serving as a "Fraction Anthem." Also, the supplementary liturgical resource of the Church of England, *Common Worship*, 2000, provides for the restoration of the Agnus Dei at the fraction in both the contemporary rite ("Order One") and the traditional prayer book language rite ("Order Two). See: electronic edition, accessed March 28, 2013, http://www.churchofengland.org/prayer-worship/worship/texts/principal-services/holy-communion/orderone.aspx.

[523] See: Hatchett, *Commentary on the American Prayer Book*, 380-81.

[524] Episcopal Church, *Enriching our Worship* 1, 69.

[525] Order of Saint Luke, *The Book of Offices and Services*, 10.

[526] ICEL, "Liturgy of the Eucharist," 2011.

[527] Reed, *The Lutheran Liturgy*, 370-71.

[528] Peter Steinfels, "Cries of Heresy After Feminists Meet," The New York Times, May 14, 1994, accessed May 3, 2015, http://www.nytimes.com/1994/05/14/us/cries-of-heresy-after-feminists-meet.html?pagewanted=all..

[529] S. Mark Heim, "Why Does Jesus' Death Matter?" accessed March 14, 2013, http://www.religion-online.org/showarticle.asp?title+2138.

[530] Wes Howard Brook, *Becoming Children of God: John's Gospel and Radical Discipleship* (Maryknoll, NY: Orbis Books, 1999), 67.

[531] R. E. Clements, "Isaiah 53 and the Restoration of Israel," in *Jesus and the Suffering Servant: Isaiah 53 and Christian Origins*, ed., William H. Bellinger and William Farmer (Harrisburg, PA: Trinity Press International, 1998), 53.

[532] Ibid., 54.

[533] Luke Timothy Johnson, "Hebrews' Challenge to Christians," in *Preaching Hebrews*, ed. David Fleer and Dave Bland (Abilene, TX: ACU Press, 2003), 27. Johnson, of course, launches his critique against the two distortions of discipleship from the perspective of the Book of Hebrews. However, the correlate and "distorted set of Christologies"(26) brought to light in his analysis of Hebrews is equally illuminated by our study of the Johannine witness to the two natures of Jesus Christ, fully God and fully human.

[534] Ibid.

[535] See page 246.

[536] Jungmann, *The Mass of the Roman Rite,* II, 338-339.

[537] Ibid., 339.

[538] LaRue, *The Heart of Black Preaching*, 20.

[539] Ibid., 21-29.

[540] Ibid., 20.

[541] Donald B. Cozzens, *The Changing Face of Priesthood: A Reflection on the Priest's Crisis of Soul* (Collegeville, MN: The Liturgical Press, 2000), 84.

[542] Brant, *John*, 63.

[543] Ibid.

[544] See: Dulles, "The Church as Servant," in *Models of the Church,* expanded ed., 81-94.

[545] Stanley Hauerwas, *A Community of Character: Toward a Constructive Christian Social Ethic* (Notre Dame, IN: University of Notre Dame Press, 1981), 50.

[546] Lowry, *The Sermon*, 64.

[547] See: Buttrick, *Homiletic*, 47-48, for an analysis of opposition in congregational hearing and the homiletical strategies for diminishing that resistance to acceptable levels.

[548] See: Allan R. Bevere, "Faith Seeking Understanding," accessed May 23, 2013, http://www.allanbevere.com/2012/01/preachers-take-note-real-world-is-not.html.

[549] Wright, *Simply Christian,* 51.

[550] Hilkert, *Naming Grace*, 52-53.

[551] Ibid., 100.

[552] LaRue, *The Heart of Black Preaching*, 22.

[553] Hickman et al, *The New Handbook of the Christian Year*, 194-95.

11 The Communion, 284-307

[554] Evangelical Lutheran Church in America, *Evangelical Lutheran Worship*, 112.

[555] Dix, *The Shape of the Liturgy*, 135.

[556] Justin Martyr, Apology I, 66, in *Early Sources of the Liturgy*, 24.

[557] Hippolytus of Rome, *Apostolic Tradition*, IV, 21, in *Worship in the Early Church: An Anthology of Historical Sources,* ed. and trans., Lawrence J. Johnson (Collegeville, MN: Liturgical Press, 2009), 1:207.

[558] Ibid.

[559] Dix suggests that the Johannine phrase resonates most fully with the witness of earlier pre-Nicene writers who identify the Eucharist as the "the medicine of immortality," (Ignatius of Antioch) or as the feast that renders our mortal bodies" incorruptible" (Irenaeus of Lyons). See: Dix, *Shape of the Liturgy*, 137.

[560] Hatchett, *Commentary*, 386.

[561] Ibid.

[562] Ibid. Hatchett notes that this idea of the body of Christ relates to the body of the communicant while the blood of Christ ministers to the believer's soul was picked up by Thomas Aquinas in his *Summa Theologica*. See: Hatchett, *Commentary*, 386-87.

[563] Thompson, *Liturgies,* 85.

[564] Ibid., 208.

[565] Thompson, *Liturgies*, 261.

[566] Hatchett, *Commentary*, 386.

[567] Methodist Church, *The Methodist Hymnal*, 1939, 531.

[568] Methodist Church, *The Book of Worship*, 1965, 21.

[569] Joseph D. Quillian, "The Lord's Supper or Holy Communion," in *Companion to The Book of Worship*, ed. William F. Dunkle and Joseph D. Quillian (Nashville, TN: Abingdon Press, 1970), 70.

[570] Episcopal Church, *Book of Common Prayer*, 1979, 365.

[571] Presbyterian Church (U.S.A.), *Glory to God.*

[572] Ibid., 12.

[573] Evangelical Lutheran Church in America, *Evangelical Praise.*

[574] Ibid., 112.

[575] The exception here being those churches within the Reformed communion where pew Communion remained the practice and everyone communed together following the distribution of the elements to the congregation.

[576] Roman Catholic Church, "*Basic Texts for the Roman Catholic Eucharist,*" Missal of 2011, accessed August 24, 2015, http://catholic-resources.org/ChurchDocs/Mass-RM3. htm.

[577] See: Paul Bradshaw, Maxwell E. Johnson, and L. Edward Phillips, *The Apostolic Tradition*, ed. Harold W. Attridge (Minneapolis, MN: Fortress Press, 2002), 88-93.

[578] Hippolytus, *Apostolic Tradition*, IV, 21, *Documents of Christian Worship*, ed. James F. White, 188.

[579] Dix, *The Shape of the Liturgy*, 137.

[580] Ibid., 136.

[581] Jungmann, *The Mass of the Roman Rite*, 2, 361.

[582] Ibid., 364-65.

[583] Dix, *The Shape of the Liturgy*, 598.

[584] Jungmann, *The Mass of the Roman Rite*, 2, 472.

[585] Ibid., 473.

[586] The 2004 United Methodist statement on Holy Communion provides for occasions when the Table will need to be extended. "The Table may be extended, in a timely manner, to include those unable to attend because of age, illness, or similar conditions." United Methodist Church, THM, 22.

[587] Cassian Folsom, "*Bene et Firmiter*: A Short History of Reservation of the Eucharist," *Sacred Architecture* 22 (2012): 15. See: "*Bene et Firmiter*," 15-17, for a survey of the architectural and doctrinal developments related to the reservation of the Blessed Sacrament from the Council of Trent to the present.

[588] Martin Luther, *Formula Missae*, 1523, Thompson, *Liturgies*, 117. *The Book of Common Prayer*, 1552, states in a rubric that both minister and people shall receive Communion in both kinds, the people kneeling and receiving in the hands. (Thompson, *Liturgies*, 281.)

[589] Reed, *The Lutheran Liturgy*, 374.

[590] Randel, *The Eucharist in the Reformation*, 181.

[591] Ibid., 192.

[592] Reed, *The Lutheran Liturgy*, 374.

[593] John Walsh and Stephen Taylor, "Introduction: The Church and Anglicanism in the 'Long' Eighteenth Century," in *The Church of England c.1689-c.1833: From Toleration to Tractarianism*, ed. John Walsh, Colin Haydon, and Stephen Taylor (Cambridge, UK: Cambridge University Press, 1993), 11.

[594] Charles and John Wesley published a collection of 166 hymns on the Eucharist in 1745. The sweep of these hymns conjoins "matters which have been long divided—catholic and evangelical, sacramental discipline and religious experience, solemnity and heartfelt joy, corporate worship and personal piety. . . ." Don E.

Saliers, "Introduction to the American Edition," J. Ernest Rattenbury, ed., *The Eucharistic Hymns of John and Charles Wesley*, xiii.

[595] John Wesley, "The Duty of Constant Communion, *Sermon 101*, 1872, accessed July 10, 2013, http://www.umcmission.org/Find-Resources/John-Wesley-Sermons/Sermon-101-The-Duty-of-Constant-Communion. For an elaboration of Wesley's arguments for constant communion, see: Lorna Lock-Nah Khoo, *Wesleyan Eucharistic Spirituality* (Adelaide, Australia: ATF Press, 2005), 14-20.

[596] John Wesley, "The Duty of Constant Communion," II, 7.

[597] See: Kenneth Stevenson, *Eucharist and Offering* (New York: Pueblo Publishing Company, 1986), 175-183, for an overview of the Tractarian Movement's Eucharistic emphases and reforms.

[598] See: Ibid., 183-187.

[599] Alexander Campbell, "Breaking the Loaf," ed., Maxwell E. Johnson, *Sacraments and Worship: The Sources of Christian Theology* (Louisville, KY: Westminster John Knox Press, 2012), 246.

[600] Khoo, *Wesleyan Eucharistic Spirituality*, 215-24.

[601] One pastor recently noted that upon his arrival at a new parish, the "bread" for Communion was regularly that of the cheddar-flavored Pepperridge Farm Goldfish. That practice, thankfully, has been set aside in favor of the use of bread for Communion bread.

[602] For a careful summary of the liturgical movement, see: Patrick Comerford, "What is the Liturgical Movement?" accessed June 28, 2014, http://www.patrickcomerford.com/2013/11/liturgy-2013-71-baptism-and-eucharist-2.html. The essay was developed for Comerford's course, "Liturgy, Worship, and Spirituality" offered in the fall semester, 2013 at The Church of Ireland Theological Institute, Dublin, Ireland.

[603] Robert R. Howard, "Son-Light for Those Who Stumble in the Dark," First Christian Church, Globe, Arizona, Dec. 20, 2015."

[604] William H. Willimon, *Peculiar Speech: Preaching to the Baptized* (Grand Rapids: William B. Eerdmans Publishing Company, 1992), ix.

[605] Ibid.

[606] Tisdale, *Preaching as Local Theology and Folk Art*, 23.

[607] Ibid., 25.

[608] All of these thematics are to be found in the Eucharistic hymns of John and Charles Wesley. See: Ratttenbury, *The Eucharistic Hymns of John and Charles Wesley*.

[609] Order of Saint Luke, *The Book of Offices and Services*, 10.

[610] James B. Foley, "One Bread, One Body," *United Methodist Hymnal*, 1989, 620.
[611] Omer Westendorf, "Gifts of Finest Wheat," *The United Methodist Hymnal*, 629.
[612] Numerous phrases in the opening lines of this move are drawn from the *Exultet*, the church's ancient hymn sung at the Easter Vigil. See: Hickman, et al., *The New Handbook of the Christian Year* (Nashville, TN: Abingdon Press, 1992), 195.
[613] Episcopal Church, *Book of Common Prayer*, 1979, 364.
[614] See: Hilkert, *Naming Grace*.
[615] Michael Monshau, "Introduction," *Preaching at the Double Feast*, vii.
[616] Evangelical Lutheran Church in America, "This is the Feast," in *Evangelical Lutheran Worship*, 101.

www.ingramcontent.com/pod-product-compliance
Lightning Source LLC
Chambersburg PA
CBHW071648090426
42738CB00009B/1458